A to Z

of Industrial Relations in
the Caribbean Workplace

A to Z

of

Industrial Relations

in the Caribbean

Workplace

George J. Phillip and Benthan H. Hussey

Canoe Press

Jamaica • Barbados • Trinidad and Tobago

Canoe Press
1A Aqueduct Flats   Mona
Kingston 7   Jamaica
www.uwipress.com

10 09 08 07 06   5 4 3 2 1

Phillip, George J.
A to Z of industrial relations in the Caribbean workplace / George J.
Phillip and Benthan H. Hussey – Rev. ed.

p. cm.

Includes bibliographical references.
ISBN· 976-8125-82-9 (cloth)
ISBN: 976-8125-83-7 (paper)
1. Industrial relations – Caribbean, English-speaking. 2. Labour unions –
Caribbean, English-speaking. 3. Industrial management – Caribbean,
English-speaking. I. Hussey, Benthan H. II. Title.

HD6961.P45 2006   331.097292

Book design by Roy Barnhill.
Cover design by Robert Harris.

Printed in the United States of America.

Contents

L

M

N–O

P

Preface

A to Z of Industrial Relations in the Caribbean Workplace is essentially a complete revision and expansion of the earlier publication of *A–Z of Industrial Relations Practices at the Workplace* by George Phillip. It comes against the background of a new era in Caribbean economic history and experience. The Caribbean Single Market and Economy has had a long gestation period, but in January 2006 the "single market" aspect became a reality, while the "single economy" will await further dialogue, deliberations and adjustments among the member states.

The new project also recognizes and highlights the modern trend in disputes resolution, the preference for conciliation and alternative disputes resolution rather than litigation. The social and economic history of the Caribbean has been fraught with conflict and confrontation and, as such, the region faces a particularly difficult challenge to use a more cooperative approach to resolving industrial relations problems. Hence, the extensive allusions to provisions of the International Labour Organization in regard to social partnerships, social dialogue and social contracting.

Another challenge for the Caribbean is the need for a focus on productivity and competitiveness, and as such, in the limited way permitted by this type of publication, these issues have been addressed.

The Industrial Disputes Tribunal and the Industrial Court of Trinidad and Tobago have been highlighted, for purposes of comparison and contrast. This feature has also been complemented by a selection of cases on industrial relations from Barbados, Jamaica, and Trinidad and Tobago, suitably summarized and commented on.

This book should therefore serve as a practitioner's guide as well as reference, even if limited, for academic purposes.

Acknowledgements

This edition owes much to the research and administrative input of several persons. Among them we must select for special mention, Dr Paul Martin, tutor in English language, media and sociology, University of the West Indies, Mona, Jamaica, and Caron Martin, personal assistant to Dr George Phillip, at ATL/Sandals Group.

The authors also wish to thank the Industrial Disputes Tribunal of Jamaica; the Employers' Consultative Association of Trinidad and Tobago; Gerry Pinard, the group human resources director of Guardian Holdings Limited of Trinidad and Tobago; and the Barbados Employers' Confederation, for providing us with case material.

Thanks also to the many students and practitioners, too numerous to mention individually, who have made suggestions and whose expressed needs have led to this revision and expanded version of Dr Phillip's earlier publication, *A–Z of Industrial Relations Practices at the Workplace*.

Industrial Relations: An Overview

Industrial relations is arguably the "Cinderella" branch or aspect of management, which over time has emerged with its own high degree of importance. It now commands greater recognition, specialized treatment and increased resource allocation at the enterprise, national and supranational levels. According to one observer, "its focus is the regulation (control, adaptation, and adjustment) of the employment relationship which is shaped by legal, political, social and historical contexts" (Salmon 1998, 3).

There are many reasons for the emergence of industrial relations as a subject matter and operational activity in its own right, both at the organizational level and as a field at the academic level. One of the principal reasons is the cost associated with disruptions and dislocations in production processes and systems over time as a result of misunderstanding and mishandling of industrial conflict.

Second, the rise of industrial relations is largely due to the gradual democratization of late-nineteenth- and twentieth-century economic and societal systems. This democratization hastened entrenchment of the trade union movement, both its employee and employer varieties (discussed in the relevant sections of this book) and supranational organizations such as the International Labour Organization and UN-related bodies (such as UNCTAD, UNIDO and the like) that incorporate political pluralism and activism in their civil and governance formats.

Several elements have combined to ensure that both the practice and theory of industrial relations are an ever-changing and dynamic endeavour: the ever-increasing complexities in the world of work, in class, gender, racial and age division of labour; rapid technological changes; internationalization of production systems; multicultural and multi-ethnic workforces (due largely to an increasingly internationalized labour market); child labour; and varied compensation and reward systems, and so on.

Despite its obvious areas of focus and application, industrial relations is not easily defined, either practically or theoretically. Given its ties to mature disciplines such as law, economics, psychology, sociology and history, any definition could quite rightly emphasize one or all of them.

Most definitions of industrial relations imply a certain shortcoming or inadequacy. For instance, Michael Salmon's suggestion, after much examination of the submissions of others, that "it is possible" to define industrial relations as "a set of phenomena, operating both within and outside the workplace, concerned with determining and regulating the employment relationship" (1998, 3), is at once agreeing to the difficulty, while at the same time attempting to be broad and all encompassing. The set of phenomena would have to be legal, economic, social, philosophical and so on, while being definitive and directional as well as motivational.

The essence of the definition is certainly correct in stating that industrial relations is "concerned with determining and regulating the employment relationship". This accords well with G.D. Green's offering that it "deals broadly with the relationships encountered by working people in their working lives (as opposed to their private lives, though the latter is not unaffected by the former)" (1991, 1). Industrial relations has to do with the individual worker and groups of workers, variously constituted and defined, and their interfacing with other individuals and groups at the workplace.

At the core of industrial relations, practice and theory, is the issue of conflict. Because industrial relations is relevant to the workplace, it is given reason and effect by the coming together of – some would argue – two disparate interests: labour and capital (through the owner[s] of the enterprise or their representative[s] as management).

Perspectives

It is precisely this issue of conflict and the manner of its origin, as well as how it is played out, articulated and resolved, that has given rise to the principal theoretical perspectives on industrial relations. There are three broad perspectives: the class conflict or Marxist perspective, the unitary perspective and the pluralist perspective.

Class Conflict or Marxist Perspective

Marxists argue that the ownership, structure and operation of the organization or enterprise are essentially patterned off the wider society. Production systems have private ownership and are managed by the owners or their agents to make profit on their behalf. In this scenario, workers are paid and treated in a manner secondary or pursuant to the motive of making profit.

In keeping with its broad theoretical tenets, the unequal relationship between workers and the owners of capital, as is the case for the wider society, will change in an evolutionary manner, often via a revolutionary process, in favour of the working classes. The conflicts that occur in the organization are symptomatic and reflective of the disparities between social groups and classes and of the change in process.

Trade unionism and employee activism, while occurring at the workplace, are nevertheless expressions of a wider social and political struggle for changing the power and reward mechanisms and improving the status of the working classes.

The principal shortcoming of the Marxists' perspective is its failure to recognize the amorphous and multifaceted working class(es), its pursuit of leadership, and also that the democratization process along with genuine collaborative initiatives have made far-reaching improvements for workers. Workers themselves, in some jurisdictions, have become "significant" shareholders, individually and en bloc, as in cases of employee share-ownership plans (ESOPs).

The Unitary Perspective

This perspective sees organizations as having single, common objectives, with everyone working towards them with loyalty by accepting the authority structure of the organization. Management's "right to manage" principle is a given and should be respected by all interests.

This united effort is maintained through good leadership and by building team spirit. If conflict arises in these situations it is because the system is not working properly and not that it is wrong.

This perspective is criticized as being impracticable, particularly for its refusal to acknowledge conflict or that conflict can be healthy, even if disruptive. Conflict may also reflect real situations of inequity, exploitation and injustice.

The Pluralist Perspective

This perspective starts out by acknowledging that society and organizations are plural or represent plural interests. The primary objective is to find accommodating conditions whereby all interests are satisfied. As opposed to the Marxist view, pluralists believe that the parties can be held in equilibrium with a gradualist approach to change rather than revolutionary action. Given this pragmatic outlook on the organization, trade unionism and other forms of activism have a legitimate and important role to play in highlighting differences and seeking rational resolutions.

New rules of organizational behaviour and engagement, under the tenets of corporate governance, require a higher level of public accountability from managers. These include new and higher levels of ethical conduct and a greater level of managerial responsibility for good management practices, particularly the obligation to honour worker/management contracts and ensure a fair and equitable system of grievance handling and efficiency.

In many countries, including the Caribbean, governments have instituted laws and regulatory machinery to ensure that management follows laid-down procedures and that they conduct their business operations with integrity and strict observance of statutory obligations, within the laws of the land.

The fast pace of current and emerging technology coupled with the extraordinary growth in communications and competition have forced management to be much more aggressive and dynamic in responding to changes in the environment. The gradualist approach, which was acceptable and commendable in the past, may be too slow to ensure effective communication. Managers must now be more proactive, creative and aggressive in responding to the demands of the market, while ensuring that the industrial relations climate, at the workplace, provides an environment of harmony, motivation and reasonable reward for the people who work there.

A common trend in industry today is to index reward to productivity. In this climate, job security is not as assured as before. The challenge, therefore, is to derive and implement management and reward distribution systems which are equitable, just, meaningful and sensitive.

The Caribbean Context

Grace Strachan, director of the International Labour Organization Sub-Regional Office for the Caribbean, in the preface to Samuel Goolsarran's *The System of Industrial Relations In Guyana*, admirably captures the essence of modern industrial relations systems, particularly for emergent economies and societies of the Caribbean, in noting:

> Industrial relations systems are being judged not only on the extent to which they deliver on traditional expectations, but also increasingly on how well they respond to the new challenges thrown up by emerging workplace trends in the 21st Century. Such trends include inter alia a growth in contingent employment, outsourcing and sub-contracting, teleworking and networking and the growing influence of multinational corporations. They are also being assessed by their contribution to broader economic and social objectives, including to the fostering of the more competitive environment required for success in the new global economy. In the Caribbean,

the case for this type of appraisal is compelling, as the countries in the region brace for the competitive challenges implicit in the establishment of the CARICOM Single Market and Economy and the Free Trade Area of the Americas. (2003, v)

Mindful of the common social and economic history of the Caribbean, particularly the English-speaking Caribbean, many references are drawn from some of the territories, particularly Barbados, Jamaica, and Trinidad and Tobago. Indeed, the addition of industrial relations case material from these three countries and a summary overview of the industrial court systems of both Jamaica and Trinidad and Tobago reflects their common history and the growing regionalism among Caribbean countries. Helpful material is also drawn from outside the Caribbean region.

Applications and Practice

A research project drawing on the experiences of twenty-eight supervisors and their subordinates on industrial relations practices first indicated that a manual of procedures on handling industrial relations issues would help to improve their job performance. This need, added to experience in the field of industrial relations, prompted the compilation of a book of procedures, the first edition of *A–Z of Industrial Relations Practices at the Workplace*, by George Phillip (1986), to assist managers and workers alike in understanding the terminologies and some of the basic industrial relations techniques.

Unclear lines of authority, indecisiveness and procrastination in handling industrial relations matters help to aggravate emotions at the workplace, frustrate production and result in unwelcome industrial action. Too often, departmental managers push industrial relations issues "upstairs" to the boss, resulting in the power or authority vested in the position being undermined. Sometimes the ambiguity that exists in defining and performing the role of the departmental manager or supervisor destroys respect between management and employees and trade union officials, resulting in a breakdown in communication and poor worker/management relationships.

Managers should use every available management tool, operate under clear lines of authority with decision-making powers, guided by a clear vision and buttressed by a proper understanding of the philosophy, role and objectives of the organization, and with encouragement from members of senior management.

Managers must boost their efforts by acquiring the basic knowledge needed to manage personnel effectively. They must learn the art of fair, just and swift decision-making; the techniques and importance of follow-up; and must acquire the ability to set clear objectives and give positive and precise directions to subordinates.

One of the main concerns of workers in any organization is the absence of clear and understandable policies and procedures for dealing with problems and concerns. In many instances, the treatment of employees may seem to be inconsistent, arbitrary and without any recognizable objectives in mind. Sometimes workers show strong resistance to punitive measures imposed by management for any alleged misdemeanour or decline in levels of performance. In such instances, workers are usually unclear about the performance standards expected. In the absence of explicit industrial relations policies and procedures, workers tend to be mistrustful of management. The result is a breakdown in the relationship between managers and workers. Mutual trust is extremely important at the workplace.

Extreme fluctuations of workers' attitude and commitment may reflect a high level of inconsistency in management's industrial relations policies and practices. While such policies and practices should not remain too rigid, management must nevertheless have clearly defined guidelines to ensure that, within the bounds of managerial discretion, some flexibility is allowed in their implementation. Many conflicts between workers and managers can be avoided if management practices in handling grievances are perceived as fair.

The Labour Relations Code, 1976 (Jamaica) (see Appendix C) clearly outlines some procedures for handling grievance matters. In addition, guidelines on the handling of disciplinary action are included in the relevant sections of this book. Several other areas which are cause for concern among managers in industrial relations are dealt with as well, under their respective headings: absenteeism, strike, fighting on the job, productivity, wage and so on.

Many employers who resist unionization of the workplace may do so on the assumption that if the workers are seeking union membership, they must be dissatisfied. This is not necessarily the case, as workers sometimes simply feel that their representation to management may be more effective if it is done on a collective rather than individual basis. Too often, managers tend to see workers as adversaries around the bargaining table, when, in fact, they may be merely protecting their rights through a collective relationship with their union. Such representation may be the workers' only alternative to individual efforts in the absence of the right climate in the manager/worker relationship.

Collective bargaining, which is a feature of unionization, may work either effectively or ineffectively, depending on the attitude of those engaged in the process. In the final analysis, collective bargaining helps to develop equitable methods of remuneration for workers and it minimizes inequalities and reduces the degree of resentment that workers sometimes feel when any act of favouritism or bias has been shown in management's allocation of benefits.

Considerable space is allotted to the matter of collective bargaining in this book, and explanations and guidelines are found under subheadings such as "Administering the Collective Agreement" and "The Communications Cycle". The fact to be borne in mind is that collective bargaining takes place in every aspect of the relationship between management and workers or their representatives. It is important that managers recognize workers as being their primary responsibility and that the provision of welfare facilities, including counselling, guidance and development, is a primary function of management. On the other hand, workers' membership in a trade union must be secondary to the primary recognition of their relationship with their managers.

The company's attitude to trade unionism and to collective representation should be clearly presented and understood by all. Furthermore, even though nothing may prevent workers from becoming unionized, sometimes an understanding attitude and a progressive approach to management can remove the perceived need for militant and aggressive representation as a means of achieving justice in attending to workers' demands. If workers feel that their needs and aspirations will be satisfied by management on its own initiative without the prodding and representation of their trade union, there is a greater likelihood that a harmonious and productive working environment will prevail.

Today, we need to approach management in a structured, scientific manner, recognizing the true value of individuals, and providing for them – with their full support and involvement – plans that will enable them to develop skills and maximize productive capabilities.

We hope that this book will help to equip the reader with tools to deal effectively with industrial relations practices at the workplace. The book is not intended to be a panacea to all industrial relations problems, nor is it a full text on industrial relations. However, it offers a number of guidelines and helpful hints that, if properly applied, will assist managers by removing some of the mystery surrounding industrial relations practices, while putting at their disposal some basic methods of handling day-to-day problems.

In regard to the academic interest, the new edition attempts to address some of the theoretical concerns, particularly of the student reader. The introductory note on industrial relations as well as a number of new terminologies, such as accountability, conflict, compensation, dependency ratio, alternative dispute resolution, labour market, productivity and unemployment benefits, have been treated in a particular manner to, first, underscore the varied nature of industrial relations and, second, to provide a more probing slant to some of the issues, thereby establishing a link between theory and practice.

A

Abandonment, of job Abandonment of a job implies that the job holder has breached the rules of engagement and deserted or left the job without the agreement or knowledge of the employer. An employee is deemed to have abandoned the job when

1. such an employee, having applied for and received leave (departmental, sick, vacation) and exhausted such leave, does not report/show up for work at the usual place of employment when said leave has been exhausted;
2. such an employee, not in receipt of approved leave (departmental, sick, vacation), fails to report/appear for work at the usual place of work for a period of three days or more (a discretionary three-day period should be allowed to ascertain whether the absence is due to illness); or
3. a seasonal employee in continuous employment fails to appear at the usual place of work in accordance with established recruiting practices.

Having determined that an employee has abandoned the job, the employer may write to or call in the employee, accepting his or her absence as an indication of voluntary resignation and apply appropriate conditions of termination for cause.

Ability Refers to the capability of an employee or potential recruit to perform particular jobs or tasks. A mix of steps, such as recruitment and selection, aptitude testing, training and orientation, and redeployment, is usually used to aid the decision of placing individuals in jobs or to perform specific tasks.

Ability to pay This term addresses the financial or economic status or viability of an enterprise and its capacity to meet the claims or demands of employees for increased wages, salaries and benefits. This is an issue that is often at the heart of negotiations between unions and business

A

enterprises. An enterprise will broadly need to satisfy two basic economic conditions, namely, ensuring the price competitiveness of its goods or services, and a reasonable return on investment.

Both price competitiveness and return on investment are important to a business. One of the accepted measures of competitiveness is that of labour cost. If the cost of labour is high relative to the competition the eventual price of the products and services may be uncompetitive. If the business is uncompetitive, it could fold.

Return on investment is also very important for two reasons. First, the shareholders are in business for a profit and to ensure that their investments pay off. Second, the return on investment ensures that the business expands and develops through reinvestments of some or all the returns.

However, if the enterprise is able to satisfy both the condition of competitiveness and that of a return on investment and also increase the welfare of its employees, then it should do so. The best way to achieve this is to tie the increased earnings and benefits to productivity improvements, which should ensure that competitiveness is not compromised, at least not on the basis of labour cost.

Absenteeism   Absenteeism may be defined as time off from the job without the prior approval of someone in authority or management. Absenteeism can become chronic and, hence, add to the overall cost of doing business. As such, it poses real challenges for management in minimizing its effect on business as well as addressing the attendant human relations aspects.

Absenteeism can be caused by many and varied factors and has implications for the proper functioning and viability of the business operation. Some factors that may cause absenteeism are as follows:

1. Poor supervision or management, resulting in employees having a free reign to do as they please
2. Lack of motivation to work for the company, resulting from one or a mix of factors, such as poor remuneration, lack of recognition for effort on the job or initiatives taken, lack of consultation in decision making, unequal treatment of employees in regard to disciplinary matters or reward for work done, and so on
3. Unsatisfying work or poor work scheduling
4. Underemployment
5. Lack of commitment to the job or spitefulness

Management, therefore, ought not to treat absenteeism lightly. The following steps should be taken to address it effectively and efficiently:

A

1. Identify absences as voluntary or involuntary: those that could have been avoided versus those that were unavoidable.
2. Identify reasons for absences under both headings at (1) above.
3. Observe any pattern (for example, illness, accident or transportation difficulties).
4. Discuss the matter with the employee(s) with the objective of obtaining a commitment to improve.
5. If deemed chronic, give a warning – verbal or written – which with counselling will help to alleviate the problem.
6. If the practice continues without acceptable reasons, the employee may lose pay or be suspended or dismissed, depending on the gravity of the situation.
7. Study the issues further to determine whether the matter is systemic and therefore warrants a more structured approach to addressing the causes, and finding solutions.

Absenteeism rate   This is the proportion of time that workers fail to report for work each day or reference period. The absenteeism rate for an enterprise or department or whatever unit of analysis is usually determined as follows:

(a)   Find the total number of hours or days of absence (that is, the number of hours or days of absence during the reference period – week, month or year).
(b)   Find the total number of available working days during the reference period. In short, determining the result of the total number of employees X {(number of working days in reference period) – (number of national holidays in reference period + sum of annual leave days of each employee during the reference period)}.
(c)   Divide the number of days of absence by the number of available working days.
(d)   Multiply the result at (c) by 100. The full process is:

$$Absenteeism\ rate = \frac{No.\ of\ days\ of\ absence \times 100}{No.\ of\ available\ working\ days}$$

A

Case: Absenteeism Resulting in Breach of Contract of Employment

Joe Brown, a delivery clerk with Panoridim Limited, was arrested and charged by the police for complicity in the theft of a goat, the property of Joseph Anderson.

Information on Brown's arrest reached the management of Panoridim Limited five days after he was arrested and held in custody. Upon investigation, the company found that Brown was not actually involved in the theft of the goat but the police arrested him when he was found in the company of others who were being arrested for the theft.

The company took the position that in view of the uncertainty surrounding Brown's involvement and in spite of the fact that he was absent from work for five days, which in their opinion was a breach of the contract of employment, they would not dismiss Brown on the grounds of absenteeism as a breach of contract, but instead allow him to continue in employment upon his release from custody.

At the trial Brown was convicted and sentenced to one year's imprisonment. The company informed him that as a result of his conviction it could no longer have any trust and confidence in his ability to perform his job and his prolonged absence was accepted as evidence that he had terminated his employment. However a clear distinction must be made between the outcome of a legal case, which may be the result of legal technicality, and the company's right to ensure that trust and confidence exist in the employment relationship.

Comment: In the above example, the conviction of Brown concluded the matter.

Accountability   Employee accountability (personal accountability) generally refers to employees' responsibility for ensuring the proper use of time, materials, machinery and other resources at their disposal for the achievement of the goals and objectives of the enterprise. As a result, many enterprises are now focused on creating policies, structures and procedures to ensure the alignment of goals and objectives between the enterprise and the respective departments or divisions and employees within them.

Employee accountability has grown in importance and prominence in human resource management and organization development processes. The increasing focus on employee accountability by organizations stems largely from an equally increasingly demanding consumer and competitive environment which emphasizes the need for individual employees to add value to the service or activity that they perform.

Such accountability is built into the broader performance management process and procedure, whereby the whole enterprise, departments and personnel, work according to predetermined vision, mission and objectives. (See **performance management**.)

A

Activity, added-value/non-added-value   Actions or steps that actually add value to an operation, production process or service delivery are *added-value* activities. From the perspective of management, these activities are justifiable and should be enhanced, as feasible, for greater efficiency and productivity. *Non-added-value* activities are those that do not improve the product or service in relation to specifications, cost efficiency, or customer needs or requirements.

Business process re-engineering or reviews take a keen interest in both added-value and non-added-value activities, with a view to eliminating or enhancing them as feasible and necessary.

Added value   Added value is an economic and accounting measure of the wealth or surplus or value created/generated by the collective effort of employees and capital providers or sources (investors, shareholders, loans and other forms of equity, and so on). It is important to note the significant difference between revenue or income or value of goods or services produced, on the one hand, and added value, on the other hand.

Whereas it is good to note and assess the revenue or income as well as the value of goods or services produced, these do not indicate the growth performance of the business or how well it is doing. Value added, on the other hand, measures the extent to which the inputs of employees, capital and so on have been improved on to realize a surplus.

Besides indicating by how much the business has improved, added value is one of the more important factors in measuring productivity. (See **productivity**.)

Measuring value added: Value added can be measured in two ways, by the addition or the subtraction method:

1. The *addition method*, also called the *wealth distribution method*, allows for value added to be determined by the following equation:

A

Added Value = Labour Cost + Interest + Tax + Depreciation + Profit

It is called "wealth distribution" because the added value so created is used to pay those who have contributed to its creation in terms of wages and salaries (labour cost) for the employees, interest on loan for capital providers, taxes to the government, depreciation for capital equipment usage and profits to the owner (National Productivity Corporation 2003, 173).

2. The *subtraction method,* also called the *wealth creation method,* is the difference between the total value of output and total cost of inputs. It is calculated as follows:

Added Value = Total Output (TO) – (Bought – in Materials and Services (BIMS))

Age dependency ratio   The age dependency ratio is a measure of the rate or extent of dependence of the aged (that is, persons over sixty-five years) on those of working age (between fifteen and sixty-five years).

The importance of this ratio does not so much reside with actual dependence of one population group on another, but more so with the implications for retirement and pension or superannuation planning, on the one hand, and for workforce replacement, on the other hand. Projections for the United States show that the age dependency ratio will increase dramatically over the next thirty to forty years.

When the aged dependency ratio is combined with the *youth dependency ratio,* which is the ratio of those less than fifteen years old to those of working age, the result is the *total dependency ratio.*

The sub-ratios of dependency are usually reflections of each other. If the youth dependency ratio is low, then there is a higher proportion of the aged, resulting in a higher aged dependency ratio. Similarly, if the youth dependency ratio is high there is the likelihood of a low aged dependency ratio.

Both ratios have their separate and combined implications for enterprises and countries as a whole. "There is a significant economic impact in the changing proportions of youth and age dependency ratios, as public sector outlays on aged people are substantially higher per head than on the young" ("A Ponzi Problem").

On the other hand, a high youth dependency ratio implies both a concern for replacement of the working population, spurring immigration initiatives or special overseas recruitment programmes by some countries, and special and expanded training and educational investments by the state to accommodate the increased numbers of youth.

At another level, when the total dependency ratio is high, it signifies that more persons are dependent on fewer working persons, thereby making it difficult for employees to meet the increased demands on them. The state then has to find ways and means to provide social assistance to both segments on the dependency side.

Aptitude   In the industrial relations context this is the sum total of the skills, ability, fitness and preparedness of an employee (management or non-management) to perform a job or set of tasks to specification.

Manpower planning today focuses much on making sure that recruitment and deployment of persons in jobs are done with strict regard to the aptitude of the recruit and the skill and general requirements of the job. Companies, therefore, make considerable investments in employee aptitude testing tools (see below) or in recruiting consulting firms to administer tests to potential recruits and even to existing personnel for purposes of promotion or redeployment.

Aptitude test   Tests devised to help assess a person's ability to undertake particular types of work or to learn particular skills. Different types of aptitude tests used in personnel selection include verbal aptitude, numerical aptitude, spatial ability or aptitude, mechanical aptitude, manual dexterity and clerical aptitude tests.

Other forms of psychological testing include integrity, intelligence, temperament and personality tests. The focus on these tests is to ensure or minimize the risks of recruiting the wrong persons for jobs and discovering this too late.

Arbitration   (see also **grievance procedure; industrial dispute**)   A process or method by which grievances, disputes, disagreements and so on are resolved. The process can range from the very formal, involving legislation and judicial hearings, to one based on simple rules agreed at the local level between potentially aggrieved parties. It could also be a graduated process of moving from the local level through a series of stages to a judicial enquiry.

A

Arbitration in Jamaica and the Commonwealth Caribbean evolved out of a determination of the governments following the Second World War (1939–1945) to provide a system within which disruptions in the essential services (light, water, transportation, shipping, hospital services, and so on) could be dealt with in a manner that prevented a disruption of the national economy (Gershenfeld 1974, 6). Jamaica adopted a law on 7 April 1952 (Law 6 of 1952), and the official name of this law was the Public Utilities Undertakings and Public Service Arbitration Law. This was commonly called the Essential Services Law.

This law defined such things as lockouts by employers, strikes by workers and other dispute-related actions. It allowed for the parties to a dispute to refer such disputes to arbitration before a breakdown occurs. The law further gave the minister of labour powers to appoint a tribunal with specific terms of reference to deal with the matter. The award of that tribunal was binding and became an implied term in the contract of employment (that is, the collective agreement where one existed). But, there was one major shortcoming of this act: It did not provide for the reinstatement of dismissed workers. Tribunals were appointed to deal with specific issues. There was no permanent body to deal with industrial disputes and no continuity in the nature of operation or consistency in the kinds of awards. Many of these awards, however, established many precedents in industrial relations that still exist as practices today.

Industrial action was forbidden, from both employers and employees, unless the Ministry of Labour failed to refer the matter to arbitration within fourteen days after the matter was first referred to them. Breaches of the law were subject to prosecution. Prosecution was, however, only possible through or with the consent of the attorney general. In a highly union-oriented society, where the political leadership is drawn primarily from the trade union movement, this should be understandable and prosecution never took place. This law was repealed on the enactment of the Labour Relations and Industrial Disputes Act (LRIDA) in 1975.[1]

Another important law that pre-dated the LRIDA was the Protection of Property Act, 1905. Under this act, a person engaged in certain essential services may be punished by fine or imprisonment for the wilful damage of property, endangering business, life or maliciously breaking a contract of employment without a lawful excuse. This law is still in force but of little relevance or effect today.

---

[1] The Industrial Disputes Tribunal (IDT) was established under the LRIDA to formalize the system of arbitration and to provide a permanent machinery.

A

The number of cases dealt with through arbitration between 1952 and 1958 in Jamaica was small – only seventeen. But, of significance in this period were some landmark awards that established precedence for current industrial relations practices. These included a case involving the Jamaica Omnibus Service (JOS) in 1958 that "marked the first time a tribunal awarded increases specified to run for a two-year period" (Gershenfeld 1974, 14). Two-year agreements are still common practice in Jamaica today.

Representation of Supervisory Personnel

Another important dispute arose in 1960 and involved the Shipping Association of Jamaica versus the Bustamante Industrial Trade Union (BITU), the National Workers Union (NWU) and the Trades Union Congress (TUC). This matter concerned whether recognition and bargaining rights for supervisory staff should be granted and, in addition, "whether the firing of five supervisors by the United Fruit Company was justifiable" (Gershenfeld 1974, 15).

The tribunal concluded that "supervisors were free to join unions and bargain, just as the companies in the Association were free to deny them recognition" (ibid., 16).

In its award, the tribunal advised that the five supervisors had been unjustifiably dismissed. Of particular significance in this award was that those sections in it dealing with the recognition of supervisory staff in July 1960 were set aside when the association appealed against the matter in the Supreme Court of Jamaica. The court held that the chairman of the tribunal "had used reference sources which had not been introduced at the Tribunal hearings as guides in reaching his conclusions" (Gershenfeld 1974, 15).

This meant that he had acted *ultra vires* in his terms of reference, as the tribunal can use as a reference evidence submitted during the hearing. Approximately two decades later, in the Reynolds case of 1979 before the Industrial Disputes Tribunal (IDT) – and later appealed in the Supreme Court in Suit No. 753 of 1979 – the tribunal awarded that all workers, including managers, were eligible for union membership. This award was later upheld on appeal in the Supreme Court.

Another award that influenced industrial relations practices was the case of the *Bustamante Industrial Trade Union (BITU) v. Johnson* (4WIR3S1, 1961). This concerned a tribunal award that rejected a claim for wage increases by the employees of the Magnet Bus Company. The employees were represented by the BITU. The court held that the Essential Services

A

Law provided that awards of the tribunal could be enforced only by each employee bringing suit individually.

The LRIDA amended this condition of employment under section 11(b) as follows: "An award shall be binding on the employer, trade union and workers, to whom the award relates . . . [and] shall be an implied term of the contracts of employment."

Another 1961 history-making award involved a matter between the Shipping Association of Jamaica (SAJ) and the unions representing port workers. A unanimous award of the tribunal granted wage increases to the workers but inadvertently omitted the retroactive date of the award. The tribunal sought to correct the error and was advised that it was not free to do so. The SAJ argued that the tribunal was empowered to correct only a clerical error and since the error in the award did not fall into that category, it was not proper for the tribunal to act on this. The Supreme Court and the Court of Appeal agreed with the contention of the association, but on appeal to the Privy Council in the United Kingdom, the council ruled that "the error was inadvertent and was correctable by the tribunal" (Gershenfeld 1974, 16–17).

Tribunals over the years have been known to offer muddled comments that have resulted in more confusion than assistance to the parties. In a 1967 matter between the Jamaica Public Service (JPS) and the BITU and the NWU, the company terminated the services of twenty-one watchmen and, instead, used an outside contractor to provide the service. The tribunal recommended that the company should employ its own watchmen, train them, install a proper system and then determine after six months whether they might want to retain the workers. The company objected strenuously to this recommendation (Gershenfeld 1974, 23). The employer felt that the tribunal was acting *ultra vires* in its terms of reference and had muddled the case. The tribunal went on to state that the then existing Master and Servants Law and the Essential Services Law could not adequately deal with the working conditions of the day. This seems to have been a case of the tribunal attempting to justify its confusion by blaming the law.

Attitude, employee   "Essentially, employee attitude refers to the manner with which employees perceive and approach their job, how they relate to colleagues and supervisors and how they react to company policy and organizational changes" (Hussey 1995, 238). There are therefore three

A

aspects or *foci* of employee attitude: the attitude to the job, the attitude to colleagues and fellow employees, and the attitude to supervisors, management, company and company policy.

An employee could have a negative attitude to the job, to supervisor(s) or to management, for whatever reason, which spills over into most or all relationships at the workplace. As such, the extent of the negative attitude or the reasons or causes of this attitude is not readily or immediately discernible. One could simply hold the view that one deserves a "better" job but because such a job is unavailable one has to retain the present one. As a result, the jobholder may see everything else in a bad light. Hussey notes: "It is generally agreed that, whatever the attitude, positive or negative, good or bad, it will pervade the work process and affect the product in like manner or in a compounded way. Therefore, the efficiency and proper functioning of the organization depends a great deal on employees having the right attitude" (1995, 238).

Negative employee attitude can be very disruptive and costly. Product or service quality, customer relations, employee relations and so on, are some aspects of a company's operations that could be affected by negative employee attitude. Because of the importance of having positive employee attitude, companies regularly conduct surveys to ascertain their employees' "attitude status" with a view to effecting improvements.

Attitude surveys   The primary objective of these surveys is to assess employees' response to changes in the working environment and the level of satisfaction in response to existing social conditions in the company, community or country.

Some companies conduct these surveys prior to the implementation of new social or community outreach programmes or the introduction of new systems, procedures or technology.

Employee attitude surveys are also conducted at the national level. Here, they are used as the barometer for determining social legislation governing workplace practices or to determine the general state of affairs in regard to industrial relations in the economy.[2]

---

[2] The late Carl Stone's *Work Attitude Survey: A Report to the Jamaican Government, 1982* (1983) is a good example of a national employee attitude survey.

B

Bargaining rights (see also **representational rights**) A trade union may be awarded or granted bargaining rights by a firm or it may win such rights through a ballot of workers on payroll at a given date. "Bargaining rights" means the right to represent workers in negotiations relating to their employment or the termination of such employment.

The first official claim for bargaining rights is submitted by the union to the company on a form shown in Appendix D, drawn from the Jamaican context. The Labour Relations and Industrial Disputes Act (LRIDA) 1975 addresses the matter of the taking of ballots to determine bargaining rights. The stipulation is:

> If there is any doubt or dispute as to (a) whether the workers or a particular category of workers wish a trade union to represent them, or (b) which of two or more trade unions should represent the workers, the Minister of Labour may cause a ballot to be taken to determine the issue. (Kirkaldy 1979)

In the event that a ballot is being taken the following procedures will apply:

1. The Ministry of Labour will advise the firm of the taking of the ballot. (See Appendix E.)
2. Each party will appoint an observer of the proceedings, preferably someone who is acquainted with the workers.
3. After the ballot has been taken, the minister of labour is required to issue a certificate setting out the results. (See Appendix F.)
4. If the union has won a simple majority of those eligible to vote, it then achieves bargaining rights.
5. Two unions may achieve joint bargaining rights if each wins 30 per cent of votes cast.
6. If the union loses the poll, it cannot apply for another ballot to be taken for a period of twelve months from the date of the last ballot unless new circumstances arise that could justify another ballot. In such a case, application for a new ballot must be made to the minister of labour.

B

Some of the circumstances that could justify a new ballot may include the following:

1. Bogus voting by union members
2. Malicious action by an employer to prevent the taking of a proper ballot: for example, the summary dismissal of employees for no justifiable reason, the forcing of employees to take an unpaid leave of absence in order to prevent them from voting on the ballot, or the use of threats or other means of discouraging employees from voting
3. Malicious action by employees, including acts of violence or disruption, which may interfere with the voting procedure either before, during or after the ballot
4. Falsification of the results by any party

This list is not conclusive. In such circumstances, the minister of labour reserves the right to direct that another ballot be taken.

Case: KGB – Redundancy and Re-employment

A joint road transportation service was set up to operate as a department of two companies. All members of staff of the department were on secondment from the two parent companies.

After two years as an operating, self-contained department, a decision was taken to change it into a limited liability company (KGB Limited) and to have all members of staff who were previously on secondment resign their positions with the two parent companies and join the permanent staff of KGB Limited. Most employees took the option to resign and were given redundancy payments for their periods of service with the parent companies.

Immediately after the acceptance of employment with KGB Limited, two unions, the National Union and the General Union, filed claims for bargaining rights on the grounds that each represented more than 50 per cent of the more than one hundred workers. A week after these claims were received from the two unions, a third union, the Transportation Union, filed a claim on behalf of the clerical and supervisory staff, whose classifications duplicated those that were also included in the claim of the other two unions.

The necessary machinery was put in place for a ballot to determine bargaining rights; but before the ballot was taken, the General Union and the National Union decided that they would seek joint representation through the General Union and contest the ballot against the Transportation Union.

This was done and the General Union won 75 per cent of the vote. Bargaining rights were granted to the General Union, which immediately advised the company that, in accepting bargaining rights, it wanted the company to recognize the National Union as joint bargaining agents for members of the bargaining unit. The company acceded to this request and joint representation was established.

The Transportation Union, however, although losing the ballot, decided to write to the company seeking the recognition of its right to be paid membership dues through the "check off" system for those members of the union who wished to continue with their membership in spite of the representational rights won by the General Union. The company responded that in light of the results of the ballot giving representational rights to the General Union, it could not accede to the request to operate a check off system for the Transportation Union.

The Transportation Union made no further representation on this issue.

Bargaining unit   The bargaining unit is usually comprised of homogeneous classifications – that is, similar classifications of workers employed in one undertaking who share a common location or workers employed in one undertaking who share a common location or work for a common employer.

A union obtains bargaining rights for an agreed number of classifications arising out of a ballot (taken by the ministry or department of labour) or as a result of a voluntary concession of representation granted by the employer. The worker engaged in any one of the classifications included in the bargaining unit is subjected to the terms and conditions agreed on through the process of collective bargaining for that classification.

There are no provisions in industrial relations practice that permit a unionized worker (while employed in his original classification) to withdraw from a bargaining unit, either individually or collectively, without the agreement of the trade union or employer. A worker who desires to withdraw from the bargaining unit may do so only in one of the following ways:

1. By agreement between his or her employer and trade union
2. By resigning the job

B

3. By having a change of classification from one which is in the bargaining unit to one which is outside of the bargaining unit
4. By gaining support from other members of the bargaining unit for a ballot to be taken immediately prior to the termination of any existing collective agreement and showing proof to the Ministry of Labour that such a ballot is necessary and justifiable, and then, being exempted by the result of the ballot

An employer faced with a request from a worker or a group of workers to withdraw from a bargaining unit should approach the matter with great caution so as to avoid being accused of union busting or unfair labour practices by the trade union or other workers. The employer should advise such workers to take up the matter with the trade union. Failing resolution, the employer should – together with the workers – approach the Ministry of Labour to have the matter resolved.

Benchmarking   Benchmarking is a process of evaluating or assessing (prototyping) work processes, such as time or materials taken to complete a task; output of a work process by an individual employee or group of employees (such as quality, quantity or value); rate of staff turnover, number of persons employed, and so on, against an established standard for an industry or a particular type of work process.

Benchmarking is a widely accepted method used by companies to measure their performance against some industry or reference standard. In job evaluation exercises, for instance, it is customary to identify benchmark jobs to be used as prototypes against which to evaluate, compare and remunerate other jobs, both within and outside the enterprise.

Benchmarking requires a free flow of reliable data and information for standards to be established. Countries, industries and enterprises which develop a culture of information exchange usually perform better than those that do not.

Bonus   Earnings paid periodically, over and above the basic pay and based on the performance of the individual or enterprise. Bonuses are intended to be incentives for production.

A bonus, being performance related, may be measured in terms of output, profits, sales or an agreed individual target. The bonus scheme should contain a "formula for relating the reward to performance" (Johannsen and Page 1975, 15). Bonus schemes should fulfil the following objectives:

B

- They must establish a clear relationship between effort and reward.
- Earnings must be high enough to provide an incentive.
- Earnings should not be subjected to wide variations.
- There must be no arbitrary changes in formula.

C

Cafeteria (flexible) benefit plans   Cafeteria benefit plans are so called because of their menu-type offerings from which employees choose their mix. Each employee is allowed a mix of benefits (including health insurance, life insurance, pension, education, disability and so on) to a certain maximum total value.

The rationale for the cafeteria benefit system is that all employees do not have the same needs or desires at the same point, which the traditional benefit packages assume. Providing for employees on an individualized basis can cost both the enterprise and the employee less, since only what is required is purchased in the cafeteria system.

Check-off   A mechanism that allows an employer to collect union dues on behalf of a union holding bargaining rights. Dues are deducted from the pay packet and sent to the union office or held in readiness for collection by the union. The procedure for establishing a check-off system is as follows:

1. A voluntary order (see Appendix G) is given to the employer by the employee authorizing the deduction. The employee may revoke this order at any time (see Appendix H). Unauthorized deductions are not permitted under law (see Appendix L).
2. Deductions from wages are made following agreement between the union and the company on the manner in which such deductions should be transmitted to the union.

There is no obligation on the part of the employer to make deductions under a check-off system. However, good industrial relations practice suggests that cooperation in this respect is vital to a harmonious relationship between company and union.

Closed shop   A system whereby every individual in a company must either be a member of a specific trade union prior to employment or must

C

become one on permanent appointment. One school of thought claims that this system is contrary to the ideal of personal freedom. It is not a practice of industrial relations in Jamaica. A closed shop may restrict a company in its ability to choose the people it thinks are best suited for the job. Alternatively, a closed shop allows the employer to select the union with greater stability, thus minimizing the reasons for irrational militancy, which is a product of job insecurity.

Co-determination   Commonly referred to as the German model of "giving wage and salary earners more freedom and growth" (Döding 1976, 5). This model includes participation in setting policy objectives, strategic planning and decision making at the senior management level of the organization.

Employees' interests are represented at board level in policymaking: at departmental and plant level in work organization, scheduling, wage-related schemes and productivity programmes.

There are many other forms of employee participation at the workplace. These include joint consultation, industrial democracy and worker participation. The Government of Jamaica introduced the system of worker participation in 1976. This model included nominal board representation; employee participation in shop-floor discussions and decision making. This model failed to achieve popular support and it faded from the workplace. One of the primary reasons offered in explaining its failure is its politically socialist character, which was symbolic of the period of the People's National Party (PNP) government of the 1970s.

There is a great deal of goodwill for a system of industrial democracy which ensures the widest possible participation of employees in the ownership, decision making and profit sharing of the enterprise. However, such a system must be carefully thought out and tailored to suit the needs of the particular enterprise and the culture of the society in which it operates. Worker participation may be said to have contained these features in the 1970s, but mistrust between business and government and lack of trade union support contributed to the failure of that experiment.

Collective agreement   The International Labour Organization Collective Agreement Recommendation, 1951 (No. 91), defines the term "collective agreements" as "all agreements in writing regarding working conditions

C

and terms of employment concluded between an employer, a group of employers or one or more employers' organizations, on the one hand, and one or more representative workers' organizations, or, in the absence of such organizations, the representatives of the workers duly elected and authorized by them in accordance with national laws and regulations, on the other" (ILO 1995, 75).

For effectiveness of collective agreements, the recommendation states:

1. Collective agreements should bind the signatories thereto and those on whose behalf the agreement is concluded. Employers and workers bound by a collective agreement should not be able to include in contracts of employment stipulations contrary to those contained in the collective agreement.
2. Stipulations in such contracts of employment, which are contrary to collective agreement, should be regarded as null and void and automatically replaced by the corresponding stipulations of the collective agreement.
3. Stipulations in contracts of employment, which are more favourable to the workers than those prescribed by a collective agreement, should not be regarded as contrary to the collective agreement.
4. If the parties secure effective observance of the provisions of collective agreements thereto, the provisions of the preceding should not be regarded as calling for legislative measures.
5. The stipulations of a collective agreement should apply to all workers of the classes concerned employed in the undertakings covered by the agreement unless the agreement specifically provided to the contrary.

Collective bargaining   A process or set of procedural rules for arriving at conditions of work, including wages, through negotiations between employers and employees or their trade union representatives. The collective agreement which results from this process is applied to all employees within the bargaining unit.

"Collective bargaining" and "collective agreement" are terms also defined in Jamaica's Labour Relations and Industrial Disputes Act (LRIDA), section 2. It is to be noted that from these definitions the law seeks to treat the worker as one in need of strength of unity with his or her co-workers. This results in – by implication of the law – disallowing

C

a worker from collectively bargaining to reach a collective agreement on his or her own.

There are various levels of collective bargaining and agreements. These include industry-wide bargaining – that is, bargaining at a national level for an industry – and company, factory or plant agreements (sometimes referred to as workplace agreements). Examples of industry-wide bargaining in Jamaica are in the building, sugar, printing and shipping industries. Agreements reached at the national level set minimum standards for workers in the relevant industry.

In Jamaica, no particular statute exists giving legal effect to collective agreements. There is a presumption here that a collective agreement is not meant to establish legal relations unless expressly stated otherwise. If the parties to the collective agreement mutually accept this, then the legal force of such collective agreement will be felt when such agreements are hereafter injected into new contracts of employment for the parties concerned.

The successful application of such agreement depends primarily on mutual acceptance, as well as on the ability of the parties to manage the agreement.

Some typical clauses in a collective agreement include the following:

- duration of the agreement
- rights and responsibilities of management and union
- hours of work (including overtime) – defining workday, work-week and scheduled time off
- vacation leave, sick leave and public holiday entitlements
- wages, premium pay and allowances
- grievance procedure – a system for handling grievances
- maternity leave – approved time off for pregnancy
- pension, provident funds and fringe benefits provisions
- redundancy and recall – a procedure for handling permanent or temporary reductions in the labour force
- check-off – voluntary deductions from pay packets to pay union dues, and so on
- disciplinary code – guide to decision making on disciplinary issues (see Appendix J)
- seniority promotion/transfers – remunerating and protecting employees with seniority and arranging their horizontal and vertical mobility

The signing of an agreement is no guarantee that either party to the agreement will honour its conditions scrupulously. Differences arise, circumstances change and so do managers, union officers and delegates; and intentions that led to certain understandings are blurred by the passage of time.

A collective agreement places a moral obligation on both parties to do that which they agreed to do. Many conflicts arise because one party to the agreement fails or is reluctant to honour a part of it. The management of a collective agreement is therefore a serious responsibility, requiring great moral strength and good management practices. Effective administration of the agreement depends on the manager, and on the cooperation of trade union leadership and the employees.

Communications Cycle in Collective Bargaining

A well-defined "communications cycle" is an important test of effective negotiations. The cycle identifies the parameters of consultation: who, when, where, why and how must be determined as part of the negotiating strategy. Failure to use a system tends to create obstacles in the setting of mandates and in the acceptance of the agreed terms of the contract.

Many negotiators fail to communicate effectively with members of their side. Such a weakness in negotiating strategy must be avoided. An inadequate consulting mechanism delays negotiations and frustrates the parties with possibly disastrous results in the form of strikes or other industrial action and a consequent loss of production.

Negotiating the Collective Agreement

Here are a few guidelines that many negotiators have found helpful:

A. Preparation

1. Upon receipt of the union's claim, study it carefully, analysing and researching the wishes and aspirations of the workforce just as a routine practice, but, particularly, prior to negotiations.
2. Document all observations – note positive suggestions and negative reactions, and complaints about working conditions.
3. Examine existing conditions of employment to determine if they are effective and efficient. If not, propose positive amendments to these conditions.
4. Discuss observations with colleagues and supervisors – seek opinions and recommendations on proposed changes in the collective agreement.

5. Prepare the company's proposal to the union and cost it. Get a mandate but ensure some flexibility in the mandate because this may be needed to arrive at a settlement. The company's proposal for determining the mandate must include the most optimistic settlement, the most pessimistic settlement and the reasonable expectations from the outcome of the negotiation statement – cost it.

6. Compare the claim with the company's proposals and against claims to other but similar companies to establish comparative advantages or disadvantages and relevance.

7. If satisfied that the union's claim is clearly understood, become conversant with the company's mandate. Submit the company's proposal to the union.

B. The Protocol for Negotiating the Collective Agreement

1. Never approach the bargaining table with a closed mind, inflexible to suggestions or change.

2. Always be in possession of facts and figures.

3. Speak the truth and do so firmly and with conviction.

4. Be clear on your role as spokesman, as failure to do so may create confusion around the bargaining table and weaken your bargaining position. Conflicting presentations from more than one spokesperson may confuse and derail the negotiations.

5. Call time out for sidebar discussions with members of your negotiating team or to simply breathe. Marshal your thoughts, review your strategy and revise if necessary.

6. Maintain accurate minutes of the proceedings, ensuring that all intentions and opinions are properly recorded. These will have to stand close scrutiny by successive negotiators in the future.

7. The attitude and behaviour of the negotiator during and after negotiations will greatly influence the quality of settlement arrived at and its acceptability at the workplace afterwards.

8. When negotiations have been concluded, draw up the heads of agreement, arrange a meeting, and sign the agreement.

9. The language of the heads of agreement and subsequent collective agreements must be clear, concise and direct. Avoid ambiguity, repetition and distortions.

C. Administering the Collective Agreement

1. Immediately after the settlement, arrange a meeting of all managers, supervisors and, if necessary, workers, and discuss the

total agreement, explaining the intentions and understandings that led to the settlement. This avoids misinterpretations, misunderstandings and neglect in the future.

2. If uncertain about an agreed condition, consult the other party, agree on a common interpretation, and exchange letters for the record.

3. Keep your colleagues and employees aware of actions being taken at all times. This is a demonstration of courtesy which must not be ignored.

4. Each administrator of the collective agreement must be issued with a copy.

D. Understanding the Collective Agreement

1. The main purpose of this section is to ensure that the agreed conditions are properly interpreted and that the intentions of the negotiators are clearly understood.

2. Read and understand the minutes and notes of the meetings – what did the parties say they meant when they considered and adopted the provisions?

3. Discuss the provisions with colleagues and members of the negotiating team.

4. Study all grievances resulting from the implementation of the provisions. How were the grievances dispensed? Are there minutes, records and opinions?

5. Research past practices. What has been the experience in the company since the provision was first agreed on?

6. Priority of clauses in agreement: Where there is a conflict between two clauses, the most important clause shall govern. For example, management may have the right to decide on the time when vacation leave is taken if the exigencies of the business demand a specified period available for vacation leave between, say, June and September. In such an event, however, adequate notice must be given to workers before implementation of the change.

7. Language of agreement: Specific language must govern over general language. In the event of layoff and recall, seniority of service shall govern where skills and ability are equal. It may not be possible to determine the exact degree of skill and ability; therefore, if there is doubt, seniority shall prevail.

C

Common law (see also **statute law**)   This may be called the everyday law of the land. Common law has developed over hundreds of years as a result of an acceptance of practices of people who have shared a "commonality" of such practices.

Whenever disputes arise and are taken to court, the judge makes a ruling. This decision lays down the precedent which becomes accepted by society as law until it is changed by the decision of other judges or until changes in the society invalidate it or constitutional changes negate it.

When a common law decision conflicts with statute law, statute law always takes precedence over common law (Vincent 1983).

Communication   This is the imparting or passing on of information and messages or an exchange of ideas or information with others. Some methods of communication include meetings, memoranda, letter writing, newsletters, counselling, discussion groups and brainstorming.

Good and effective communication is essential to the corporate health of an organization. Every organization must have a practical, workable structure that is understood by all so that each individual knows to whom he or she reports and who reports to him or her. The employee must understand the functions that he or she performs and to whom he or she is accountable for those functions. Failure to provide such direction and information relieves the individual of the obligatory responsibility and accountability for assigned functions and is tantamount to a dereliction of duty by those responsible for the overall management of the organization. A lack of understanding of one's role creates confusion and frustration and is counterproductive. The importance to the organization of an effective system of communication that encourages and allows the free flow of information up and down the ladder and at all levels cannot be overemphasized.

One of the most common means of communication is a staff meeting. The following are guidelines for conducting effective meetings:

1. A chairman or coordinator must direct and control the activities of the meeting.
2. A suitable meeting room must be chosen – one that is properly ventilated but sound-proof.
3. A certain amount of time must be set for the meeting and should be rigidly observed.

4. An agenda or objectives, formal or informal, must be stated and agreed at the commencement of the meeting.
5. Opportunity must be given to all who wish to speak to do so.
6. The chairman of the meeting must make a summary of the proceedings.
7. The meeting must be adjourned promptly when the issues have been dealt with.
8. Disruptions by participants entering and leaving the meeting room should be discouraged.

Factors that create a "bad" meeting are as follows:

- cross-talk
- lack of direction
- indecisive chairmanship
- unclear objectives
- poor ventilation
- an inadequate audio system
- use of cellular phones, especially by the chairperson

Compensation (see also **wage**) Compensation is the monetary as well as non-monetary reward offered by an employer to an employee in exchange for assistance rendered in the production of goods or provision of services.

Monetary reward can be direct as well as indirect. Direct pay relates to the actual amounts an employee receives. Indirect reward relates to the benefits and support assistance received, but which is not immediately quantifiable. Examples of indirect reward include health insurance, pension, childcare and personal development.

Modern compensation management practices also recognize and apply *mental* and *social* or *psychic wage* elements to supplement the monetary earnings. "Mental wage" is a term used to describe recognition and appreciation systems or gestures to employees for outstanding services or performance rendered. "Social wage" refers to subsidized or fully paid facilities such as recreation and health services available to the employee at the community level.

Importance of Understanding and Managing Compensation

Compensation management is perhaps the most important aspect of human resource management. Most medium to large companies commit

C

over 50 per cent of their operating expense to salaries and wages. This level of outlay requires serious planning and management to ensure a return on investment.

However, compensation systems and amounts paid do not only affect the company but also affect, in a cumulative way, the economy in general. Andrew Downes states:

> An important aspect of the productivity-investment drive in the Caribbean has been the role of wages and salaries. The need to link wage and salary increases to productivity growth has been seen as an important element in the drive to enhance international price competitiveness, especially where the country adopts a "fixed" exchange rate regime. In addition, the level of wages and salaries adjusted for productivity effects has been a major consideration in foreign investment decisions. (1997, 33)

Compensation Systems

There are two broad compensation systems. The traditional or *fixed* pay compensation systems essentially pay based on the value or worth of the job. *Variable* or performance-based systems pay entirely or partly on the basis of performance of individual employees or groups of employees.

Competitiveness   Generally refers to the wellness of a business or economy in terms of its ability to compete for market share of goods and services produced. Although it is feasible and practical to assess the competitiveness of enterprises against competition within local markets, it is external competitiveness that is usually considered the litmus test of how well an enterprise or an economy is doing.

There are three principal levels at which competitiveness can be assessed. These are enterprise, industry and economy or national levels. "In effect, competitiveness refers to the ability of the enterprise/sector/country to produce and sell goods and services in domestic and foreign markets at prices and quality that ensure long-run viability and sustainability" (Downes 2003, 12).

The presence of rival producers of similar or substitute/alternative goods or services forces enterprises to ensure that their design, price and service quality are comparable or better than the competition.

Competitiveness at the industry level addresses the question of whether or not there are opportunities for investments that will attract an acceptable return.

One of the many ways available for measuring external competitiveness is by computing the *relative real unit labour cost of production* (RULC), which is the ratio of the real wage rate to labour productivity.

C

Conflict   As noted earlier, conflict is at the core of industrial relations. Regardless of the perspective taken on industrial relations its focal point is on the issue of conflict, its (conflict) origin, inevitability, persistence or continuity and mechanisms to lessen or manage it.

Experience and documentation indicate that there is, in the industrial relations and organizational context, a set of terminologies which are unwisely used interchangeably to mean conflict. They are perhaps better described as stages of industrial conflict rather than as absolutely industrial conflict. The terminologies are *difference, concern, complaint, grievance, dispute* and *conflict* itself.

Causes of Conflict

There are many causes of conflict, or, perhaps more to the point, many factors that tend to encourage conflict. Some of these factors are as follows:

1. *Social,* such as class, colour, race, creed, gender, sexuality and envy. Quite often it is factors such as these, largely external to the organization, which, nevertheless, cause conflict in the organization. Policies of non-discrimination and inclusiveness can go a far way in minimizing conflict emanating from them.
2. *Organizational,* such as insensitive and inappropriate rules; inequity with respect to treatment and rewarding of individuals and groups; inadequate or inappropriate communication policies and practices; procrastination with making decisions and handling grievances and complaints; and high handedness. All of these or any combination of them can be very costly to an organization in so far as they cause and prolong conflict.
3. *Personal,* such as attitude to work, offensiveness, poor hygiene, and being intimidating are also very high on the list of factors which cause and exacerbate conflict.

Conflict management   This speaks to the policies, procedures and approaches used in managing conflict. For purposes of organizational

C

stability and productivity, conflict management strategies should be pre-ventive – that is, they should ensure that all organizationally potential causes of conflict are minimized, controlled or eliminated where feasible.

Conflict management should be expeditious, efficient, non-personal, equitable and decisive, to allow for the business of the enterprise to go on with the minimum of disruption.

Consumer price index (also called **cost of living or inflation index**)   This index (CPI) is intended to measure changes in the prices paid by families and individuals for a list of goods and services sometimes called a "basket of goods" in a given place and at a given time. These families and indi-viduals are wage and salary earners. Of primary interest is the amount of income spent on each item among the goods and services.

In Jamaica, the "basket of goods" comprises over 260 items including housing, transportation, food and clothing. The CPI analyses differences in the movement of costs of items in the "basket of goods" in urban and rural areas of the country.

Contractor (also called **independent contractor**; see also **employee**)   One who undertakes a contract to provide a service to the specific plans or terms of the contract – that is, construct a building, repair a motor car and so on.

The terms and conditions of the relationship between the parties must be expressly stated.

A contractor is not a contractor when he or she is an individual whose conditions of work are laid down and enforced by an employer without the right, responsibility or authority to determine how, where and under what terms the job is to be performed. Such an individual is an employee who is entitled to all the rights and privileges and responsibilities of other employees.

Customary practice   A well-known voluntary tradition in industrial relations. Most of the accepted norms in industrial relations today have resulted from practices that became custom with the passage of time. Consequently, all changes in custom or practice must (1) be properly recorded in minutes for future reference; and (2) explain the circumstances that led to the introduction of the practice or its change.

C

A periodic review of such customs and practices must be undertaken to ensure current application. These reviews may take place prior to the renewal of the collective agreement or changes in policies, rules and regulations.

It is important to note that although most of these practices may be informal and unwritten, they are often held to be as binding as any clause in a collective agreement or rules and procedures, and as such a breach by any party may be interpreted as a breach of the contract of employment.

Case: Industrial Action Arising Out of Interpretation of Rules and Regulations

The Johnson Hotel has been operating for thirty years in Jamaica's south-west. One of the rules of the organization is that employees are required to enter the premises through a wooden door located adjacent to the kitchen. Employees are also required to leave by that same door. The staff locker room is located near to a side entrance adjacent to the main dining room of the hotel. Over the years, all members of staff, including managers, entered the premises through the side entrance and not through the wooden door designated for this purpose.

A new manager, on joining the company, immediately reinforced the rule requiring all members of staff to enter through the wooden door next to the kitchen. In addition, he had that door painted black as part of an overall facelift of the premises. The members of staff immediately took industrial action on grounds that the new manager, Mr Johnstone, was discriminating against them by:

1. painting the door black; and
2. forcing them to enter by this "back door", as they referred to the staff entrance, instead of the customary side door which was closer to their lockers.

Questions of racial prejudice (Mr Johnstone was a white American), victimization, abuse of the rights of staff and repressive management tactics were all discussed at the various meetings between the union representing the hotel staff and the management of the hotel. Eventually, Mr Johnstone resigned his job in disgust, claiming that he was merely enforcing a rule that had always been in existence and was never rescinded and that the union was discriminating against him.

The union claimed that the staff complaint was based on a deviation from the custom and practice: although the staff entrance was so designated some time ago, the practice of the staff had been to use the side entrance.

C

Members of management had also condoned and supported this practice by using the same side entrance for entering and leaving the premises over the years.

The hotel abandoned the use of the disputed staff entrance and permitted the staff to use the side entrance, as had become their custom and practice.

Comment: The above example resulted from a situation whereby custom and practice superseded established rules and regulations. A meeting between the parties prior to the re-enforcement of the rules and regulations might have enhanced the probability for an amicable agreement to implement the change of staff entrance.

D

Decision making The continuous function of choosing between several courses of action. A decision is a conclusion or settlement of a matter. Good decision-making skills are a function of training and experience. Here are a few guidelines on making good, snap decisions:

- Know that you might "blow it"
- Know that you can change your mind
- Don't get hung up on fact finding
- Break out of your usual thought patterns
- Respect your hunches
- Check your values
- Ask around
- Then ask the experts
- Go on a solution search
- Calculate your risk extremes
- Let someone else decide
- Refuse to decide
- Know when to slow down and proceed with caution

Note: The origin of these guidelines is unknown, but the tips are helpful. Irrespective of the strategies used, making a decision is a critical function of business success.

Delegate, union The terms *union delegate, shop steward* (in Europe) and *union steward* (elsewhere) mean the same thing. The delegate is the worker selected by union members as their representative on the shop floor. The union delegate must be a union member in good standing to effectively represent the interest of the union and its members. The delegate performs some or all of the following functions:

1. Recruiting new union members
2. Raising and handling issues between the shop floor and full-time union officials

D

3. Negotiating with management on most of the day-to-day issues on the shop floor
4. Sitting as participant in the union's negotiating team

Time off for union delegates: A reasonable amount of time off with pay must be given to a union delegate to attend union meetings and to handle union business during working hours. This is a discretionary management decision.

Study time: From time to time the union may request permission for a delegate to attend a course of study. Such time off is granted at the manager's discretion, but permission should not be unreasonably withheld.

Points to Note

1. It is the union's obligation to advise the company, in writing, whenever a delegate has been elected or is changed.
2. If the union fails to do this, such recognition must be established at the first meeting arranged between the union and management.
3. Where there are several delegates in the plant, the union usually appoints a chief delegate as the senior shop-floor representative.
4. It is imperative that an atmosphere of cooperation, mutual trust, respect and understanding be developed as a condition of good industrial relations. By the very nature of their respective functions, a supervisor and a delegate are bound to be on opposite sides of many issues. They are not expected to co-manage. Nevertheless, cooperation and understanding must be the hallmark of their peaceful coexistence on the shop floor.

Disciplinary action   Action taken, usually against an employee, arising out of a breach of rules, regulations or accepted standards of conduct or behaviour. Every manager would like to exercise the right of disciplinary action without the inevitable objection from the union. However, the union is the employee's representative and it has the responsibility of ensuring that any action taken is fair and just. Sometimes fear of reprisal is in direct proportion to the degree of uncertainty surrounding the circumstances that led to the disciplinary action being taken.

It follows, therefore, that disciplinary action should be taken using certain clear guidelines:

D

1. Objectivity in analysing the facts and arriving at the decision
2. Thoroughness in conducting an investigation into the circumstances of the case
3. Careful consideration of all circumstances
4. Consultation with others more knowledgeable or informed on the issue
5. Proper documentation of the case (corroborated statements and copies must be sent to the union)

Disciplinary action against a worker may be oral or written and may be in the form of a warning, suspension or termination, depending on the severity of the offence and as guided by a grievance schedule or the collective agreement. Copies of all correspondence on disciplinary action involving unionized workers should be sent to the appropriate union officer. (See Sample Disciplinary Code, Appendix J.)

Some Legal Principles on Disciplinary Action

1. When an employee has been accused of committing a criminal offence, guilt beyond reasonable doubt does not have to be established before a disciplinary decision can be taken and implemented. However, the rules of "natural justice" may be adhered to by the employer and accordingly:
   (a) The employee should be advised of the nature of the offence which he or she has allegedly committed.
   (b) The employee, having been so advised, should be given an opportunity to defend himself.
   (c) Any decisions taken in connection with the above should be the result of an impartial and fair hearing.
2. The test when deciding whether or not an employer was justified in terminating an employee for gross misconduct is whether or not the employer:
   (a) Carried out reasonable investigation into the matter as outlined in 1(a) to (c) above.
   (b) Having undertaken these steps, still "entertained a reasonable suspicion amounting to a belief in the guilt of the employee of that misconduct at the time" (Mr Justice Arnold, 1980, *British Home Stores v. Burchell*).
3. An employee who has been dismissed before his criminal case comes up for trial has no grounds for claiming reinstatement

D

once he or she is acquitted. The reason for this is the difference between the tests to decide guilt in criminal proceedings versus reasonable suspicion in disciplinary and arbitration proceedings.

Points to Note

1. Management has the right to direct and control the activities of its workers during working hours. Management must therefore exercise its right to discipline workers.
2. Peace and order must be maintained at the workplace.
3. A worker must not be disciplined on the grounds of union membership, race, colour, creed, sex or national origin – although management may discipline a worker for a misdemeanour committed as a result of any one of these factors.
4. A disciplinary code (see Appendix J) guides decisions that may be taken in the event of the commission of certain misdemeanours. However, it must not be followed slavishly in exercising disciplinary control or taking action; good sense and objective judgement must prevail.

Dismissal for cause   An employee's services with an enterprise may be terminated on the basis of "cause". Causal dismissal may vary from the committing of an offence to a loss of trust and confidence in the worker's ability to perform the job.

The Employment (Termination and Redundancy Payments) Act (1995) of Jamaica vests the employer with the right, as he or she had before the passage of this act, to dismiss an employee without notice for misconduct or "cause". Examples of such misconduct or cause include the following:

1. Insubordination or wilful disobedience in carrying out a reasonable order under a contract of employment
2. Breach of confidence in disclosing trade or other secrets
3. Impaired capability or non-performance as a result of drunkenness or use of drugs (not medically prescribed)
4. Failure to display a reasonable degree of competence in the skill professed

However, the right to summarily dismiss an employee must be exercised within four weeks of the employer becoming aware of the worker's misconduct or failings which justifies termination. Failure by the employer to dismiss within the period will entitle the worker to be given payment in lieu of notice.

D

Points to Note

1. All statements of cause must be corroborated.
2. All entitlements due to the worker up to the time of dismissal must be paid at the time of separation.

Dismissal, constructive   Normally it is the employer who has the authority to decide to and actually dismiss employees, for whatever reason. However, constructive dismissal may occur whereby the employee initiates a claim for such. G.D. Green (1987, 253) explains it as follows:

> In certain circumstances an employee can serve notice to leave and then claim constructive dismissal. The grounds for doing this are that the employee was no longer able to continue working for the employer under the prevailing circumstances. This may be due to victimization, harassment, being overlooked for promotion, the employer not fulfilling promises made, etc. If the employer's conduct shows that they no longer intend to be bound by an essential term in the contract, then the employee has grounds for giving notice, leaving and claiming unfair dismissal. The procedure followed is then the same as for a normal claim for unfair dismissal.

From a Caribbean perspective, constructive dismissal opens up a new and broader horizon in industrial relations for the practitioner, employer and employee alike, as well as the whole traditional process of disciplining.

Case: Dismissal of Workers Based on Allegations of Involvement in Theft of Goods

Two workers, Wilson and Adams, were dismissed by Associate Importers Limited when the company was informed by the police that these two men were suspected of being part of a gang that stole a ton of wheat from the company's warehouse.

D

Wilson was sent a letter from the company stating, "in view of your 'involvement' in an illegal act, the company has decided to terminate your services". Adams, on the other hand, was given a differently worded letter stating, "in view of your participation in an illegal act, the company has lost all trust and confidence in your ability to perform your job as a delivery clerk and is, therefore, terminating your services with immediate effect".

The police charged both men and the matter was taken to court. Several witnesses failed to show up to give evidence at the trial and as a result the matter was dismissed by the courts.

In the meantime, twelve months had elapsed during which both employees were off their jobs.

Upon the dismissal of the case by the courts the union immediately sought full reinstatement of both workers without loss of pay. The company responded by saying that they were both guilty of a breach of contract and, consequently, there were no grounds for reinstatement.

The matter was referred to the conciliatory machinery of the Ministry of Labour and both sides decided to maintain their original positions on the issue.

The matter remained unresolved until the parties came to a compromise in the form of a financial settlement, which concluded the matter.

In spite of the settlement, the company still felt that its decision was justified.

Comment: In this matter, a decision to terminate the services of the workers should not have been based on conviction for an illegal act or allegations of the commission of an illegal act, but instead, on the loss of trust and confidence in the individual in the performance of his or her job. This would have warranted dismissal for cause. Furthermore, the wording of both letters of dismissal should not have differed, particularly in terms of reasons stated for dismissal. Whenever employees are being dismissed from their jobs for the same reason, and on similar grounds, their letters of dismissal should be explicit and consistent.

Dismissal Notices

In many respects, managers write dismissal notices without taking into account the implications of these notices and whether or not such notices can be justified under close scrutiny or when challenged legally. Due care and attention must be exercised in handling dismissals. This is one of the most testing and serious management decisions.

Case: Dismissal – Involvement in an Illegal Matter

D

Feeds of Jamaica dismissed a delivery clerk on the grounds that he was on duty at the time when a truckload of fertilizer was removed from the premises through the delivery gate without permission.

The letter read:

Dear Mr Jonathon:

We wish to advise you that we have decided to terminate your services with immediate effect for being involved in the illegal removal from the premises of a certain quantity of fertilizer on 20th August.

Signed: _____.
                    Management

The police, following a statement from a known felon that he was an accomplice to the removal of a quantity of fertilizer from the company's premises, arrested Jonathon, the delivery clerk involved.

The matter was sent to the courts and was dismissed by the magistrate when the arresting officer failed to show up to give evidence. A period of one year had elapsed between Jonathon's dismissal and the trial. When the courts dismissed the matter, Jonathon immediately applied to the company through his union for immediate reinstatement without loss of pay for the time he was off the job.

The company refused to acknowledge his claim for reinstatement on the grounds that it had lost faith and trust in Jonathon's ability to perform his job and for gross neglect in discharging his duties. The union argued that Jonathon was dismissed not for "loss of trust and confidence" but, rather, for his involvement in an illegal act, and that because the court had dismissed the matter, the company no longer had any justifiable grounds for dismissal.

The company argued that this may have been so, but there were certain legal principles involved whereby, "when deciding whether or not an employer was justified in terminating an employee for gross misconduct, the true test is whether or not the employer entertained a reasonable suspicion amounting to a belief in the guilt of that employee of that misconduct" (attorney's opinion).

The matter was referred to the Ministry of Labour after all attempts to settle at the local level had failed. The Ministry of Labour conciliated the matter but no settlement was reached. The parties agreed, however, to settle the matter "out of court" with a financial settlement to Jonathon amounting to a sum equal to his redundancy pay entitlement as specified by the existing formula in the collective agreement.

D

Comment: Jonathon's dismissal should have been handled in a more positive and conclusive manner. In its submission to the courts, the company had no witnesses to support any claim that Jonathon either knew about the stolen fertilizer or that he was involved in its wrongful removal from the premises. Consequently, the company issued a letter of dismissal based on the statement of a doubtful source that Jonathon was guilty of an illegal act, and not on the grounds of loss of trust and confidence in him as someone occupying a position of trust and responsibility – that is, a delivery clerk. Furthermore, Jonathon's supervisor was not disciplined for neglect in the performance of his duties.

No discussion took place between the company and the union in respect of the company's decision. The company seemed to have been persuaded by its lawyer that Jonathon's arrest for complicity in the matter was sufficient evidence to dismiss him on the grounds that he had allegedly committed an illegal act.

It is of paramount importance that managers take every precaution to clearly define the reasons for dismissal. An act of dismissal should take place only after thorough and careful investigation of the circumstances involved. All cases involving unionized workers must be communicated to the relevant union officer as soon as possible after the action has been taken. In a non-unionized undertaking, consultation and fair play must guide managers in resolving all issues of discipline.

Dismissal, wrongful   A term used to describe the unjustifiable dismissal of an employee. If wrongful dismissal is proved through negotiations or awarded by arbitration, the worker must be reinstated from the effective date of dismissal without loss of pay or related benefits to which the worker would normally have been entitled. These do not include incremental and discretionary benefits such as overtime pay or premiums paid for productive time.

Dispute, labour (see also **industrial dispute**)   According to the International Conference of Labour Statisticians, "a labour dispute is a state of disagreement over a particular issue or group of issues over which there is conflict between workers and employers, or about which grievance is expressed by workers or employers, or about which workers or employers support other workers or employers in their demands or grievances" (ILO 1997).

D

Dispute resolution   The term could address the processes leading to, or, the actual cessation or conclusion of a dispute.

Dispute resolution, alternative (ADR)   Generally refers to any and all means of settling disputes outside the judicial process or courtroom. ADR procedures were originally largely related to settling disputes relating to commercial transactions. However, its appeal has expanded its application to much wider scenarios, particularly because of lengthy delays in the court systems and the high costs of litigation. The Honourable Justice Lensley H. Wolfe, OJ, chief justice of Jamaica, is eloquent on this point, stating:

> Society has, over the years, become more litigious. The increased amount of litigation has resulted in a clogging of the justice system. It has therefore become necessary to employ alternative methods of resolving disputes with a view to disposing of matters more expeditiously. One such method is arbitration. Arbitration provides a credible and readily accessible alternative to dispute resolution in courts. This method is in fact being increasingly utilized on a global basis. (2001, xiii)

Aside from arbitration, other forms of ADR available include non-binding arbitration, mediation, conciliation, mini-trial and short-hearing rules.

The field of industrial relations has certainly bought into alternative disputes resolution procedures and techniques. The conciliation and arbitration facilities within ministries of labour are examples of ADR at work, seeking to avoid disputes escalating to the point of the court system. Indeed, the industrial relations system of Barbados retains the conciliation format for ultimate resolution instead of the industrial relations court systems of Antigua and Barbuda, Jamaica, and Trinidad and Tobago.

The Dispute Resolution Foundation of Jamaica is one such body which seeks to resolve disputes before they escalate to violence or legal mechanisms. Stoppi (2001, xvii) outlines the advantages of arbitration over litigation as follows:

- There is less formality than in the courts.
- The arbitration award is final. There is no appeal (except in exceptional cases) as there is in the courts, always provided no "special case" is to be stated.

D

- The time and place of hearing can be fixed to suit the convenience of the parties.
- Disputes are settled by experienced technical people of integrity who understand the complexity of problems presented to them for adjudication.
- It is quicker than the present legal process of litigation.
- It may be less expensive.
- It is private.

Double jeopardy   Double jeopardy means punishing an employee twice for the same offence. An employee should not, for example, be suspended twice without pay for the same offence. Suspension may, however, precede dismissal for an offence provided that it is expressly understood that such suspension without pay is an interim disciplinary measure pending further investigations into the matter, which may or may not lead to dismissal.

E

Education in industrial relations   The field of industrial relations is now
very well established. Most leading universities currently offer training
in it as a fully fledged discipline, leading to certificates and degrees to
doctoral level. Other programmes of study, particularly in management
or, more specifically, human resource management, offer industrial relations as a component.

Less formal training in industrial relations is conducted through sem-
inars and workshops, locally and abroad. However, whether or not one
received academic introduction to industrial relations, one of the best
ways of learning it is through on-the-job training and experience.

Employee assistance programmes   These are employer-initiated and
administered programmes to assist employees to overcome personal and
work-related problems. These programmes have two underlying bases.
First, as management becomes more humanistic and concerned for the
welfare of employees, more and more resources and facilities are made
available for the personal maintenance and development of employees.

Second, as it becomes increasingly apparent that employee wellness
and motivation affect the bottom line of businesses and the realization of
overall objectives, enterprises are assessing and countering the effects of
absenteeism, lateness for work, malingering on the job, procrastination,
employee friction, on-the-job accidents and general downtime as possible
main causes or symptoms of these.

Some employee assistance programmes extend beyond the employee
to the employee's family. The programmes are broadly counselling and
advisory and are entirely voluntary, both for the employee or his or her
family. However, some programmes go beyond providing advice and
counselling by providing material assistance, as required, feasible and
practicable.

Employee assistance programmes, in their organization and operation,
must inspire confidence and confidentiality. They must be structured and
operated on an extremely professional basis, especially in respect to the
quality of the counselling of personnel and the use and management of
information.

Because of their growth in importance, employers the world over are now fashioning complete corporate employee wellness programmes. Research by the Interlock Employee Assistance Program of Queensland, Australia, indicates two broad categories of issues presented at counselling sessions with employees. The categories are *personal issues* (accounting for 80 to 85 per cent of all issues presented at the sessions) and *work-related issues* (15 to 20 per cent) (Interlock 2005).

Interlock breaks out the issues and sub-issues as follows:

PERSONAL ISSUES

Presenting Issue Group	Types of Issues
Alcohol and Drug	Alcohol dependency syndrome
	Alcohol related with no dependency
	Smoking and tobacco
	Other drug addictions
	Other drug related with no dependency
Emotional	Anxiety and depression
	Non-work related stress
	Loss or grief
	Suicidal thoughts and behaviours
	Post trauma stress reactions
Family and Relationships	Family issues
	Marital and de facto relationships
	Gay and lesbian issues
Financial	Financial problems
	Gambling issues
Health	Medical and health problems
	Psychological disorders
Legal	Legal advice information service
Interpersonal	Social skills deficit
	Loneliness
	Self-esteem

WORK-RELATED ISSUES

Presenting Issues Group	Type of Issues
Administrative	Difficulties with personnel-related matters
Equal Employment	Discrimination and all other EEO issues
Opportunity Environment	Physical environment
	Shift work
	Overload/underload

E

Harassment	Threats
	Misuse of power
Interpersonal Conflicts	Conflicts with managers and supervisors
	Conflicts with peers and other staff
Performance	Productivity
	Absenteeism
	Accidents
	Behavioural issues
Stress	Severe stress reaction related to work
Vocational	Vocational choice
	Job satisfaction
Retirement or Redundancy	Choice
	Acceptance
	Career issues

Severance package: Compensation given to an employee upon termination in an attempt to prevent financial hardship until other employment can be obtained.

Employee (see also **contractor** and **vicarious liability**)   An employee is employed under a "contract of service" as opposed to a "contract for services" which pertains to the contract of an independent person. Tests attempting to accurately define who is really an employee have been changing over the years. In the judicial decision of *Short v. J.W. Hederson Limited* (1946), Lord Thankerton stated that there were four indications of a contract of service:

1. The master's (employer's) power of selection of his servant (employee)
2. The payment of wages, or other remuneration
3. The master's right to control the method of doing work
4. The master's right of suspension or dismissal

It has been felt that the above is not a conclusive test in itself. Lord Justice Denning's famous statement in the case of *Stevenson, Jordan and Harrison Limited v. Macdonald* (1952) is a more helpful guideline in establishing what constitutes a contract of service:

It is often easy to recognize a contract of service when you see it, but difficult to say wherein the difference lies. A ship's master, a

E

chauffeur and a reporter on the staff of a newspaper are all employed under contract of service, but a ship's pilot, a taxi man and a newspaper contributor are employed under a contract for services. One feature, which seems to run through the instances, is that under a contract of service, a man is employed as part of a business and his work is done as an integral part of the business; whereas under a contract for services, his work although done for the business is not integrated into it but is only accessory to it.

It would follow that an employer would have disciplinary control over the conduct of his or her employee, but not over conduct of an independent contractor.

A more exhaustive discussion on who constitutes an employee was stated by Justice MacKenna in the case *Ready Mix Concrete (South East) Limited v. Minister of Pensions and National Insurance (United Kingdom)*. He felt that a contract of service exists where

1. the servant agrees that, in consideration of wage or other remuneration he will provide his own work and skill in the performance of some service for his master;
2. he agrees expressly or impliedly that in the performance of that service he will be subject to the other's control in a sufficient degree to make that other, master; and
3. the other provisions of the contract are consistent with it being a contract of service.

Many believe that a more complete and general test does not exist than the above.

Employers' associations   Workers have trade unions; employers have associations. Employers' associations are groups of employers formed to regulate and control relationships between employers and unions, between government and employers and between employers and employees. In Jamaica, several employers' associations are registered as trade unions. The Shipping Association of Jamaica, the Gasoline Retailers Association, the Master Builders Association, the Jamaica Employers' Federation and the Jamaica Farmers Union are some of them.

E

Employers' federation/confederation/organizations   Employers have
formed organizations and associations at both the local and international
levels, partly to counter the effectiveness of their industrial relations coun-
terpart, the trade unions, and partly to be more effective in providing
assistance and general service to their member organizations and companies. The Barbados Employers' Confederation, the Jamaica Employers'
Federation and the Trinidad and Tobago Employers' Consultative Association are three of the more active employer organizations in the English-
speaking Caribbean. A brief summary of their origin and purpose follows.

Barbados Employers' Confederation

The Barbados Employers' Confederation was formed on 31 July 1956. It was
registered as a trade union with a voluntary membership. At the time of its
establishment, the confederation consisted of five member companies and
six officers. In the past, the confederation dealt mainly with labour-related
matters (for example, rates of pay and conditions of employment and labour
legislation). Today, the range of activities developed by the confederation
has expanded to training, management training, statistical managerial
advice and other social affairs. The government, the trade unions and international institutions recognize the confederation as the most representative
of employers in Barbados dealing with industrial relations matters.

Functions

The confederation provides members with the following services:

- Advisory and negotiation services in collective bargaining – the
  range of these services covers consultation and advice on the formulation of offers of substantive terms and conditions of employment negotiating procedures, strategies and tactics, leadership
  during negotiations, research and preparations of relevant case
  material, formalization of records and documentation of agreements reached, including the drafting of collective agreements
- Technical advisory services, built upon members' request for
  advice, guidance and information on questions relating to
  employment legislation, personnel policies and procedures, and
  good industrial relations practice
- Advice and direct assistance in the settlement of employee-
  grievances and collective disputes involving employer/employee
  rights under collective bargaining agreements

E

- Organizing and delivering training courses on personnel management practices, industrial relations and related matters
- Publication of a newsletter containing information on organizational activities, developments in collective bargaining (especially changes in wages and conditions of employment), new labour legislation and other topical information on industrial relations matters which should be of interest to employers (for example, developments in collective bargaining, employment standards, inflation, employment legislation and judicial decisions in the field of labour law in the Caribbean region and elsewhere in the world)
- Representation on government bodies and committees dealing with labour and social questions and at the regional and international levels

The confederation is represented on many boards and committees at the national level related to economic policy and international relations; education, training and employment; occupational safety, health and environment; social security and welfare; conditions of employment; and the private sector agency (which groups all the private sector organizations of employers in Barbados).

Affiliations

The Barbados Employers' Confederation is affiliated to the International Organisation of Employers (IOE) and to the Caribbean Employers' Confederation and represents all Barbadian employers in the activities of the International Labour Organization (ILO). For further details visit http://www.barbadosemployers.com

Jamaica Employers' Federation

A trade union of employers established in 1958 to "protect and advance the interests of employers in all matters affecting relations between employers and the government".

With the growth of the trade union movement it was felt necessary for employers to organize themselves into an association to safeguard and promote their interests in all matters affecting relations between employers and employees. Listed among its objects are the following:

E

- To provide its membership with information as to policies, conditions, rates of wages and general and specific practices in the fields of employment and industrial relations
- To facilitate, promote and provide for joint consultation between members
- To represent employers on various bodies locally and overseas

The objects have broadened with the passage of time and its mission statement could be summed up as follows: "to actively advance the interests of employers in their relations with employees and other stock holders through the provision of a range of professional services geared towards the development of human resources and fostering of industrial peace".

Jamaica Employers' Federation is a member of the IOE and of the Caribbean Employers' Confederation. It represents all Jamaican employers in ILO activities (see http://www.ioe.org). For more details visit http://www.jamaicaemployers.com.

The Employers' Consultative Association of Trinidad and Tobago

The Employers' Consultative Association (ECA) was established on 17 December 1959 and was set up originally to enable employers to match the strength of the trade union organizations, which had grown into well-organized, powerful institutions since their early stirrings in the 1950s.

Employers in Trinidad and Tobago had traditionally been represented by other organizations more directly concerned with special interests (for example, the Wholesale/Retail Provision Dealers' Association, the Chamber of Commerce and the Shipping Association). At the time, however, there was no single employers' association possessing the expertise, the knowledge or the responsibility for industrial relations for all employers.

Since its establishment in 1959, the association has devoted itself to facilitating smooth labour relations by representing employers at the national and international levels, assisting national legislation and the government's formulation of policy as a tripartite member, arbitrating pending labour disputes, modernizing human resources management and providing information and training programmes. The association has thereby become the first organization on industrial relations matters in the country and is recognized by the government as the national employers' representative.

E

Functions

- Research and publications. The provision of information is central to all ECA's activities. The research section of the ECA provides information on request to members on wages and conditions of work and labour legislation. Information is also provided via publications such as
  - summaries of collective agreements
  - summaries of industrial court judgements
  - summaries of seminar proceedings
- Industrial relations consultancy service and representation at industrial court and collective bargaining negotiations
- Training programmes to members on various subjects
- Environment; occupational health and safety. Since the 1980s the environment has been part of the ECA's mandate. The ECA's director in 1991 was appointed Environmental Focal Point for the Caribbean region.
- Representing employers' interests at the following national boards and committees: Minimum Wages Board; National Emergency Management Agency; National Insurance Appeals Tribunal; National Insurance Board; National Training Board; Pesticides and Toxic Chemicals Control Board; Registration, Recognition and Certification Board; Standing Tripartite Committee on Economic Matters; and Standing Tripartite Committee on Labour Matters

Affiliations

ECA is a member of the IOE and of the Caribbean Employers' Confederation. It represents Trinidad and Tobago employers in ILO activities. For more details visit http://www.wow.net/community/eca.

The more broad-based employers' affiliations, of which Caribbean associations are a part, are the Caribbean Employers' Confederation and the International Organisation of Employers.

The International Organisation of Employers: Since its creation in 1920 the International Organisation of Employers (IOE) has been recognized as the only organization at the international level that represents the interests of business in the labour and social policy fields. Today, it consists of 139 national employer organizations drawn from 134 countries from all over the world.

The mission of the IOE is to promote and defend the interests of employers in international fora, particularly in the ILO, and to this end it works to ensure that international labour and social policy promotes the viability of enterprises and creates an environment favourable to enterprise development and job creation. At the same time, it acts as the secretariat to the Employers' Group at the ILO International Labour Conference, the ILO governing body and all other ILO-related meetings.

In order to ensure that the voice of business is heard at the international and national level, the IOE is actively engaged in the creation and capacity building of representative organizations of employers, particularly in both the developing world and those countries in transition to the market economy.

The IOE is the permanent liaison body for the exchange of information, views and experience among employers throughout the world. It acts as the recognized channel for the communication and promotion of the employer's point of view to all United Nations agencies and other international organizations (http://www.ioe-emp.org).

Caribbean Employers' Confederation: For details, visit http://www.cec.com.

Employee share-ownership plan (ESOP)   Employee share-ownership or stock option plans are legal trusts in which blocks of a company's shares are placed for ownership by its employees. There are specific rules of management, distribution, financing and resale of these shares by employees, which are designed to ensure the integrity of the block of shares as the property of the current set of employees.

ESOPs are used for various purposes. They may be used as deferred or retirement income, a form of pension or they could be used by companies having cash-flow problems as payment in lieu of negotiated increases in pay. ESOPs can also be genuine attempts by companies to have employees participate in the ownership of the enterprise.

ESOPs should be distinguished from special share options offered by companies to select groups of employees annually or other regularities. The real difference is in the manner of financing and management of the shares. A board of trustees and proper financing must direct ESOPs and a disposal plan be put in place for the shares in the trust.

The Government of Jamaica, on 1 April 1995, passed into law the Employee Share Ownership Plan Act (the Act). The act provides the opportunity for greater participation of workers in management and ownership of economic enterprises.

E

Employment   The 1982 international definition of employment (ILO) suggested that the *employed*

comprise all persons above the age specified for measuring the economically active population, who during a specified brief period (one week or one day), *usually referred to as the survey week/day or reference period*, were in the following categories:

- *Paid employment* (1) "at work": persons who, during the reference period, performed some work for wage or salary, in cash or in kind; (2) "with a job but not at work": persons who, having already worked in their present job, were temporarily not at work during the reference period but had a formal attachment to their job;
- *Self-employment* (1) "at work": persons who, during the reference period, performed some work for profit or family gain, in cash or in kind; (2) "with an enterprise but not at work": persons with an enterprise, which may be a business enterprise, a farm or a service undertaking, who were temporarily not at work during the reference period for some specific reason. (Hussmanns, Mehran and Verma 1990; emphasis added)

Enquiry, boards and commissions of   In Jamaica, "the Minster of Labour has powers under the Labour Relations and Industrial Disputes Act, 1975, to set up a board of Enquiry to enquire into any industrial dispute relating to economic conditions in Jamaica" (Kirkaldy 1979, 47).

A board of enquiry is empowered to enquire into a matter and make recommendations to the minister. A board may consist of a sole enquirer or a panel of enquirers comprising such members as the minister may think fit. The recommendations are not binding except in circumstances where parties expressly accept this as a prior condition in the spirit of good industrial relations practice.

Similar powers exist for the appointment of a commission of enquiry. The presentation of witnesses and records may be demanded by enquirers to assist in their deliberations.

Boards and commissions of inquiry should state their findings comprehensively, and by so doing set guidelines to assist the parties in improving the quality of industrial relations practice.

Enquiries must be impartial, and the boards' findings and recommendations must reflect this impartiality. To do otherwise is to corrupt the important role of an enquiry and forever damage the image and credibility of enquiries into labour matters.

E

Enthusiasm, loss of   This term was introduced into industrial relations by airline pilots of the British West Indian Airways (BWIA or commonly called BWEE) to describe their feelings towards their employer during a dispute in 1978.

Loss of enthusiasm by employees is thus interpreted as a work-to-rule form of protest, which disturbs the normal workflow.

Essential services   The Labour Relations and Industrial Disputes Act, 1975, of Jamaica, empowers the pertinent minister to prohibit industrial action in disputes wherein an "essential service" is involved. What service constitutes an "essential service" is set out in the first schedule of the act as being the following services:

A. Water services
   Electricity services
   Health services
   Sanitary services
   Public passenger transportation services
   Fire fighting services
   Correctional services
   Overseas telecommunication services
   Telephone services

B. Services connected with
   1. loading and unloading of ships;
   2. the storage and delivery of goods at or from docks, wharves, operation in connection with docks and wharves; and
   3. oil refining and the loading, distribution, transportation or retailing of petroleum fuel for engines or motor vehicles or aircraft.

E

C. Any business whose main functions consist of
  1. the issue and redemption of currency;
  2. the issue and redemption of government securities and the trading in such securities;
  3. management of the official reserves of the country;
  4. administration of exchange control;
  5. providing banking services to the government;
  6. air transport services for the carriage of passengers, baggage, mail or cargo destined to or from Jamaica; or
  7. civil aviation services.

F

Factories act   See **safety at work.**

Fair play   A philosophy and practice in management, industrial relations and trade relations that accords equitable treatment to all parties involved. The rights and interests of others – indeed, of all parties – are respected and taken into consideration in making decisions and imposing discipline.

Good industrial relations practice demands fairness in the treatment of individuals or groups having differences, conflicts or disputes. Different interests or parties to conflict or potential conflict always pay attention to the outcomes experienced by each other in an effort to assess the fairness of not only the outcomes but also the procedures that give rise to these outcomes (hence the related terms of procedural justice, also called natural justice, and interactional justice).

Procedural justice refers to the fairness of the methods and systems used to arrive at a resolve or outcome, while interactional justice speaks to the manner in which the outcome is implemented, ensuring privacy, sensitivity, respect and so on.

Fighting, on the job   This is physical exchange of a violent nature between two or more employees causing, or intending to cause, bodily harm to each other. The disciplinary action for this misdemeanour is summary dismissal in most cases.

Before taking action, however, circumstances must be thoroughly investigated – witnesses summoned, statements recorded, corroborated, and discussed and placed on personal/individual files.

Summary dismissal in this case means dismissal without notice or without payment in lieu of notice, but other monies earned must be paid: for example, unused vacation leave time actually worked, pension contributions (refund) and so on.

In cases where provocation was the primary cause, the victim may be treated less harshly than the provocateur. Mitigating circumstances must not be ignored. It is important to bear in mind that the matter at hand is an industrial relations issue and there can be no hard and fast rules in applying justice and fair play.

F

Fighting, off the Job

If the worker was, at the time of the fight, acting as an agent of the company, for example, as an outdoor salesman or deliveryman, disciplinary action as for fighting on the job will apply. If not, then consideration ought to be given to the effect that such behaviour might have on the company's image and reputation, and action taken to match the degree of the offence.

Arrest and Detention

When the police have been involved and the individual detained, another issue – breach of contract – is raised, if the individual, as a result of detention, is absent without permission for a period of a few days. Here again the punishment must fit the crime. If absence is prolonged the individual may be disciplined for committing a breach of contract through absence without permission, abandonment of job or dereliction of duty.

Case: Hollywell Company Limited – Dismissal

Hollywell Company operates a public warehouse. The company employs about twenty warehouse men who load, off-load and stack cargo in the warehouse. Two of them were engaged in a fight and the company dismissed both of them. During its investigation, the company found that Jones, a union delegate, had instigated the fight by threatening bodily harm to Thompson. When Thompson failed to respond to the threat, Jones pushed him and Thompson retaliated, resulting in a violent physical exchange.

Most of the other workers felt that the company's decision to dismiss Thompson was harsh as he was the victim. The company, on the other hand, said that the fight took place between two people and despite the circumstances – with one as instigator and the other as victim – both should be and were dismissed.

Comment: In this matter, the decision to dismiss both men was the right course of action, based on the disciplinary code in force. However, mitigating circumstances proved Thompson to be a victim of circumstances and, consequently, a lesser punishment may have been better for morale in the company. Workers' opinions and mitigating circumstances must be taken into account before making decisions on disciplinary action, and special care must be taken to ensure that the union is informed of all developments throughout the investigation and decision-making stages.

F

Fringe benefits   Those benefits which are paid or granted in excess of normal wages and which may be integral to a wage package are called fringe benefits. Such benefits include membership in health schemes; life insurance schemes; pension schemes and maternity leave benefits; subsistence allowances for meals and travel; housing; education for children; and uniform allowances. In unionized companies many of these benefits are negotiated between the companies and the trade union, and the benefits vary from company to company.

Frolic of his own (see also **vicarious liability**)   An employee is deemed to be responsible for his or her actions that result in damage, loss or injury, where such an employee

1. has wilfully disobeyed the terms of his employment and acted on his or her own; and
2. even though committing such damage, loss or injury during the hours of employment, he or she is still responsible as a result of (1) above.

Where an employee's behaviour is in the manner as described above, he or she is said to be on a frolic of his (or her) own and general principles, such as vicarious liability, will not apply. In such a case, an employee will have to accept the full consequences of this "frolic".

G

Garnishment, wage   Wage garnishment is a legal procedure in which the courts authorize an employer to withhold a proportion of an employee's earnings for debt payment to a creditor or for social and economic obligation such as child support.

The procedure is for the creditor to get the garnishment order from the court, which is then submitted to the employer for action. The garnishment order, "which has the force of law, requires the employer of the debtor to deduct some portion of the debtor's pay and to deliver it to the creditor" (Wallace, Marc and Fay 1988, 138).

Garnishment practices have been a part of the industrial relations landscape of the United States for nearly four decades. The Consumer Credit Protection Act of 1968 provides for the protection of the rights of both the creditor and the employee. "Prior to the passage of the law, some employers simply fired any employees against whom a garnishment order had been obtained" (Wallace, Marc and Fay 1988, 138).

However,

> Title III protects employees from being discharged by their employers because their wages have been garnished for any one debt and limits the amount of employees' earnings that may be garnished in any one week. It does not, however, protect an employee from discharge if the employee's earnings have been subject to garnishment for second or subsequent debts.

> Title III applies to all individuals who receive personal earnings and to their employers. Personal earnings include wages, salaries, commissions, bonuses, and income from a pension or retirement program, but do not ordinarily include tips. (http://www.legal-help-usa.org/wage_garnishment.htm)

Good industrial relations   This relates to the quality of life at work. Good industrial relations are the product of effective communication, acceptable conditions of work, job satisfaction, acceptable levels of productive output and a positive working environment.

G

Go-slow   A go-slow – that is, a deliberate act of slowing down or obstructing production by workers – is interpreted as industrial action and is a breach of the contract of employment.

Guidelines to Follow in the Event of a Go-Slow

1. Record the productive output during the go-slow versus prior production norms.
2. Call in union delegates to notify them that industrial action is in progress and the reason for the action.
3. Advise the union and the Ministry of Labour that the workers have taken industrial action.
4. If life, limbs, machinery, equipment, raw materials or other assets are in danger of injury or damage, lock down the premises to safeguard them.
5. Initiate an early meeting between company and union to settle the grievance that caused the go-slow.
6. Summon the "leaders" to meetings to settle the matter.

Graveyard shift   The term normally used to describe a late-night shift, say, between 10:00 p.m. and 6:00 a.m.

It is assumed that an employee on a graveyard shift sacrifices his or her night-time sleep and social pleasures. Night-time is generally considered to be more taxing on the physical well-being of an employee. Night-time work in certain sectors such as medical services, security, power, light, water, communication, securities trading, is, however, compulsory.

Usually workers on the graveyard shift enjoy a special pay premium indexed to the rate of pay to compensate for working nights.

Grievance   A grievance may be described as any matter that mentally disturbs an employee in his or her place of employment. This grievance may be real or imagined and it may be expressed or silent. Among the symptoms of a grievance are ill temper, moroseness, absenteeism, insubordination, negligence and ultimately a fall in the level of productivity.

A grievance under a collective agreement is an allegation that the contract has been breached, intentionally or otherwise, resulting in an improper interpretation or application.

G

Whereas a negotiated grievance procedure is applicable to the bargaining unit it covers, the procedure should be applied to all employees for reasons of equity and fair play in industrial relations practice. Here are a few suggested steps in handling a grievance:

1. The first step is usually informal, and it allows the supervisor and employee to settle the matter quickly. Failing settlement,
2. The union delegate with the manager or department head takes up the matter. Failing settlement,
3. The union takes up the matter officially with the chief executive officer or the human resources manager. Failing settlement,
4. The matter is referred to the Ministry of Labour (Conciliation). Failing settlement,
5. The minister of labour refers the matter to arbitration.

Where union representation is non-existent, a meeting is called between the management and the aggrieved persons. An independent "friend in court" may participate to provide balance in the proceedings.

Throughout the various steps in the grievance procedure, minutes must be taken of proceedings, witnesses called as necessary, and statements recorded and corroborated.

Handling Grievances

Among the many problems that confront a manager at the workplace is the difficulty in handling grievances.

Many managers, and sometimes union officials, take the view that some grievances are too trivial to warrant immediate action. Perhaps the worker is worrying unduly and needs counselling sessions to identify the source of the grievance and, where possible, to explain the causes that may be at the root of the problem. Such an explanation can lead to a significant reduction in the cause for worry.

Broadly speaking, there are several types of grievances which may be summarized as follows:

1. Those arising out of a collective labour agreement
2. In the absence of an agreement, those grievances arising out of terms and conditions of employment
3. In-house or domestic grievances

Common causes of grievances include the following:

G

- Pay adjustments that either were not done at the appropriate time or, if done, were wrong or appear to have been wrong
- A promotion that occurred prior to fulfilling promotional guidelines, or jealousy over the promotion of a colleague, or the absence of plans for promotions
- Division of labour that may appear to have been arbitrary, resulting in a heavy workload allocation to some whereas others appear to have little work to do
- Any bias or favouritism by a manager resulting in jealousy of the particular worker to whom the bias is being shown
- A manager's attitude in dealing with the workers that may be interpreted as arrogant, officious, rude or derogatory
- Problems in the home that have been transferred to the workplace
- A breakdown in relationships between workers leading to conflict at the workplace
- Sexual harassment
- Broken promises by management
- Manager/employee conflicts in their relationship

Irrespective of the type of grievance or cause of such grievance, it must be handled with decisiveness and speed. The object is to arrest the grievance and to allow every opportunity for employees involved to air their views on the matter.

Every attempt must be made to have an appropriate investigation into the matter and such investigation should be done privately. Adequate notes must be taken during all interviews and these notes should be reread to the employees concerned so that they can be verified. Any action taken in such instances should be prompt and any promise made, kept. Any failure on the part of management to keep a promise should be explained to an employee with reasons given for the failure. In every instance where a manager is incapable of reaching a decision on a matter, he or she should consult others in the organization immediately to obtain appropriate guidelines to assist him or her in decision making.

Usually, failure to communicate with parties involved in a grievance matter and with others whose interests may be affected, such as the trade union official, colleague managers and union delegates, results in a breakdown in the relationship between the management and workers, thereby creating a mushrooming effect, whereby what should have been a simple matter is transformed into a major industrial dispute. Consultation is, therefore, of paramount importance in the handling of all grievances.

Points to Note

1. Good communication is the best preventive measure against grievances. Keep workers informed of what is going on in the organization.
2. Look out for causes of grievances. Honour your agreement; if you cannot do so for any reason, call in the union. Discuss the matter.
3. Be impartial in your delegation of work and in recognizing good performance.
4. Be objective and consistent in handling issues.
5. Constructive changes in work organization are necessary to progress – and they must be explained and discussed prior to implementation.
6. Be diplomatic and show by example that management is an art, which is learnt by practice.

Proper investigation and objective decision making put meaning to the saying that "Justice must not only be done but must manifestly be seen to have been done". Do not guess. Investigate.

Case: Grievance – Fighting on the Job

Shipping Services, Inc., is engaged in the business of providing an agency service to several shipping lines. It employs about twenty workers in various classifications including administrative, sales, marketing, and accounting.

One day the manager of Shipping Services heard a commotion in the office outside his door and on looking out he saw two male workers in a fight. He immediately went out, stopped the fight and escorted both workers to his office, asking each to explain his side of the story.

One worker was a union delegate and a member of the sales staff and the other a member of the accounting staff.

James, the salesman, told the manager that Wilson, the accounting clerk, was provoking him, and after repeated pleas from James for Wilson to stop the provocation he lost his temper and attacked Wilson. Wilson concurred.

The manager fired Wilson for fighting on the job and suspended James for one week, for indiscipline.

Members of staff thought the action by the manager was inequitable and unjust on the grounds that both employees should either have been dismissed or both suspended. The manager took the view that the cause

G

of the fight was provocation and the person responsible, the provocateur, was dismissed. Persistent representation from other workers continued and the manager compromised by paying a gratuity equal to redundancy pay entitlement as a form of compensation to Wilson for not contesting the dismissal while allowing the decision of suspension of James to stand.

Comment: The issues in the above matter may be summarized as follows:

1. A proper investigation of the matter was not undertaken and statements were not collected from witnesses to the incident.
2. Although mitigating circumstances may persuade a manager to mete out two levels of punishment to two workers engaged in the same misdemeanour, ultimately the important consideration is the degree of involvement of both workers in committing the misdemeanour.
3. The payment of severance pay to one worker establishes a precedent for handling future grievances of a similar nature, especially if there is strong representation from the members of the workforce in respect of any decision taken by the manager. This should not be encouraged.
4. Where union delegates, or even past delegates, are involved, immediate consultation between the management and the union is a most desirable course of action to maintain good relations between both parties.

Grievance procedure   An important working condition in all collective agreements is a grievance procedure with an accompanying disciplinary code. These procedures outline certain steps to be taken in the event of a grievance. Usually the steps are as follows:

1. The matter is taken up by the worker with his or her supervisor. Failing settlement,
2. The matter is taken up by the worker and his or her union delegate with the management of the company. Failing settlement,
3. The matter is referred to the conciliation machinery of the Ministry of Labour. Failing settlement,
4. The minister may refer the matter to the next level, in Barbados's case, the prime minister, and in Jamaica's case, the Industrial Disputes Tribunal (IDT) for arbitration.

H

Heads of agreement   A summary of points agreed to during collective bargaining. Statements are brief and factual. This agreement allows for the immediate implementation of agreed upon guidelines of working conditions before the main collective agreement is drawn up.

Points to Note

1. Draw up heads of agreement immediately after completing negotiations.
2. Have heads of agreement signed by both parties before implementing any condition contained in it, unless otherwise agreed.
3. All administrators of the agreement must be issued with a copy after it has been discussed with them.

Upon completion of negotiations, heads of agreement are prepared as a quick summary of the points agreed on to conclude negotiations. However, heads of agreement are merely summaries of the working conditions and they should not be regarded as the full collective agreement. As soon as possible after concluding negotiations, a comprehensive document must be prepared and signed by all parties in order to provide a more complete statement of the conditions of work and a proper guide to both managers and employees on the interpretation and implementation of the collective agreement.

Exhibit: Heads of Agreement

The parties agreed on the following amendments to the existing collective agreements:

1. Duration of Agreement: 16th September, 20__ to 15th September, 20__
2. Subsistence – Office Staff: Subsistence allowance will be paid as follows:
   a. Monday to Friday – $200.00
      (for work between 4:00 p.m. and 7:00 p.m.)
   b. Saturdays, Sundays and Public Holidays – $300.00
      (for work between 9:00 a.m. and 3:00 p.m.)

H

3. Meal and Transportation Allowance: The meal and transportation allowance for the graveyard shift will be as follows:
   Meal – $200.00 per shift
   Transportation – $200.00 per shift
4. Meal Allowance – Consecutive Shifts (Mondays to Fridays):
   That the meal allowance be increased to $250.00.
5. Uniform:
   a. One pair of safety boots will be supplied every two years to those members of the operations staff whose work determines the necessity for safety boots.
   b. Five pairs of trousers will be supplied to each member of staff.
6. Reclassification: An industry-wide job evaluation exercise is currently being undertaken and therefore:
   a. No additional reclassification exercise will be undertaken at this time;
   b. Upon receipt of proposals from the job evaluators, the parties to this contract will meet to discuss and agree on the implementation of the recommendations; and
   c. Arising out of the recommendations of the job evaluation exercise, where parity is demanded between classifications, parity adjustment will be addressed.
   All parity adjustments will be effected no later than the effective date of the succeeding contract, particularly in respect of clerical workers.
7. Redundancy Payments: Travelling allowance will be added to basic salary for computing redundancy payments up to a maximum of 65 weeks' pay.
8. Vacation Leave: No change.
9. Salaries: The following increases to basic salary for computing payments up to a maximum of 65 weeks' pay.
10. Laundry Allowance: This will be increased by $200.00 per week.

The above items represent a full and final settlement of all claims submitted by the union.

SIGNED FOR AND ON   SIGNED FOR AND ON
BEHALF OF (company)   BEHALF OF (union)

Honorarium   A special or honorary payment, usually to professional persons, for services rendered. The circumstances would normally determine the amount and nature of the payment. For instance, a university

H

lecturer or a senior functionary in an establishment may render a service (such as a presentation, conducting research or providing advice on specific issues), but by virtue of their already being employed, or because of the emphasis on the "provision of service", implying a "voluntary" input, an honorarium is paid rather than a fee.

In regular circumstances on the job as well, an honorarium is paid when an officer who is not eligible for overtime rates of pay is assigned duties extraneous to his or her normal duties, and is therefore expected to work in excess of normal hours over an extended period, provided of course that the officer carries out his or her normal duties as well.

Hours at work (working hours)   The period of time during each day when employees are normally expected to work and for which they are paid by the employer, on a straight time basis. Usually, any hours worked outside of this time frame are considered overtime and employees receive a higher premium rate per hour for such periods.

A clause in a collective agreement stipulating hours of work does not guarantee that the employers must provide work. This clause defines the workday and establishes a schedule as one of the conditions of work. Failure to be present during the stipulated hours may result in disciplinary action being taken against the absentee.

This clause may also set out overtime and premium rates for working on weekends and public holidays, depending on the nature of the business.

Provision is also made for lunch breaks, shift work and time off.

I

Incentive schemes   These schemes are intended to index earnings to performance and productivity by providing a monetary outcome or motivation to workers for above normal performance or productivity.

The examples in the exhibit below are just a few of the many schemes in existence. Several publications on the subject of incentive schemes are available in bookshops.

Exhibit: Incentive Schemes

Halsey or Weir System: This is a British system that allows for a time allocation to perform the job and for a proportionate part of the time saved to be paid to the worker. There is, of course, a guaranteed basic time rate. It is usual to pay one half of the time saved in addition to the time taken to do the job.

Example: If time allowed for a job is 100 hours and time taken 80, then time paid for is 90. Thus,

$$Time\ Taken + \frac{Time\ Saved}{2} = 80 + \frac{20}{2} = 90$$

It should be pointed out that the wage cost per unit is reduced as the time taken decreases. Let us say that the time allowance on a job is 20 hours and the rate is $0.50 per hour. If the job is done in 16 hours, the cost will be $9.00; if done in 12 hours, it will be $8.00. The hourly earnings of the worker will, however, increase from $0.552 in the first case to $0.666 in the second.

Scanlon Plan: This is an American plan employed by a number of enterprises where salaries are linked to variation in turnover and the number of employees. It is necessary to establish a conversion factor. This is done by selecting the average sales for a period, dividing this by the number of employees to establish the average sales per employee. The result is the conversion factor. The normal arrangement in this type of plan is for the employees to share on a fifty-fifty basis any increase in turnover.

Example: Let us assume that the average sales for a month were $500,000 and the employees numbered 100. The average sales per employee were

$$\frac{\$500,000}{100} = 5000$$

I

Assuming that the basic wage is $20.00 per week, the conversion factor would then be

$$\frac{20}{500} = 0.04$$

If the sales for the following month rise to $700,000, the increase in sales would be $200,000, and in accordance with the arrangements, $100,000 of this would go to *the employees*. By applying the conversion factor of 0.04 we find that the new salary of the *employee* for that week would be:

Average employee per month × *conversion factor* =

$$\frac{\$(500,000 + 100,000)}{100} \times 0.04 = \$24$$

The Priestman Bonus: This is another British scheme which is used for group plans. It is based on the principle that if a given number of men in a given time under normal conditions are capable of producing so much (referred to as the standard output), then if by greater collective effort the output is increased (with time limit and number employed remaining the same) they should benefit by the same percentage of increase on the standard output (Kirkaldy 1979, 87).

Industrial action   Any action, by an organization or employer or groups of employers, by employees or groups of employees, or by trade unions, which results in a disruption of the production process. Such action may be in the form of a strike by employees, lockout by an employer, or any form of action that disrupts production and is taken in furtherance of an industrial dispute.

In the event of industrial action by workers, you may pursue the following:

1. Talk to the union delegate to find out the reason for the industrial action.
2. Advise the union official and seek a meeting to discuss the matter.
3. Advise the conciliation department of the Ministry of Labour.
4. Document all statements, changes in production schedules, output and reactions of parties.

5. When the meeting has been convened, insist on normality before discussion.
6. Approach the meeting with an open mind.
7. Minute all discussions at the meeting.
8. Leave the meeting with an agreement. At all times try to alleviate tension between the parties.

Industrial dispute   A dispute between one or more workers or organizations (for example, trade unions, staff associations) representing workers and one or more employers or organizations representing employers over an issue or group of issues relating to terms and conditions of employment, disciplinary action against one or more workers or regarding matters relating to rights and privileges of workers. (See Appendix A for notes on the tribunals in Jamaica and Trinidad and Tobago.)

Industrial Disputes Referred to Jamaica's IDT

In the Jamaican context, the minister of labour, under the following conditions, refers a dispute to the Industrial Disputes Tribunal:

1. If the minister is satisfied that attempts were made, without success, to settle the dispute by such other means as were available to the parties; or
2. If, in the minister's opinion, all the circumstances surrounding the dispute constitute such an urgent or exceptional situation that it would be expedient so to do.

The procedures for dealing with an industrial dispute referred for arbitration to the IDT are as follows:

1. The secretary of the IDT advises parties (union or individual versus firm) that the minister of labour has referred a matter with stated terms of reference to it.
2. Parties may be summoned to a preliminary hearing (usually on a mutually agreed date). The hearing is conducted by a panel consisting of a chairman, two other members (usually representing employer and trade union interests), a secretary, and one or two recording stenotypists. Undertakings from both parties are given to supply written briefs within a specified time. Alternatively, the

IDT may, by letter, invite the parties to submit briefs within a specified period. In the event either party cannot prepare a brief by the deadline date, an extension of time must be sought in writing from the IDT.

3. The company or union may wish to be represented at the hearing by an attorney-at-law or consultant. All pertinent facts must be supplied to the representative to ensure accuracy of detail in preparing briefs. Submissions may be elaborated upon verbally at hearings. Written briefs must be concise and accurate.

4. After the briefs have been submitted, the tribunal will schedule a meeting. Opening submissions from the aggrieved side, usually the union, will begin the hearing.

5. Witnesses may be summoned, documents presented and all relevant evidence submitted in support of the case.

6. Upon completion of the hearing, an award is handed down. At least two members of the panel (a simple majority) must sign the award to make it binding.

7. Clarifications of the award may be sought through the chairman of the panel, who may sit alone or with other members, inviting all parties to the sitting. The panel may, in writing but without a sitting, also provide clarification.

8. Awards from the IDT are binding on all parties.

9. IDT awards may be appealed in the Supreme Court on the following grounds:
   a. Breach of law
   b. Insobriety of one or all panellists
   c. Insanity of panellists

10. The Supreme Court's decision on appeal is binding on the parties, but there are provisions for further appeals through the judicial machinery to the Privy Council in the United Kingdom, which is, constitutionally, for the time being, Jamaica's and the Commonwealth Caribbean's highest court of justice.[1]

---

[1] The Caribbean Court of Justice (CCJ) is the proposed regional judicial tribunal to be established by the Agreement Establishing the Caribbean Court of Justice. It has a long gestation period commencing in 1970 when the Jamaican delegation at the sixth Heads of Government Conference, which convened in Jamaica, proposed the establishment of a Caribbean court of appeal in substitution for the judicial committee of the Privy Council (Duke Pollard, Caribbean Community Secretariat, 17 April 2000, http:www.caricom.org/archives/ccj-q&a.htm). The Trinidad-based court held its first hearing in the summer of 2005.

11. An award may be retroactive but it must not precede the date when the dispute first arose. (See Appendix B for a specimen of an IDT award.)

Exhibit: Typical Letter from the IDT Informing Parties of Matters Referred to It

Re: Dispute – XYZ Limited and the National Union

I am advised that the Honourable Minister of Labour has referred to the Industrial Disputes Tribunal for settlement, the dispute between XYZ Limited and the National Union in accordance with section 11A (1)(a) of the Labour Relations and Industrial Disputes Act.

The terms of reference to the tribunal are as follows: "to determine and settle the dispute between XYZ Limited on the one hand and certain unionized workers employed by the company and represented by the National Union on the other hand, over the dismissal of Mr J.K. Public".

I am requesting that the parties submit within nine days of the date of this letter eight copies of a brief outlining the cause of the dispute. As soon as the brief is received a date will be arranged for hearings to commence.

Signed: Secretary
Industrial Disputes Tribunal

Industrial relations   The interaction between people at work, their complex relationships, which are common features of the workplace on a daily basis. Many describe industrial relations as "common sense". Common sense to one person is not necessarily common sense to another. Usually during a strike called by a union, common sense to its members could be considered a flagrant disregard of good taste and logic to the affected employer and his or her shareholders.

Points to Note

1. Industrial relations is about people and their relationships.
2. People must understand industrial relations as an important area of day-to-day practice.
3. Plan systems and procedures for dealing with people.

I

Industrial relations policy   A decision of the board of directors made, on behalf of the management, on industrial relations functions in the company. The policy should reflect the culture of management practice in the company. In some instances involving collective bargaining, there is a strong preference for mandates to be handed down from top management to negotiators who are expected to carry them out. This mandate must allow some degree of flexibility to the negotiator so that there would be no "walking away" from a settlement at a crucial stage of the negotiations.

On the other hand, the approach could be consultative. This implies a more democratic style of management. The consultative approach assumes that the negotiators are allowed more flexibility in arriving at agreements by using their own skills, knowledge, initiative and negotiating style at the bargaining table. Both approaches can work effectively depending on the skill of the negotiators in exercising their functions.

Points to Note

1. The industrial relations policy must be in writing.
2. The policy must be authorized and supported by the chief executive officer.
3. The policy must be consistent in concept and application.
4. The policy must be made known to all personnel.
5. The policy must be structured and applied within the boundaries of the law and guided by custom.
6. The policy should be reviewed periodically and amended as necessary.

The Government of Jamaica issued a Labour Relations Code in 1976 and this is a useful guide to all organizations for the establishment of effective industrial relations policy and practice.

Industrial union (see also **trade union**)   This union organizes its membership from among the workers in a particular industry. Although there are no exclusive industrial unions in Jamaica, some near examples may be the Petrol Service Station Attendants Union, the Electrical and Construction Workers Union and the Jamaica Union of Bank Employees.

Inflation   In its simplest understanding, inflation is a condition of rising prices and devaluing money and the impact on the purchasing power of personal income. The condition portends that the purchasing power in a given territory is constantly running ahead of the output of goods and services, with the result that as incomes and prices rise, the value of money falls. Inflationary spiral obtains when prices move upward, partly as a result, and partly the cause, of increases in wages and salaries, dividends, interest rates and so on.

Insubordination   Insubordination, according to *The Living Webster Encyclopaedic Dictionary* means "not submitting to authority; wilfully disrespectful or disobedient; rebellious". An accusation of insubordination, which is a commonly used term in industrial relations, must therefore be substantiated by clear evidence of an employee's failure to obey instructions, of being rude and disrespectful to his or her supervisor/manager or behaving in a rebellious manner, thus causing a breakdown in relationships or frustrating the productive process.

An employee found guilty of insubordination would be subject to summary dismissal – that is, dismissal without notice or pay in lieu of notice. However, all other benefits to which the employee is entitled, such as unused vacation leave and pension refunds, are due and payable at the time of termination.

Disciplinary action taken against an employee for insubordination may vary in degree from suspension to dismissal, depending on the gravity of the offence committed.

International Labour Organization (ILO)   The ILO was founded in 1919 to advance social justice and better living conditions throughout the world. In 1946 it became the first specialized agency associated with the United Nations. It is a tripartite organization, in that workers' and employers' representatives along with governments take part in its work with equal status and recognition. The number of ILO member states was 174 on 1 February 2000.

The ILO uses the vehicle of *conventions* and *recommendations* as the basis of communicating acceptable labour standards and, through the process of ratification of the said conventions and recommendations and country

I

by country information gathering, to monitor countries for their confor-
mity to these standards.

In 1994, the Governing Body decided upon a tailoring of the ILO's
supervision of ratified ILO conventions. *The designation of four conventions as priority conventions was among the decisions taken.* One of
the changes to the regular system of reporting was the decision to
require regular reports from governments every five years on most
ratified conventions, but once every other year on the fundamental
and priority conventions. Part of the rationale for this decision was
the essential importance for labour institutions and policy formulation of the subjects covered by these conventions.

Eight ILO conventions have been identified by the ILO's governing body as being fundamental to the rights of human beings at
work, irrespective of levels of development of individual member
states. These rights are a precondition for all the others in that they
provide for the necessary implements to strive freely for the
improvement of individual and collective conditions of work. (ILO
1996–2004)

Conventions

The following are considered by the ILO to be *priority* conventions:

The Labour Inspection Convention, 1947 (No. 81)
The Employment Policy Convention, 1964 (No. 122)
The Labour Inspection (Agriculture) Convention, 1969 (No. 129)
The Tripartite Consultation (International Labour Standards) Convention,
    1976 (No. 144)

The following are considered to be *fundamental* conventions:

Forced Labour Convention (The Abolition of Forced Labour), 1930 (No. 29)
Freedom of Association and Protection of the Right to Organize Conven-
    tion, 1984 (No. 87)
Right to Organize and Collective Bargaining Convention, 1949 (No. 98)
Equal Remuneration Convention, 1951 (No. 100)
Abolition of Forced Labour Convention, 1957 (No. 105)
Discrimination (Employment and Occupation) Convention, 1958 (No. 111)
Minimum Age Convention (The Elimination of Child Labour), 1973 (No.
    138)

Worst Forms of Child Labour Convention, 1999 (No. 182)

Other conventions include the following:

Right of Association (Agriculture) Convention, 1921 (No. 11)
Weekly Rest (Industry) Convention, 1921 (No. 14)
Forty-Hour Week Convention, 1935 (No. 47)
Holidays with Pay Convention, 1936 (No. 52)
Right of Association (Non-Metropolitan Territories) Convention, 1947 (No. 84)
Weekly Rest (Commerce and Offices) Convention, 1957 (No. 106)
Termination of Employment Convention, 1982 (No. 158)
Vocational Rehabilitation and Employment (Disabled Persons) Convention, 1983 (No. 159)
Home Work Convention, 1996 (No. 177)

Recommendations

Holiday with Pay Recommendation, 1936 (No. 47)
Cooperation at the Level of the Undertaking Recommendation, 1952 (No. 94)
Weekly Rest (Commerce and Offices) Recommendation, 1957 (No. 103)
Reduction of Hours of Work Recommendation, 1962 (No. 116)
Communication with the Undertaking Recommendation, 1967 (No. 129)
Equal Opportunities and Equal Treatment for Men and Women Workers: Workers with Family Responsibilities Recommendation, 1981 (No. 165)
Termination of Employment Recommendation, 1982 (No. 166)

An expanded list of ILO conventions and recommendations appears in Appendix M. See full details at http://www.ilo.org/ilolex/english/.

International labour standards   These are conventions and recommendations adopted by the International Labour Conference, covering a broad range of matters in the field of social and labour matters.

What Are International Labour Standards?

Universal international labour standards are those embodied in the conventions of the ILO. Some debate has focused on the idea of which ILO conventions constitute a "core" which could serve as a social clause in international trade agreements. Opponents of a social clause have sought to confuse the issue by arguing that proponents are promoting a varying set of ILO conventions on wages, working hours, benefits, or health and safety regulations as core conventions. It is also noted that the ILO itself does not formally identify a category of core conventions. The international trade union position on this matter is clear. Together with other international and national trade union organizations, TUAC has all along proposed that only the following seven ILO conventions constitute core labour standards:

- ILO Convention 87 – freedom of association
- ILO Convention 98 – the right to collective bargaining
- ILO Conventions 29 and 105 – the prohibition of forced labour
- ILO Conventions 100 and 111 – covering non-discrimination in employment and remuneration
- ILO Convention 138 – minimum age for employment – to eliminate child labour

All governments have already explicitly committed themselves to the implementation of these labour standards in the Declaration of the World Summit on Social Development, held in Copenhagen in March 1995.

These ILO conventions constitute basic human rights applicable to all countries, irrespective of their level of development. Furthermore, membership in the ILO demands adherence to the principles of freedom of association and collective bargaining. The governing body of the ILO has recently discussed the implementation of these core conventions. It has specifically noted that they belong to a set of conventions which are not in need of revision even though in this context some divergent views on Convention No. 138 were expressed. Proposals have been made on how to strengthen the supervision of Conventions No. 29 and 105 on forced labour, and No. 100 and 111 on discrimination. One real possibility is the establishment of a committee to deal with the violations of these conventions in the same or a similar way as the governing body committee on the freedom of association does concerning violations of Conventions No. 87 and 98.

Child labour has received increased international attention. From the fundamental labour standards' point of view, Convention No. 138 has posed some problems, as its nature is more technical and not quite comparable to the others which are human rights conventions. In any event, the ILO has begun work on a new convention, aimed at eliminating the exploitation of children in working life. This will run in parallel with but not replace Convention No. 138 (ILO 1996).

J

Job description Describes the content of a job. A necessary tool of management, the job description spells out essential areas of job functions. It cannot contain all the functions that must be performed by an individual, but it is a guide to the main duties and responsibilities of a job.

In a well-organized and effectively managed organization, every job holder is issued with a job description that has been discussed and understood by all parties concerned. A job description is an important tool in performance appraisal and assessments.

Some of the subheadings may include the following:

- title of the job
- duties and responsibilities – main functions of the job
- skills and knowledge required
- disciplinary authority (that is, decision-making authority over conduct and performance of subordinates)
- other working conditions including economic factors
- accountability – to whom and for what responsible

Job evaluation Job evaluation is the systematic determination of the relative worth of the jobs in an organization based on their demands on the jobholders and importance to the work or business of the organization. The result is a ranking in the order of jobs, providing the basis of an equitable wage structure, which is acceptable to the individuals or groups concerned and the organization as a whole.

Job evaluation is an integrated process comprising the following:

1. Job analysis
2. Establishing the relative rather than the absolute values of jobs
3. Grouping/classifying jobs hierarchically and establishing minimum and maximum wages for them

There are two broad types of job evaluations – the quantitative and non-quantitative types. Both types, in turn, have two sub-types: the quantitative evaluations fall under the point system or the factor comparison system. On the other hand, the non-quantitative evaluations include the ranking system and the grade description system.

J

Certain minimum conditions should be met before a job evaluation exercise is undertaken. These include the following:

1. Receiving the commitment and support of senior management
2. Receiving the necessary resources, technical and material, in order for it to be done properly
3. Being done for the right reasons and not simply to satisfy personal, group or political objectives
4. Pointing employees in the direction of the organization's objectives and values, such as customer satisfaction, performance, productivity, efficiency and quality
5. Gaining the support of important groups

Job analysis is central to the whole job evaluation exercise: it is the basis on which the respective jobs are ascribed numerical and relational values. Job analysis is the process of determining and reporting pertinent information relating to the nature of a specific job. It is the determination of the tasks which comprise the job and the skills, knowledge, abilities and responsibilities required of the worker for successful job performance.

The steps in an analysis may include the following:

1. Title of job – identifies the job
2. Duties and responsibilities – shows, as far as possible, a breakdown (by tasks) of the job
3. Skills and knowledge – identifies the basic skill and knowledge required by someone to do the job effectively
4. Working conditions – describes the conditions under which the job is to be carried out
5. Economic conditions – outlines the rates of pay, fringe benefits, bonuses, holidays and vacation leave, and other elements

---

Job rate (rate for the job)   A job rate is the rate paid to workers for a given job. This may be a single rate or the minimum in a range of rates.

Job security   Layoffs and redundancies at best destroy morale in an organization. It is desirable, therefore, that such programmes be carefully analysed and implemented with good and clearly understood reasons.

They have the negative effect of reducing the quality of performance of all the employees in the organization. Ultimately productivity falls, resulting in serious financial losses to the company. Decisions on layoffs and redundancies should be swift and properly communicated to all employees and those members of staff who are not involved in the programmes should be told as quickly as possible after the decision has been taken.

Job specification This important tool of management sets out the personal qualities required in an individual to achieve the standards set for the job.

Some of the criteria in a job specification include the following:

- Health and fitness – state of health
- Motivation – What factors will motivate the individual?
- Qualifications – Are they relevant?
- Relationships with others – Is he or she a leader, and so on?
- Past experience, and so on – Is it relevant?
- Knowledge and skills – Are they appropriate?

A job specification plan helps in personnel selection, including promotions and transfers. It is a useful exercise to undertake prior to any form of selection as it provides a scientific basis for choice while minimizing the pitfalls of instinctive decisions.

Joint bargaining The practice over the years has been to hammer out agreements around the bargaining table, rather than to use the facilities of arbitration, or the courts. In some cases, particularly through the joint industrial councils and in such industries as bauxite and sugar, there are systems of joint bargaining, where such a practice is deemed beneficial to the industry on the whole. Joint bargaining may come about voluntarily on agreement between the parties, or through the joint industrial council, or joint representation of a bargaining unit by two or more trade unions each representing not less than 30 per cent of the bargaining unit as provided for under the LRIDA section 5, subsections 1 (b) and 6:

> The result of the ballot shows that each of two or three of these trade unions received the votes of not less than thirty percent of the number of workers who were eligible to vote . . . the minister, shall at

J

the request of not less than two of the trade unions, that they wish to be recognized as having joint bargaining rights, inform the employer, who shall recognise these trade unions accordingly.

Joint consultation The communication of work-related matters between management, workers and their representatives. Such matters may include workers' welfare, production schedules, changes in production systems and methods and change of geographical location of plant.

Appropriate committees are established with specific objectives and guidelines of operation to ensure an effective joint consultation programme. Consultation at all levels of an organization is a desirable feature of effective management and should be encouraged and nurtured to ensure viability and success.

Joint industrial council Councils set up to negotiate working conditions on an industry-wide basis. The establishment of these councils arose out of a report from the Whitely Committee (1916) of the British government. The committee recommended the establishment of an organization comprising representatives of employers and employees with the objective of offering regular consideration on matters affecting the well-being of the trade from the point of view of those engaged in it. Such consideration should be consistent with the general interest of the community. The Ministry of Labour sets up councils and guides them until they are firmly established. Each joint industrial council has an approved constitution. The council must always act in the interest of the industry. (See Appendix K.)

Representation on the joint industrial council is made through employers' associations and trade unions.

The oldest established joint industrial council in Jamaica was set up for the shipping industry in 1952. Joint industrial councils also exist in the building and printing trades, and cane and banana farming.

Just and proper cause What is just and proper cause? A "no" answer to any one or more of the following questions normally signifies that just and proper cause did not exist – that is, that the disciplinary decision contains one or more elements of arbitration, it was capricious, unreasonable and/or discriminatory, or it warranted an arbitrator to alter the decision.

1. Did the company give the employee forewarning or foreknowledge of the possible or probable disciplinary consequences of the employee's conduct?
2. Was the company's rule or managerial order reasonably related to the orderly, efficient and safe operation of the company's business?
3. Did the company, before administering discipline to an employee, make an effort to discover whether the employee did in fact violate or disobey a rule or order of management?
4. Was the company's investigation conducted fairly and objectively?
5. At the investigation, did the "judge" obtain substantial evidence that the employee was guilty as charged?
6. Has the company applied its rule, orders and penalties even-handedly and without discrimination to all employees?
7. Was the degree of discipline administered by the company in a particular case reasonably related to
   a. the seriousness of the employee's proven offence, and
   b. the record of the employee in his or her service to the company?

Juvenile employment (see also **International Labour Organization** and **international labour standards** and ILO convention 138)   The Juvenile Act monitors and prohibits the employment of juveniles. A "child" is deemed to be *a person who is less than sixteen years old*. A child is forbidden to do work in an industrial undertaking. An even younger child of less than twelve years, in addition to being prohibited from the above, also must not do night work. However, a child can be employed to do light domestic, agricultural or horticultural work if with the parents. "Night work" is defined in the act as work in any industrial undertaking during any portion of a period of eleven consecutive hours, between the hours of 10:00 p.m. and 5:00 a.m.

K

Kaizen   Used frequently in South East Asian territories, perhaps because of its grounding in Japanese philosophy, "kaizen" means continuous improvement, a gradual unending improvement of everything in the business. The incremental change strategy and process of kaizen is usually compared with innovation, which involves more radical or large-scale improvement.

Kicked upstairs   This is an act of promoting an employee out of a position of inefficiency where his or her presence is creating problems for the company. Some companies use this method as a form of "reward cum punishment" to create opportunities for older employees with long service, for members of the owner's family or for employees who may have been injured or become ill on the job or are incapable of performing at acceptable standards.

Killing time   This is otherwise known as idling. Care has to be taken to ensure that what may be interpreted as killing time is not a failure by management to organize alternative activities for workers during machine breakdowns, power outages, water lock-offs or other occurrences which result in a stoppage of work.

On the other hand, idling is the favourite pastime of some workers and appropriate disciplinary action must be taken against those who waste company time. Such action may be

- a verbal or written warning;
- suspension for repeated idleness; or
- dismissal for chronic idleness.

In any event, the manager should

- notify the trade union of the decision; and
- record the decision on the employee's file.

K

Knocking-off time   The time of day when a shift ends.

Knowledge economy   An economy or organization which not only believes in the acquisition, distribution and utilization of knowledge, but has done so as the basis for improving its well being and that of its citizen or personnel. Education and training are investments in growth and development.

Knowledge worker   "Ideally one who possesses both technical know-how and intuitive skills. Good knowledge workers at any level should have a combination of 'hard' skills such as structures knowledge, technical abilities, and professional experience, with 'softer' traits, i.e. a sure sense of the cultural, political, and personal aspects of knowledge" (National Productivity Corporation 2001, 50).

L

Labour competitiveness   This indicates the comparability of the industry in producing products or services at the lowest possible labour cost. Three such indicators are:

1. *Added value per labour cost:* A low ratio would mean high prevailing labour cost, and would not be supportive of added-value creation.
2. *Labour cost per employee (average remuneration per employee):* A high ratio would indicate that individual employees, on average, are earning well, and vice versa.
3. *Unit labour cost or the proportion of labour cost to total output:* Obviously, a high ratio indicates high labour cost, which could be due to one or a mix of a lack or shortage of skilled labour or poor mix or deployment of labour or an oversupply or underutilization of labour.

Labour cost (LC)   Defined as payments in the form of gross salary and wages, bonuses and other cash allowances paid to employees, plus salaries, allowances, fees, bonuses and commissions paid to working directors, plus fees paid to non-working directors for their attendance at the board of directors meetings, plus payments in kind to paid employees, plus value of free wearing apparel provided, plus employer's statutory contributions.

Labour laws   These are used to regulate various aspects of life at the workplace. They address areas ranging from benefits such as leave of all kinds to the obligation of the employer to provide certain physical facilities in respect of safety and physical working environment. In terms of industrial relations, the main act which sets the tone for this in Jamaica is the Labour Relations and Industrial Disputes Act (Jamaica) 1975 (LRIDA).

L

Jamaica's main labour laws are as follows:

- The Employment (Termination and Redundancy Payments) Act, 1974, as amended in 1986
- The Employment (Termination and Redundancy Payments) Regulations, as amended in 1986 and 1988
- The Holidays with Pay Law, 1947
- The Holidays with Pay Order, 1973
- The Labour Relations and Industrial Disputes Act, 1975, as amended in 1978, 1986 and 2002
- The Labour Relations and Industrial Disputes Regulations, 1975, as amended in 1978
- The Employment (Equal Pay for Men and Women) Act, 1975
- The Minimum Wage Act and The National Minimum Wage Order, 1975
- The Maternity Leave Act, 1979
- The Trade Union Act, 1919
- The Factories Act, 1943
- Factories Act, Rules (under section 5 (7))
- The Factories Appeal Rules, 1950
- The Factories Regulations, 1961
- The Building Operations and Works of Engineering Construction (Safety, Health and Welfare) Regulations, 1968
- The Docks (Safety, Health and Welfare) Regulations, 1968
- The Employment Agencies Regulation Act, 1957
- The Employment Agencies Regulations, 1957
- The Foreign Nationals and Commonwealth Citizens (Employment) Act, 1964
- The Foreign Nationals and Commonwealth Citizens (Employment) Exemptions Regulations, 1964
- The Apprenticeship Act, 1955
- The Arbitration Act, 1900, as amended 2004

These laws should be studied and explanations sought from qualified personnel before applying any of the clauses.

Labour market[1] The labour market is the interaction between economic activities and supply of skills and expertise. That is to say, the economic

---

[1] A modified version of this definition appears in Hussey 2000.

L

activities within a jurisdiction, manufacturing, construction, services, and so on, existing and prospective or projected, essentially dictate the skills and capability requirements which are, in turn, provided by the population supply pool, channelled through or processed by the education and training facilities. The interplay can be structured or unstructured.

The formal sectors of the economy tend to be structured and inter-linked. Recruitment and selection of skills and expertise are, to some extent, coordinated with the suppliers and the relationships are, in varying degrees, somewhat highly formalized.

Notwithstanding that the definition essentially addresses particular jurisdictions or areas, the reality is that, given the internationalization of trade and business and employment opportunities, the labour market has to be viewed as having extended operational features or international dimensions.

The three aspects to the labour market – the *supply side,* the *demand side* and the *institutional, regulatory aspect* – are inexorably linked, forming a dynamic trilogy.

In the trilogy, the state plays a multifaceted role as an employer (in Jamaica's case, the single largest employer), the single most important supplier of trained personnel and also in being the dominant partner in providing the regulatory framework for employer and employee interac-tion as well as the climate and conditions for investment.

The market will operate effectively and efficiently if the supply and demand sides are aware of and respond expeditiously to the needs and requirements of each other.

The Demand Side

The demand side constitutes the broad mix of economic and social activ-ities that are undertaken, temporarily or on an ongoing basis, in the public and private sectors, as well as in non-governmental organizations (NGOs), requiring skills and competencies for their execution.

In addition, the demand side includes umbrella representative bodies such as employers' associations, local, regional and international institutions.

The Supply Side

The supply side involves the broad mix of skills and capabilities within the subject economy or designated economic area, seeking or aspiring to work for pay or other types of reward.

L

This supply side would also include representative bodies and associations which bargain/negotiate for employees and prospective employees or assist in setting rates of pay and conditions of employment.

The Regulatory and Support Systems

The third, seemingly sedate, aspect of the labour market is the state and other regulatory bodies. The government, in an almost omnipresent way, from the standpoint of its policies, regulatory and legislative responsibilities, plays a very critical role in the structure and functioning of the labour market. Legislation, procedures and initiatives such as wage guidelines, minimum wage(s), general conditions of employment, fiscal and monetary policies together prescribe the context and rules of the interface between employers and employees as well as their representative agencies.

The ILO, trade unions/confederation of trade unions, local and international, employers' federations/confederations, local and international, are important parts of the institutional, regulatory side of the operations of the labour market, especially in the context of local, regional or international conventions, social contracts, or memoranda of understandings between the main players to elicit cooperation and concerted action on important issues or processes. The labour market structure and operation are graphically summarized in the figure on the opposite page.

Labour market indicators   Labour market indicators are "sign posts" or signals of the conditions or state of the labour market in an economy. They are proxies of the demand, supply, regulatory and support services aspects of the market. Individual indicators can be useful in providing particular details of the market but are not by themselves sufficient to describe the labour market fully. Collectively, though, they provide an overall picture of the structure, nature and operational dynamics of the market. It is, therefore, important that a sufficiently broad spectrum of indicators is chosen to provide the range of information and activities that are representative of the market in the particular jurisdiction or area.

The ILO developed and disseminated a set of twenty key indicators of the labour market (KILM) to guide national efforts in developing their own indicators and labour market information systems.[2] These are:

---

[2] For full details please consult ILO 1999 or http://www.ilo.org/public/English/employment/strat/kilm/

The Labour Market

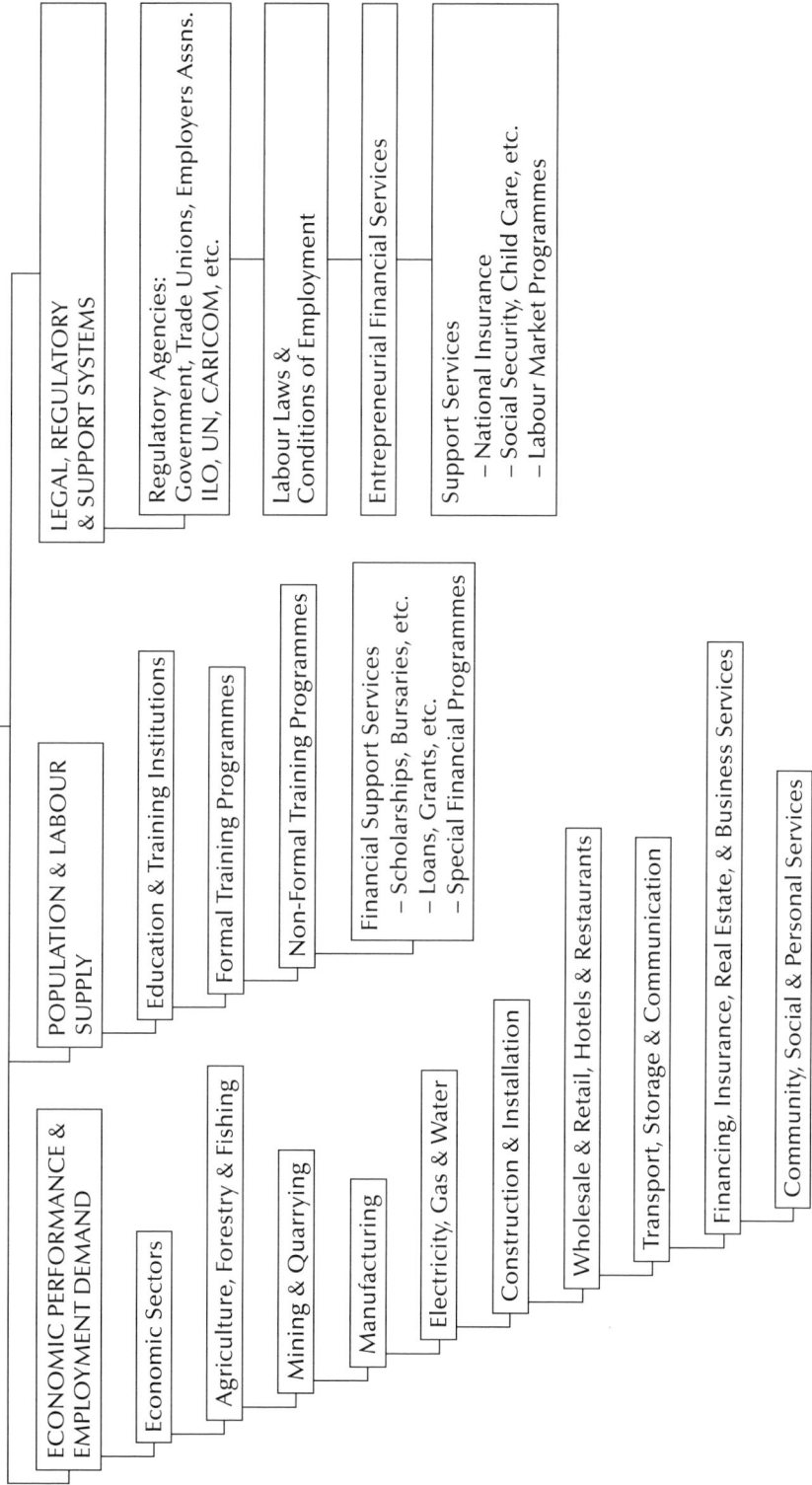

ECONOMIC PERFORMANCE & EMPLOYMENT DEMAND

- Economic Sectors
  - Agriculture, Forestry & Fishing
  - Mining & Quarrying
  - Manufacturing
  - Electricity, Gas & Water
  - Construction & Installation
  - Wholesale & Retail, Hotels & Restaurants
  - Transport, Storage & Communication
  - Financing, Insurance, Real Estate, & Business Services
  - Community, Social & Personal Services

POPULATION & LABOUR SUPPLY

- Education & Training Institutions
- Formal Training Programmes
- Non-Formal Training Programmes
- Financial Support Services
  - Scholarships, Bursaries, etc.
  - Loans, Grants, etc.
  - Special Financial Programmes

LEGAL, REGULATORY & SUPPORT SYSTEMS

- Regulatory Agencies: Government, Trade Unions, Employers Assns. ILO, UN, CARICOM, etc.
- Labour Laws & Conditions of Employment
- Entrepreneurial Financial Services
- Support Services
  - National Insurance
  - Social Security, Child Care, etc.
  - Labour Market Programmes

L

1. Labour force participation rate
2. Employment-to-population ratio
3. Status in employment
4. Employment by sector
5. Part-time workers
6. Hours of work
7. Urban informal sector employment
8. Unemployment
9. Youth unemployment
10. Long-term unemployment
11. Unemployment by educational attainment
12. Time-related underemployment
13. Inactivity rate
14. Educational attainment and illiteracy
15. Manufacturing wage trends
16. Occupational wage and earning indices
17. Hourly compensation costs
18. Labour productivity and unit labour costs
19. Labour market flows
20. Poverty and income distribution

Labour market information system (LMIS)   Labour market information systems are mechanisms, electronic or otherwise, which provide information concerning the dynamics, that is, the size, composition and changes in the labour market, or any part of it. The way the market, or part thereof, functions, the problems and opportunities which it portends, and the legal and institutional parameters are critical elements of an LMIS.

Jamaica and other Caribbean territories, under the guidance and assistance of the International Labour Organization and the United States Department of Labour, since the late 1990s, have been fashioning individual and combined labour market information systems. Jamaica's LMIS can be found at http://www.lmis-ele.org.jm while Barbados's is located at http://www.labour.gov.bb.

Labour relations code   See Appendix C.

L

Labour turnover   The number of employees leaving a company over the course of the year, expressed as a percentage of the total number of employed over the same period. High labour turnover is expensive. When labour turnover is high as a result of resignations or dismissals, it could mean that all is not well within the company or department.

Exit interviews help to identify the reasons why people leave a company. These reasons should be noted and corrective action taken. A zero turnover may not always be a good thing either. This could mean that the labour force is unemployable elsewhere or that jobs are unavailable. On the other hand, zero turnovers make it difficult to recruit new and possibly better-qualified staff.

When a worker leaves the job, experience, training and skills go with him or her. Recruitment of new skills usually costs the company more, especially if such skills are scarce. Retraining new workers and acclimatizing them to new work situations are costly endeavours.

Layoff and recall   This is a temporary measure undertaken to reduce the workforce owing to a cutback in production, machinery breakdown or temporary closure of operations. Workers are laid off without pay during the period of layoff.

In implementing this measure, the following steps should be taken:

1. Advise the union delegate and employees, giving notice of the layoff.
2. Inform the union official.
3. Pay employees up to the date of the layoff.
4. Vacation leave with pay may be substituted for the layoff period.
5. Employees remain on payroll without pay during the layoff. At management's discretion, certain fringe benefits may remain in force during the layoff.
6. The layoff period should not normally exceed 120 working days but may be extended for a further period of up to six months. However, the employee may elect to be dismissed by reason of redundancy if the period of layoff is in excess of 120 working days. A written request must be sent to the employer seeking redundancy not less than fourteen days or more than sixty days after the date of the notice. Such notice shall have effect as if it has implemented a dismissal of the employee on the grounds of

L

redundancy (Employment [Termination and Redundancy Payments] Act [Jamaica], as amended, 1986).

7. Recall: Advise the union and start the recall programme. This should be done on the basis of need, that is, skill and ability or seniority depending on the circumstances. Letters of recall must be issued.
8. Employees do not suffer loss of seniority during a layoff.
9. Where skill and ability are equal, length of service (seniority) should be the deciding factor in recalling employees.

In some instances, the system of last in, first out (LIFO) and last out, first in (LOFI) is used to determine the procedure in a layoff and recall programme. In such cases, "last" means that employees with the shortest service will be laid off first and, conversely, employees who were laid off first and, conversely, employees who were laid off last (those with longer service) should be recalled first.

Exhibit: Layoff Clause in Collective Agreement

If temporary layoff becomes necessary, the employees will be given one week's pay in lieu of notice. Selection of employees to be laid off will be on the basis of skill and ability and where these are equal, seniority shall be the deciding factor.

Letters of reference   Letters of reference are testimonials given to individuals based on personal knowledge of the person's honesty, integrity, skill and ability. It is illegal to knowingly give a false or misleading reference on a current or former employee to a prospective employer.

Liquidation (see also **winding up**)   Liquidation or winding up are two terms with the same meaning. These terms represent the process by which the existence of a company is terminated. Liquidation may be voluntary or involuntary.

Voluntary liquidation takes place when the members of a company pass a resolution to wind up. In the event of liquidation, liabilities are ascertained and assets apportioned to stakeholders.

L

Lockout   This is a form of industrial action taken by *employers* in furtherance of a dispute. It is "a total or partial temporary closure of one or more places of employment, or the hindering of the normal work activities of employees, by one or more employers with a view to enforcing or resisting demands or expressing grievances, or supporting other employers in their demands or grievances" (ILO 1997).

This action excludes workers from their places of employment by suspending work or by summarily terminating the services of a group of workers by physically "locking the doors".

In pursuing such a course of action, management must take the following steps:

1. Workers and their union must be notified.
2. The Ministry of Labour's conciliation department must be notified.
3. Advance notice of restoration of normality or discontinuance must be given to workers, union and the Ministry of Labour. This should be done in writing.

M

Manpower statistics Every organization should properly document its manpower data. This is best done using an inventory system, which must be updated from time to time. Similar to an inventory of stocks and other assets, the inventory will include the following:

- number of employees
- qualifications of employees
- linguistic abilities – languages spoken
- skills
- job performance by job-family groupings, that is, marketing, production, clerical, administrative, and so on
- schedule of wages
- age distribution, by classification – to help assessment of potential for promotion, training, and so on
- labour turnover

Such an inventory is useful for assessing manpower strength and capability in order to plan the future of the organization.

Maternity leave Time off granted to a pregnant female worker to deliver and give post-natal care to her newborn baby. The period of maternity leave may vary from twelve weeks upward to any time fixed by the employer or agreed between the (female employee) union and employer.

The following conditions are essential when granting maternity leave in the case of Jamaica:

1. The worker must have completed fifty-two weeks prior to going on maternity leave. Seasonal workers must have worked for a total of not less than fifty-two weeks during the five years immediately preceding the leave.
2. The leave entitlement is twelve weeks. This may be extended to as many as fourteen weeks with a medical certificate. Further extension may be granted on medical advice at the employee's cost, that is, without pay.

M

3. Right to return to work: The worker has the right to return to work in the same capacity and place and with the same terms and conditions she enjoyed before going on maternity leave. She must, however, give her employer three weeks' notice of her intention to return to work.
4. Maternity pay: The worker is entitled to pay for the first eight weeks of her twelve-week maternity leave, but pay will not be granted if she has been given leave for three or more pregnancies.
5. Seasonal workers: Workers on piece or task rates or on commission shall be paid at the rate of one-third of the aggregate "normal wages" earned during the last thirteen normal working weeks.
6. Replacement: During the absence of a female employee on maternity leave her position may be filled by a temporary worker who will be employed on the clear understanding that her employment may be terminated at the end of the maternity leave of the pregnant employee.
7. During her absence on maternity leave, an employee should not suffer the loss of
   a. seniority of service, or
   b. fringe benefits – other than during the unpaid period. This includes entitlement to pension and to medical and group life insurance, unless expressly stated in the contract of employment or collective agreement.

Managers must be aware that pregnant employees might be sickly. Consequently, managers will need to show understanding and compassion during periods of pregnancy.

Medical scheme   A fringe benefit provided by the employer to assist the worker in maintaining good health and to provide medical services during illness. There are several types of medical schemes. The fully provided scheme is paid for by the employer at no cost to the worker. The partially funded scheme is paid for jointly by employer and employee, usually on a fifty-fifty basis. The dependents' scheme covers the worker's dependents and may be fully or jointly funded. Most schemes are operated through insurance companies and premiums paid either by the employer or jointly by the employer and individual employee.

M

Merit increase   A merit increase is an increment paid to a worker in addition to normal wages in recognition of an acceptable or above-average level of performance on the job.

Merit increases take into account the skill level and value placed on the quality of performance. Consideration is given to the pay scales of comparable jobs and skills, the ability of the company to pay and the relative importance of the job. However, a merit increase does not necessarily change the job rate because such increases are individually related and not job related.

Minimum wage   The minimum amount that must be paid to an employee in a classification as set out in the statutory Minimum Wage Law of a jurisdiction.

Motivation   The drive, initiative and self-direction of an individual, which encourages production at optimum levels.

Points to Note

1. A manager can motivate a worker through encouragement, persuasion and incentives.
2. A motivated worker is an asset to the organization.
3. Lack of motivation should be investigated and dealt with immediately after the cause has been identified. Motivation may be achieved through training, incentives, encouragement and effective management.

N–O

Natural justice   See **fair play.**

Negotiations (see also **collective bargaining**)   The process of bargaining between employers and employees, their association or trade unions about conditions of work and related issues. The underlying principle is that the parties should arrive at an agreement through this process of give and take. Mutual trust, confidence and respect are vital. If these are in place and both parties bargain in good faith, realizing that negotiations are not a game to be won or lost, the resulting agreement is likely to be supported even though one side may give up more than the other.

Points to Note

1. The company must have a clear policy on all negotiations.
2. Negotiators must be given a clear mandate, that is, they must know beforehand how far management is willing to go and what it wants to achieve.
3. A negotiating team must develop a strategy for negotiations, such as
   a. who will lead;
   b. who will discuss the various topics;
   c. how much room is there for compromise; and
   d. who calls the breaks, and so on.
4. Appropriate minutes must be kept of all meetings.
5. Minutes must be circulated to all parties for study prior to the meeting.
6. Meetings must be started on time.
7. Banter and small talk have their place sometimes, to establish rapport and ease tension, but should not be overdone. One should always remember that the discussions are concerned with people's welfare.
8. At the conclusion of negotiations, heads of agreement must be prepared and signed.

N

9. Agreed conditions must be implemented as soon as they become effective.
10. A copy of the collective agreement should be accessible to all members of the bargaining units.

Night work   Usually referred to as the graveyard shift, that is, between 8:00 p.m. and 6:00 a.m. the following day. This period normally attracts a special night premium, which is added to the normal wage. All night shift premiums must be established or agreed to between the parties (where a union is involved) before implementation.

Non-standard employment   The British management scholar Charles Handy predicts that all competitive firms and institutions of the future will have three types of workers. Handy uses the term "shamrock organization" to describe the organizational structure he envisions, with each type of worker representing one of the leaves in a shamrock.

1. The first leaf of the shamrock is made up of the *professional core.* It consists of professionals, technicians and managers who possess the skills that represent the organization's core competence. Their pay is tied to organizational performance, and their relations will be more like those among the partners in a professional firm than those among superiors and subordinates in today's large corporation.
2. The next leaf is made up of *self-employed professionals* or *technicians* or smaller specialized professionals who are hired on contract, on a project-by-project basis. They are paid in fees for results rather than in salary for time. They frequently telecommute. No benefits are paid by the core organization, and the worker carries the risk of insecurity.
3. The third leaf comprises the *contingent workforce*, where there is no career track and often routine jobs. These are usually part-time workers who will experience short periods of employment and long periods of unemployment. They are paid by the hour or day or week for the time they work (Handy 1992, 153; cited in "Making Career Sense").

N

Standard jobs are traditionally life-long (or with some degree of permanence), single employer type, career oriented, full-time and stable, and attract standard welfare and benefits. Most employees are perhaps still embraced in this category. However, the labour market is rapidly changing to challenge both traditional notions of employment and how work is organized, carried out and rewarded. In short, there is non-standardization of working arrangements. This is often viewed as a revolution in work, heralding the end of secure long-term employment for practically everyone.

Working-time arrangements (discussed elsewhere in this book) are one of the most obvious areas of work-life to be affected in this grand change. Longer workdays and shorter workweeks, reduction in overtime, part-time, temporary, just-in-time labour and so on, are some of the ways in which work-time is being revolutionized.

Telecommuting is another significant way in which work is being non-standardized. This is a changing of working arrangements whereby work is carried out at a location other than the conventional office or work site, at home or somewhere closer to home.

Many reasons are provided for this particular direction. On one hand, especially in large cities, where air pollution is a concern, telecommuting is said to aid clean-air objectives and to reduce traffic.

Telecommuting is also argued to have potential for increasing productivity, through improvements in staff morale and better use of company and personal resources. There have been suggestions that it also enhances "recruitment and retention of quality employees, and decreases absenteeism".

On the personal side, telecommuting "establishes a family-friendly work environment that enhances quality of life".

There are caveats for the establishment of telecommuting work programmes. For instance, the *Los Angeles County Board of Supervisors Policy Manual* states:

- This program is a management option, not a universal employee benefit. Department heads may implement telecommuting when it is deemed mutually beneficial by both the department and the employee.
- Telecommuters can be selected from among either represented or non-represented employees. However, they should be selected on a voluntary basis by both supervisors and employees. Selection criteria should be based on suitability of employees' jobs, an assessment of the likelihood of their success as

N

telecommuters and an assessment of their supervisors' ability to manage remote workers.

- A Telecommuting Agreement should be entered into by both the County [read *company*] and the employee that requires compliance with established telecommuting standards, guidelines and conditions.
- The terms and conditions of employment for the telecommuter and the supervisor remain unchanged. Work hours, overtime, compensation and vacation schedules must conform to the county code, to MOU (Memorandum of Understanding) provisions and to terms otherwise agreed upon by the employee and the supervisor.
- All telecommuters shall comply with the County's Telecommuting Standards, which address policy issues related to worker's compensation, use of County equipment, telephone costs, tax implications, and other issues deemed appropriate by the County. (Los Angeles County 1989)

Normality (normalcy)   The restoration of normal work after industrial action. Normality assumes that all productive efforts have been restored to the levels that existed before disruptions.

Points to Note

If other parties were notified about industrial action, restoration of normality should also be announced to the union, government officials, customers, and so on.

Normal wages   All remuneration paid as regular wages except pay for overtime work, premiums and special allowances such as meals and transportation.

Notice of termination   Contracts of permanent employment usually contain an exit or termination clause, which stipulates the minimum amount of time that either party (employer or employee) should give to the other to end the working relationship. Notice is important to both

O

sides to assist in ensuring that a minimum amount of dislocation or disruption occurs in the enterprise or in the affairs of the employee. (See Employment [Termination and Redundancy Payments] Act, 1975 [Jamaica].)

If an employer wishes to terminate the services of a worker (excluding probationers and casual workers) who has worked continuously for four weeks, the following period of notice is required:

1. Not less than two weeks for service of less than five years; or
2. Not less than four weeks for service of five years or more but less than ten years; or
3. Not less than six weeks for service of ten years or more but less than fifteen years; or
4. Not less than eight weeks for service of fifteen years or more but less than twenty years; or
5. Not less than twelve weeks for service of twenty years or more.

The period of notice to be given by the employee, regardless of length of service, is two weeks.

However, nothing in law prevents the employer and the employee from

- waiving notice and accepting payment in lieu;
- waiving notice on the employee's side; or
- accepting notice of a longer duration.

Notice is intended to give the employee sufficient time to find alternative employment while being paid. The longer an employee serves an employer, the greater is the obligation of the employer to ensure that adequate notice with pay is given to alleviate the economic hardship of the employee while in search of a new job.

The employer, too, expects reasonable notice to allow sufficient time to find a suitable replacement where one is needed.

Overtime   Hours in excess of normal hours of work for which premium rates are agreed to, and paid, periodically. By agreement, overtime rates may vary between time-and-one-half basic pay for work done during the normal workweek to double- and triple-time pay for work done on Saturdays, Sundays and public holidays.

O

If the employee resides ten miles (for residents of the rural area) or five miles (for residents of the Corporate Area) from his or her place of work, the company, on retrenchment, must provide suitable transportation to his or her home plus any reasonable subsistence.

Points to Note

1. Managers must record actual overtime hours worked.
2. Too much overtime could mean
   a. a shortage of staff
   b. poor work organization and planning
   c. poor supervision
   d. rising labour costs
   e. low productive output
3. All overtime work should be authorized by management beforehand.

P

Pay   The amount of money paid to an individual as wages (sometimes referred to as salary), commission or otherwise, as compensation for work done on a regular basis, for example, daily, weekly, monthly.

Pay Increases

These are negotiated, periodically, between management and workers and, when added to existing rates of pay, become the new rate of pay until changed again through negotiation, or given by management to non-unionized workers. Increases may be expressed in monetary or percentage terms. Increases may be given as follows:

- on a "step" basis; that is, increments added at the beginning of each pay year. This amount may be expressed in actual money to be paid or as a percentage of current rates of pay; or
- across the board; that is, a fixed percentage of the quantum which is added to pay at the effective date of the contract and is not subject to further adjustments throughout the life of the agreement.

For example, on a salary of $1,000 per month, a 15 per cent per annum increase on a two-year agreement will be as follows:

First year:	Monthly salary	= $1,000.00
	Add 15% increase	= $ 150.00
	Total	$1,150.00
Second year:	Monthly salary	= $1,150.00
	Add 15% increase	= $ 172.50
	Total	$1,322.50

During the second year of the agreement, the monthly salary will be $1,322.50. This may be compared with the alternative formula which may grant a fixed increase of $150 per month instead of a percentage increase for a two-year contract. Although the quantum increase in the first year is the same, the across-the-board increase in wage cost changes as shown below:

First year:	Monthly salary	= $1,000.00
	Add $150 increase	= $ 150.00
	Total	$1,150.00

P

$$\text{Second year:} \quad \begin{array}{lr} \text{Monthly salary} & = \$1{,}150.00 \\ \text{Add } \$150 \text{ increase} & = \$ 150.00 \\ \text{Total} & \$1{,}300.00 \end{array}$$

The monthly salary during the second year will be $1,300.

Although the object in using both of the above formulas may have been the same, the results are different. The second option costs less. In the first example, the across-the-board equivalent increase for the two-year contract will be $161.25 per month, while in the second example it will be $150 per month.

Wages Policy

A policy on wages is an important guide to management and an important tool of communication. A policy must stipulate the desired quantum of increase; the categories and amount to be given to each worker; industry-wide comparability; and rationale for current policy. A compensation progamme should reflect three objectives:

1. Solve the pay problems of the firm
2. Make strategic contributions to the achievement of set goals
3. Contribute to the overall development of the organization

Pay Policy

A policy on pay should take into account the following important factors:

1. Policies, procedures and practices that help managers to solve their daily pay problems
2. The importance of communicating information on pay to all employees (this will help to improve the understanding and acceptability of the company's compensation package)
3. The need to maintain a proper balance between basic pay; fringe benefits; premium payments; and pay for idle time and other indirect payments
4. The need for proper records to help managers make proper pay decisions
5. The need to conform with the prevailing tax laws and other statutory and legal obligations
6. The need to maintain rational and acceptable pay relationships between different categories of workers to avoid anomalies that are likely to create dissatisfaction

P

Pay for public holidays (see also **vacation leave**)   A worker who works on the day before and the day after a public holiday is entitled to pay at straight time (basic rate) as if he or she had worked on the public holiday. Failure to report for work without permission and without justifiable reason on the day before or the day after a public holiday repudiates the right to pay for the public holiday. If the worker is required to work and report for work on a public holiday, he or she is usually granted another day off with pay in lieu of the public holiday. This is in addition to payment of any premiums that he or she may be given for working on the public holiday.

Payment, methods of   System or bases on which workers are paid for work done. Broadly speaking they fall under two headings:

1. Payment according to time worked
    Hourly rate: Payment is calculated on an hourly basis and deduc-
        tions made for any shortfall in time actually worked.
    Weekly rate of pay: Payment is based on a scheduled workweek. The
        occasional absence for good cause does not always necessitate a
        prorated reduction in pay.
    Monthly pay: Payment is based on annual income divided by twelve
        and payable monthly in equal amounts.
2. Payment linked to production
    Piece or task rate: Payment is based on the number of units produced
        or assigned jobs completed.
    Payment by results: A piece-rate – payment is based on set targets.
    Commission: Payment is based on the achievement of stipulated
        production or sales targets.

Pension   This is an income which is earned or becomes due to a former employee or his or her appointed beneficiary upon the employee's retire-ment from regular employment, or if and when the employment relation-ship ends for whatever reason, such as death of the employee or inability to continue employment on medical grounds. This income is paid either as a lump sum or on a periodic basis, usually monthly, depending on the pension plan and arrangements for payment under the plan.

P

Dependents/appointees may be paid a pension on behalf of a deceased worker, for a limited or stipulated period.

Methods of calculating pension benefits vary and may be based on average salary, money purchase, life annuities and assurance schemes. Every individual should try to understand the rules of his or her pension scheme to avoid disappointment, embarrassment, and conflict at maturity of the scheme.

Pension plans have become extremely useful mechanisms for assisting companies in their human resource management programmes. If these plans are attractive enough, they help in ensuring that the companies bearing them recruit and retain highly skilled and competent persons. Studies show that employees who are socially secured are less agitated about their economic future and are therefore more satisfied and productive in their companies.

Pension fund   A system of saving and investment of contributions from the employer or employee, singly or combined, on a regular basis to provide a pension for the employee on retirement. Contributions are usually dependent on the rules of the scheme (determined through proposals, negotiation, actuarial projections, and so on), the type of scheme and its funding requirements, and on the generosity of the employer.

As such, the actual amounts contributed by the employer could range from 5 per cent to 15 per cent of the employee's pensionable salary, while the employee's contribution (where the scheme is a contributory one) could vary from 2 per cent to 10 per cent of their pensionable salary. In some pension schemes there are provisions for additional voluntary contributions (AVCs) by the employee, in order to accumulate the pensions faster. After retirement, the pensioner receives a regular payment in the form of a pension.

Pension plan   "A pension plan or pension scheme is simply an arrangement between an employer and his or her employee/employees in which an amount of money is set aside, periodically, during the period of employment and goes into a pension fund. This fund is used (under specified conditions) to provide benefits at retirement" (JTURDC 1986, 1).

There are two broad types of pension plans:

P

1. Money purchased or defined contribution plans
2. Defined benefit, which can be career average or final salary plans

Pension plans are usually tax-deferred or tax-exempted, depending on the jurisdiction. That is to say, the employer and the employee (in the case of contributory schemes) put money (proportions of the employee's pensionable salary) into a pension plan on behalf of the employee, instead of paying him or her the amount as additional income (in the case of the employer) or having portions of earnings deducted (in the case of the employee), each week or month, as relevant. The money in the plan accumulates tax free, and, on retirement of the employee, is withdrawn, as a lump sum or periodically over the remainder of the life of the retiree, and paid to them.

The plan, by its nature, forces employees to save money now and pay taxes on it later in life during their "golden years" when they are in a more advantageous tax bracket; it is therefore regarded as a tax-deferred savings plan. On the other hand, the money at retirement may be tax-empted as a goodwill gesture to the retiree/beneficiary on the part of the state.

As is obvious, there are a number of really important *terms relating to pension planning and administration,* which should be understood and noted by the employee as well as the employer. Some of these are described below.

Annuity: This term is another name for pension, essentially indicating a series of payments deriving from a pension scheme or plan.

Annuity rate: This is a crucial factor that determines the amount of pension or annuity that actually accrues. The actuary calculates this rate based on a number of subsidiary factors such as age and sex of members, salaries of members, pensionable service, pre-scheme or administrative service, interest rates (present and future), population dynamics, especially life expectancy, inflation and so on. Annuity rate is also affected by early or late retirement.

Contributory and non-contributory plans: A contributory pension plan is one in which contributions are made by both the employer and employee. As noted above, contributions of either party will vary depending on factors such as negotiation, funding requirements, and employer generosity. A *non-contributory plan,* on the other hand, is one in which the full funding requirements are paid by the employer on behalf of the employee.

A pension schemes' manual produced by Jamaica's Joint Trade Unions Research and Development Centre states:

P

There are several arguments as to whether the cost of a pension scheme should be shared by employee and employer. Persons in favour of the non-contributory scheme argue that pension contributions are a part of the wage package and, thus, employers should bear all costs.

On the other hand, it can be argued that the advantages of a contributory scheme are:

    i. an employee who takes part in contributions takes a greater interest in his pension scheme;

    ii. a more generous scheme could be implemented if the cost were shared;

    iii. a contributory scheme, which is a joint venture, fosters good relationship between management and staff; and

    iv. that the employee can receive a lump sum if he terminates his service before retirement age. (JTURDC 1986)

A *defined benefit plan* is one in which, upon retirement, the pensioner/beneficiary will receive a defined or known monthly income or lump-sum payment. The benefit will be based upon a specific formula, which includes the number of years of pensionable service with the company and the salary at the time of or nearing retirement (final three or five years, as negotiated or agreed). Two types of defined benefit plans are the *career average* pension plan and the *final salary* pension plan (that is, average of final three or final five years of pensionable salary).

The *career average* pension is the average of the pensionable salaries with the particular plan multiplied by the accrual rate. For instance, if the total pensionable salary over the life of the employee with the company is $5,000,000 and the pensionable service was twenty-five years, the career average earnings would be $5,000,000/25 = $200,000. With an accrual rate of, say, 2 per cent, the annual pension benefit would be $200,000 × .02 × 25 = $100,000.

With a *final average scheme* (say, final three years), and accrual rate of 2 per cent and pensionable service of twenty-five years and pensionable salary as follows,

Year 1	$2,000,000.00
Year 2	$2,500,000.00
Year 3	$3,000,000.00
Total	$7,500,000.00
Average salary	$2,500,000.00

the pension benefit would be 2 per cent × $2,500,000 × 25 = $1,250,000 per annum.

The *defined contribution plan,* on the other hand, is one in which the contributions to the plan account are known or defined. For example, 10 per cent of his or her weekly salary is deposited into an account established within the plan specifically for the employee. However, whereas the contributions are known, the actual pension benefits or the total amount of money to be distributed at retirement (or at other junctures, as may become necessary) is unknown and will depend on how effectively the contributions are invested.

With the defined contribution plan, the pension benefits are determined by three factors:

1. The contributions (single or joint)
2. The investment portfolio or plan
3. The cost of purchasing or administering the plan

An example of the benefits available under such a plan is as follows:

Accumulated contributions of employee	=	$100,000.00
Accumulated contributions of employer	=	$200,000.00
Total available to purchase pension	=	$300,000.00
Annuity rate (see below)	=	7.50
Pension per annum		
(total available/annuity rate)	=	$ 40,000.00
Or, monthly (annual pension/12)	=	$3,333.00

Cost-of-living adjustment (COLA): A cost-of-living adjustment is a small incremental rise in retirement benefits, granted to retirees by a plan in an attempt to keep such benefits in line with inflation.

Individual retirement account (IRA): An account established by an individual with a bank or other financial institution which is funded by the individual to save for retirement. IRAs are not employer related.

Joint and survivor annuity: The pension holder retires and receives less than the maximum monthly retirement benefit so that upon his or her death, a survivor annuity is paid to the designated survivor for the remainder of that person's lifetime. This type of benefit option is often referred to as a husband-and-wife benefit and is typically payable under a defined benefit plan.

Matured plan: A plan that is presently providing benefits to the employee/former employee or designated beneficiary.

P

Mortality discount: An adjustment or modification to a present-value figure in consideration of the possibility of the premature death of the pension holder.

Non-vested benefit: A benefit which will not be paid by the plan unless the vesting requirements are met by the employee.

Qualified domestic relations order (QDRO): A written set of instructions which explain to the plan administrator that a portion of an employee's benefit is subject to distribution due to a divorce. In order to qualify, it must be in the form of a court order and meet various other requirements.

Qualified pre-retirement survivor annuity: This is a benefit which is paid under a qualified plan to a beneficiary on behalf of the pension holder/participant, in the event such pension holder/participant should die prior to retirement.

Unvested (non-vested) plan: A plan in which the employees would lose their rights to the benefits in the event of a termination of employment.

Valuation date: The date which is used as the reference for the interest rate that is to be used in determining present value, thereby establishing value as of such date.

Vested plan: A plan in which the employees would not lose their rights to the benefits in the event of a termination of employment.

Performance appraisal   A formal system of periodic evaluation of the job performance of employees. The appraisal system for employees must identify both strong and weak points: areas of performance that are acceptable along with areas that need improvement. A simple format with defined and clear criteria is best. Appraisals must be discussed with the employees concerned and an understanding reached between assessor and employees on all areas concerned, including future plans to improve or maintain levels of performance.

As mechanisms which measure employee work performance, identify weaknesses in capability and application and recommend improvement strategies, performance appraisals are therefore to be used to build a better workforce through motivating and improving quality. Performance appraisals are to be used as developmental tools and productivity improvement measures and not opportunities for managers to punish employees or to "even the score" with employees who do not meet with their approval.

Benefits of the Performance Appraisal System

P

If structured and conducted properly, these systems can have the following effects:

1. Eliminate uneven standards that can vary from manager to manager and department to department.
2. Remove the temptation to judge employees by their personalities. When every manager ranks employees by the same specific standards, appraisals are focused on qualities that are related to job performance, and not on the manager's perception or likes or dislikes of the employee.
3. Motivate employees. Since employees know that appraisals are an important aspect of decision making in regard to promotion and level of salary and so on, if they believe they are judged fairly, they will respect the system and view appraisal as a way to improve their performance.
4. Help to create a productive workforce. Appraisal standards that are objective and measurable ensure that managers recognize and reward employees for skills that further the goals of the organization.

Performance management   Performance management is a process whereby the goals and objectives of an enterprise or organization are carefully and practically incorporated in the management and utilization of the human and material resources of the enterprise. Its four basic steps include the following:

1. *Planning* and *agreeing* on the work to be done
2. *Monitoring* the work being done against objectives or work agreed
3. *Measuring* the work done relative to objectives or work agreed
4. *Rewarding* the work done according to agreement

The process, therefore, obliges managers to work closely with their employee constituencies to ensure appropriate deployment of personnel, appropriate measurement tools and methods and motivation of employees through commensurate rewards.

Performance management processes and programmes usually operate in tandem with other human resource management systems such as performance appraisals and pay for performance systems.

P

Permanent worker   An employee who is engaged on a permanent basis, enjoys all benefits and works under conditions stipulated by the company through an agreement with the union or as otherwise agreed.

Points to Note

1. Permanent workers must be given letters of appointment outlining conditions of work and benefits to which they are entitled.
2. Appropriate records of personal data must be maintained in an updated condition.
3. Termination of employment must be supported by clear reasons and just causes.
4. By law, redundancy provisions must be observed.

Personnel files/records (see also **record keeping**) Appropriate files must be kept with comprehensive data on each worker. All written communication between the company and a worker or communication about such a worker must be placed on the worker's personal file. Each worker should be granted access to their personal file for good and responsible use. Such a privilege must be exercised with discretion on both sides. The worker may not be permitted to remove the file from the Human Resources Office without permission.

Physical (working) conditions   Many employers and trade unions pay very little attention to the physical environment in which employees have to work. For example, the cleanliness of bathrooms, lunch rooms, yards, factory floors or premises is sometimes not taken into consideration when planning production schedules, rewards and production targets. A poor physical environment can be very depressing. A well-lit factory, brightly painted, with a little piped-in music and a landscaped yard, would create a happier and more enjoyable working environment. Cleanliness refreshes the soul and the mind and it is very important that the working environment be kept clean if optimum levels of productivity are to be attained. A clean and attractive environment promotes a high level of motivation among members of staff, and good housekeeping should be emphasized as an obligation of all staff members.

P

Picketing   The word "picket" is derived from the French "piquet", which means a stake. Picket, in the industrial relations sense, means the blocking of gates by workers to prevent or impede entry to the workplace during a strike, in furtherance of an industrial dispute.

Points to Note

1. The police can arrest picketers for offences such as obstructing a police officer while doing his or her duty, assaulting a police officer, or damaging company property.
2. Secondary picketing is against the law – for example, where an industrial dispute is at Company X and the workers decide to picket Company Y, a client of Company X against whom there is no dispute.

Premium payments   Payments made in excess of normal wages for working extraordinary hours on days such as Sundays and public holidays or for working in hazardous conditions, such as underground, or above ground level. Some examples of premiums are shift premium, night-work premium and height premium – paid to workers in some industries such as construction for working at certain specified heights.

Points to Note

1. "Premiums" are negotiated rates payable under agreed conditions of work.
2. Changes in basic rates do not necessarily mean automatic changes in premium rates unless such premiums are tied by percentage to basic rates of pay.

Probation   Probation is the initial period of permanent employment – usually a period of ninety days – during which the preliminary assessment of an individual's suitability for a job is determined.

The initial period of permanent employment, usually three to six months, is called a probationary period. During this period, the contract of employment may be terminated by either side without notice or payment in lieu of notice.

P

Productivity   Productivity can and ought to be defined or argued in both descriptive and mathematical terms as they complement each other and, when combined, provide a rounded appreciation of productivity. Productivity is "getting more bang for the buck" or "doing things right". It entails the efficient conversion of inputs, such as labour, capital, management and technology into outputs of goods and services, such as agricultural produce, manufactured goods, health-care delivery, passengers transported, products delivered, waste reduction/minimization.

Mathematically, productivity is "a ratio, of what is produced and what is used to produce it", or outputs divided by inputs. Outputs must be multiples of inputs in order to yield high productivity.

Output and Input Measures

Outputs are quantifiable or countable values resulting from direct, identifiable economic activities. For productivity assessment purposes the values or units of output measurement must be homogeneous.

Measures of outputs may be gross monetary or value added of the production or business process or the quantity of physical units produced, sales volume, and so on. In the case of a single-product production/business scenario, the output will simply be either the value of the goods produced, the value added to the goods produced or the total sales for a particular period. However, for a multi-product/service entity, output has to be converted to a common value such as the total value or value added of all the goods or services produced.

Inputs are regarded as the factors of production, the elements that go into making or contributing to the production of goods or services. Depending on the type and sophistication of the business, inputs are categorized as labour, capital, energy, materials, management, and so on.

Labour is measured in one of three ways: number of persons employed, cost of labour or the number of hours worked. Capital is treated either as fixed capital assets, capital consumed or in terms of all non-labour costs.

Measuring and Interpreting Productivity

Productivity is all about ratios. In its simplest mathematical formulation productivity is as follows:

$$Productivity = \frac{Output}{Input}$$

$$Productivity = \frac{10 \text{ units}}{10 \text{ units}} = 1$$

$$Productivity = \frac{20 \text{ units}}{10 \text{ units}} = 2$$

As shown above, in the first example the productivity ratio is 1, which means that output and input are of equal value. Expressed another way, the production/business process has not been efficient enough to add value to the input factor. It is basically a break even scenario, rendering the business incapable of new investments or expansion outside of injection of new input resources. In other words, the business process has not improved on its input factor(s) to facilitate growth in the business or the welfare of the main players.

In the second scenario, the productivity ratio of 2 suggests that the business process added value to or improved on the input factor(s). This outcome presents options of reinvestments, of expansion or otherwise for the business. By virtue of the value added productivity ratio, many more options are available to this business than is the case with scenario 1.

Types of Productivity Measurement

Input measures can be combined to provide different types of and refinement to productivity measurement. The productivity outcome(s) would therefore be a function of partial factor, multi-factor or total factor inputs. These are explained below.

- *Total factor productivity* (TFP) uses all factors of production that feature in producing/deriving the output. It is therefore the ratio of value added (or output) to the total value of all factor inputs.

  Although a very useful measure of productivity, it is not used as widely as it perhaps should be. "Many large, diversified

P

companies, however, now use all four inputs (labour, capital, materials and energy) to determine . . . Total Factor Productivity."[1]

Through a system of weighting, TFP measures allow for a determination of the respective contributions of the input factors to the growth in productivity. In other words, the actual contribution of labour or capital, and so on, can be determined and tracked over time. This provides the opportunity to policymakers to address problems or circumstances hindering optimal contributions to productivity of respective input factors.

- *Multi-factor productivity* (MFP) uses more than one input factor, such as labour and capital combined. It has very strong appeal and is preferred over single or partial factor measures. The most common multi-factor inputs are labour and capital.

Depending on how capital is measured, the MFP could approximate TFP measurement. For instance, as is customary with the Singaporeans in their well-established MFP measurements, capital is measured as all non-labour input factors.

As in the case of TFP, MFP measures allow for zeroing in on the respective contributions of input factors to productivity growth.

- *Partial-factor productivity* uses a single factor of input, such as capital or labour. It is therefore interpreted as the amount of

---

[1] The Bell system has developed a sophisticated productivity programme and integrated it into its overall budgeting and planning activities.

Bell uses two partial productivity measures – volume of business per employee and number of phones served per employee. Both measure labour productivity. Bell also uses three total factor productivity (TFP) measures to determine overall corporate performance.

One TFP measure emphasizes total output, the others gross and net value added.

Bell's TFP inputs are capital, labour and materials. All are reported in current dollars, deflated, weighted, averaged, and indexed to arrive at a single total input index. Because of the great variety of Bell products and services, output is measured in current revenues, not physical units. Again, the revenue dollars are deflated. All categories of revenues are then added to arrive at a total dollar output figure. That total is indexed to arrive at a single total output index. Finally, the output index number and the resulting figure is the total factor productivity index for the company. The percentage change over time in the TFP Index is Bell's key measure of the entire company's productivity.

Bell uses this TFP model to track productivity trends, to compare them with industry norms, and to plan long term. They also combine productivity with traditional financial analysis to determine the impact of net income, productivity growth, price change and many other variables (Productivity Management, http://www.bizmove.com/general/m6g.htm, 3).

value added/output to a single unit of capital or labour input. Although this measure has very strong appeal, it should be used with caution and interpreted properly.

Labour Productivity

Labour productivity is perhaps the commonest partial-factor productivity measure in use. There are three different measures of labour productivity. They are unit labour productivity, unit labour time productivity and labour cost productivity.

$$Unit\ Labour\ Productivity = \frac{Output/Value\ Added}{Number\ of\ Employees}$$

$$Unit\ Labour\ Cost\ Productivity = \frac{Compensation\ of\ Employees}{Output/Value\ Added}$$

$$Unit\ Labour\ Time\ Productivity = \frac{Output/Value\ Added}{Total\ Number\ of\ Hours\ Worked}$$

Unit labour productivity is simply the amount or value of output achieved by each employee. Unit labour cost productivity is the employee cost for each unit of output or value added. Unit labour-time productivity is the amount of output or value added for each hour worked.

There are two basic shortcomings associated with labour productivity measurement. In the first place, it does not capture the specific contribution of labour to productivity outcome. Instead, it assumes some of the contribution made by other factors such as capital, intermediate consumption and technology.

Second, labour productivity can increase or decrease purely on the basis of adding or improving on non-labour input factor(s).

Nonetheless, the labour productivity measurement is very useful, because it is easy to calculate and it is, perhaps in most instances, the single largest input factor in value terms.

Productivity bargaining   A system of indexing or increasing earnings relative to individual or group productivity. This system may be related to a particular method of payment such as a bonus or productivity incentive scheme, piece rates or profit sharing.

P

Productivity incentive schemes   These are mechanisms designed to off-set lagging production, to increase efficiency of labour and capital, and to raise the earnings base of individual plants and the general economy. In other words, these schemes are meant to rationalize and improve the system of production in terms of a more efficient use of resources.

Promotion   The act of moving an employee upwards in the organization. Promotion is a form of recognition of individual performance. When an individual is being promoted, it is a time of praise and congratulations. A manager who refuses or neglects to give public recognition of a pro-motion may appear to be unsure of his or her decision and judgement. Perhaps the manager is not committed to the decision to promote the individual or does not wish to publicize it in case the decision has to be rescinded for any reason. Such fears should not be allowed to obstruct proper and acceptable procedures of effective management.

Points to Note

1. The employee concerned should be notified about promotion, both orally and in writing.
2. If promotion is to be meaningful, it must be accompanied by a simultaneous increase in pay or improvement in benefits.
3. When unionized workers are being promoted, the union should be officially notified.
4. In all cases of promotion, every member of staff – especially in payroll and human resources departments – must be notified.

Public holidays   Some of the recognized public holidays in the Carib-bean are as follows:

Emancipation Day	Jamaica, Trinidad
New Year's Day	All states
Second New Year's Day	St Lucia
Ash Wednesday	Jamaica
Carnival Monday	Dominica, St Lucia, Trinidad and Tobago
Carnival Tuesday	Dominica, St Lucia, Trinidad and Tobago

P

Pagwah Day	Guyana
Good Friday	All states
Easter Monday	All states
Labour Day	All states
Whit Monday	Antigua, St Lucia, British Virgin Islands, Barbados, St Vincent, St Kitts, Dominica
Corpus Christi	Grenada, St Lucia, Trinidad and Tobago
Queen's Birthday	Antigua, St Lucia, British Virgin Islands, Dominica, St Kitts, Montserrat
Kadooment Day	Barbados
Independence Day	Jamaica, Grenada, St Kitts, Trinidad and Tobago, Antigua, Suriname, Barbados, Dominica, St Vincent
August Holiday	All states except Jamaica and Suriname
CARICOM Day	Dominica, Grenada, Barbados, St Lucia, St Vincent
Republic Day	Trinidad and Tobago, Guyana
Thanksgiving Day	St Lucia
UN Day	Barbados
National Heroes Day	Jamaica
Divali	Trinidad and Tobago
Indian Arrival Day	Trinidad and Tobago
Eid-Ul-Fitr	Trinidad and Tobago, Suriname
Liberation Day	Montserrat
Prince Charles's Birthday	British Virgin Islands
National Day	St Lucia
Christmas Day	All states
Boxing Day	All states
Old Year's Day	Montserrat

Q–R

Recall   See **layoff and recall.**

Receivership   Receivership involves the appointment of a receiver or manager to carry on the company's business with the aim of managing the company's assets so as to pay debts owing, primarily to debenture holders. A receiver may be appointed by the court pursuant to the Companies Act.

Record keeping   Employers are required to keep, in relation to each worker, records containing the following particulars:

1. The name and address of the employer
2. The name and address of the employee
3. The date on which the employment or re-employment commenced
4. An accurate description of the place at which the employee was ordinarily resident when he or she was engaged under the contract of employment
5. An accurate description of the place at which the employee was present when the offer of employment was made to him or her by any other means than by advertisement or at which the contract of employment was made
6. Where the contract of employment of the employee has been terminated, particulars as to
   a. the relevant date (that is, date of termination)
   b. the period ending with the relevant date of employment or, if he or she were engaged in seasonal employment, the number of consecutive years of engagement in continuous seasonal employment
   c. the amount of redundancy payment (if any) paid to him or her
7. Training obtained prior to and during the employment (this includes history of educational attainments)

R

Red circle   Red circle is a term applied to the freezing of a prescribed rate of pay. Such a rate may have been the result of annual increments to an individual over a prolonged period but bears no logical or reasonable comparability to rates paid to similar classifications in the company. In other words, a red-circle rate is a special rate of pay associated with an individual's length of service or special talents.

A red-circle rate may remain fixed until similar categories catch up with it after which it may be adjusted according to established practices.

Redundancy (see also **notice of termination**)   Under Jamaica's Employment (Termination and Redundancy Payments) Act, 1975, a worker may be made redundant in the following circumstances:

1. Where there is a change in production methods
2. Where business has contracted or intends to be contracted
3. Where the worker, when offered alternative employment, refuses and opts for redundancy
4. Where a worker has suffered personal injury or disease on the job

The rate of redundancy pay was amended by the Employment (Termination and Redundancy payments) – Amendments Regulations 1988. (See **notice of termination.**)

Redundancy pay is also applicable to seasonal workers who have worked for two or more years, consecutively. To qualify for such redundancy pay, the seasonal worker must go to the usual place of employment and the employer must fail to provide him or her with work.

Non-Entitlement

A worker is not to be paid redundancy pay under the following conditions:

- resignation (unless he or she was forced to do so by the conduct of the employer)
- termination (breach of company rules and regulations) (see **dismissal for cause**)
- refusal of an offer to renew a contract of employment under the same terms and conditions
- such an employee retires

Qualifications for Redundancy

R

On completion of 104 weeks' service, an employee may qualify for redundancy pay. Casual or temporary workers qualify for redundancy pay if they have worked for an employer for two consecutive years. Two weeks' pay for seasonal workers means 2/104 of the aggregate normal wages earned during the last two consecutive years preceding the date of termination of employment.

Report   A concise, factual account of an event or project. In relation to industrial relations practice, it is required that dates, place and times of events should be noted as well as witnesses.

Points to Note

1. Be precise.
2. Be factual.
3. Include salient facts and figures.
4. Address the report to the persons for whom it is intended.
5. Summarize contents.
6. Send copies to all parties concerned who need to know.
7. Follow up all recommendations in the report.

Representational rights   See **bargaining rights.**

Retroactive pay   Amount of outstanding pay owed to an employee for past service. Outstanding payments may be due to a number of factors. They could result from a shortfall in pay arising from miscalculations; additional payment arising from protracted negotiations; pay reviews resulting in upward revaluation in pay; court awards for retroactivity, and so on.

From a collective bargaining standpoint, retroactive payment terms and conditions are usually agreed to in collective or other agreement schedules. Retroactive pay may be paid in a lump sum or in any form as agreed between the parties. However, retroactive pay is subject to all statutory deductions applicable to normal pay. These deductions include, for example, income

R

tax; education tax; National Housing Trust contributions; and contributions to medical and pension schemes.

Rights and interests   See **industrial dispute.**

S

Safety The Factories Act of Jamaica, which provides for the registration and supervision of factories, requires that adequate measures be taken to ensure that

1. workers are properly and appropriately attired;
2. safety goggles and other head gear are worn on the job;
3. floors are clean and the atmosphere free of injurious chemicals, fumes, odours, pollution;
4. all moving parts on machinery are properly protected;
5. physical working areas are properly ventilated;
6. fences are erected to protect workers against moving machinery, pits or vessels containing dangerous liquids;
7. women and young persons do not clean machinery while it is moving; and
8. young persons are trained and properly supervised before being allowed to work on dangerous machinery.

Initially, the act covered premises where steam, water, mechanical or electric power was being used in any commercial manufacturing process. An amendment to this act has now widened its coverage to include, in addition to the above, operations on docks, ships and the building and construction industries.

Employees have the responsibility of wearing all protective gear provided. They must also comply with all the company's rules and regulations governing the use of equipment and protective gear and all other safety measures. Clear notices or rules, which should be placed in strategic locations, must be read by employees. Failure to read or to enquire about a rule or measure is no justification for breaching it. Responsibility for safety is a dual one and the rules of safety must be rigidly enforced and strictly obeyed by all.

Often, an injury caused by carelessness on the part of the individual is interpreted as reflecting an uncaring and insensitive attitude on the part of the company, when in fact the company has taken all necessary precautions to prevent injury.

S

Safety maintenance includes the following:

- regular inspection of hoists, lifts, chains, ropes or lifting tackles at least twice yearly
- annual examination of cranes
- regular inspection of floors
- precautions taken against gassing and explosions
- frequent examination of steam boilers and air receivers

Salary (see also **wage**)   Salaries are customarily paid weekly, monthly or annually. Usually, salaried employees are defined as white-collar or professional managerial types, while wage earners are termed blue-collar or hourly paid workers. Salaried employees may receive the same pay whether for less or more than the stipulated scheduled hours of work.

Seasonal employees   Seasonal employees work for not less than ninety days or earn at least the equivalent of ninety days' pay at the going rate in any season, or their names appear on the seasonal payroll for at least sixteen weeks per year.

For seasonal employees, two weeks' pay means 1/104 of the aggregate normal wages earned by the employee during the last two consecutive years preceding the date of the termination of employment. To qualify for redundancy pay, they must have worked for at least two consecutive seasons with the same employer.

Gratuity Payments – Casual Employees: Entitlement

At or before the end of each qualifying year of employment (that is, each twelve-month period commencing on the day of employment), a casual employee shall be paid a gratuity

1. if he or she has worked with his or her employer for not less than 110 days during the qualifying year; or
2. where the number of days worked in a qualifying year cannot be ascertained, if he or she has earned a sum equivalent to 110 times the daily rate for the category of work where there is an established daily rate for the category in the area of his or her employment; or

3. where the basis for calculation cannot be established as in (1) or
    (2) above, if his or her name has appeared on the pay bills of his
    or her employer for not less than twenty weeks during the qual-
    ifying year.

Casual Employees – Sick Benefits: First-Year Entitlement

Any worker employed as a casual worker will be entitled to sick leave
benefit for the period of his or her illness or for the first ten days thereof
where the total period of illness exceeds ten days, during the first year of
his or her employment if he or she becomes ill after

1. he or she has worked for not less than 110 days; or
2. where the number of days cannot be ascertained, if he or she has
    earned, as normal wages, a sum equivalent to 110 times the estab-
    lished daily rate for the category or work in the area; or where
    there is no such established rate his or her name has appeared on
    the pay bills of his or her employer for not less than twenty weeks.

Shift premium   A shift premium is an amount paid in excess of normal
wages to those employees who work on a shift. This premium is a negotiated
amount and is usually calculated as a percentage of basic straight-time pay.
Shift premiums are included in the total pay package and are taxable. Before
implementing a shift premium, the following should be considered:

*   the desirability of implementing a shift premium
*   a careful study of industry-wide comparisons to help determine
    appropriate rates
*   its impact as a motivating factor in the productive effort
*   the cost to the company and whether the company can afford
    to pay this additional cost; and
*   whether it would be paid as a percentage of wages or as a fixed
    sum (for example, 20 per cent or $0.20 per hour)

Sick leave   The Holidays with Pay Order (as amended) refers to absence
due to illness, which may be either certified by a medical doctor or uncer-
tified. Under this law, and subject to any agreement between trade unions
and management:

S

1. An employee qualifies for sick leave after having worked for one full year.
2. Payment for sick leave is based on normal wages earned, excluding overtime or any premium or special allowances, but including a bonus, where this forms part of the regular paid remuneration.
3. If a worker falls ill before completing one year's service, provided that that worker has completed 110 days' work, he or she is eligible for paid sick leave on the basis of one day for every 22 days worked.
4. The normal annual entitlement of each employee in succeeding years of employment is two normal working weeks with pay.

Sick Leave without Pay

An employee is not entitled to be paid any sick leave benefit when

- he or she is being paid sick benefit or employment injury benefit under the National Insurance Scheme (NIS) or compensation under the Worker's Compensation Act; or
- he or she fails to notify the employer of his or her illness within the first working day after its occurrence and to furnish the employer with a certificate from a registered medical practitioner after the third day of illness.

Sick Leave for Casuals

A casual employee becomes entitled to a total of 10 working days' sick leave in any qualifying year after working for 110 days, or earning wages equal to 110 times the established daily rate for the category, or appearing on the pay bill for at least twenty weeks.

The minimum daily pay in respect of sick leave granted in any qualifying year is 1/10 of 3 per cent of a casual employee's earning, calculated from the start of the qualifying year to the day before becoming ill, in the case of the first illness; or in the case of the second or any subsequent illness, from the day of resuming work after the last illness to the day before such illness occurs. To qualify for this benefit an employee must notify the employer of the illness not later than the second day of absence through illness. If absent for more than three days, the period of absence should be noted.

Qualification for Leave

When calculating a worker's qualification for leave, the following are regarded as days worked:

1. Any day of holiday with pay granted
2. Any day of sick leave with pay granted if the employer would normally have required the worker to work on that day
3. Any public holiday on which the employer would have required the worker to work

A worker is regarded as having worked a full day even though the actual time worked was a part of that day.

Sit-in   Commonly regarded as industrial action involving a stoppage of production with the employees sitting at their usual work stations. A sit-in is also a taking over of a factory or plant by employees in an effort to keep it open when management wishes to close it down for any reason. In some cases, the employees may keep the plant open by working for nothing; they may put out the owner and turn it into a cooperative; or they may organize and manage it themselves.

Points to Note

1. In the event of a sit-in as a form of industrial action, follow the procedures laid down under **industrial action.**
2. If the sit-in is a workers' takeover, the board of directors will have to take action.

Sleeping on the job   Sleeping on the job is an offence which is subject to disciplinary action. Such behaviour may endanger the life and well-being of the company and its employees.

Employees on watchman service or whose job entails long, non-productive hours should operate in properly ventilated surroundings and be subjected to periodic supervisory visits to avoid drowsiness and lethargy and to maintain alertness. Idleness induces sleep. Wherever possible, such employees should be rotated frequently during the course of a shift.

S

Social partners   This is the term used to refer to employers' and workers' organizations engaged in dialogue or partnership with the government in the determination of social and labour policies. Indeed, the ILO itself is structured on this basis, with each social partner having equal status and importance to others in policy formulation. Because it is a structure of three partners, the process of decision making has become known as *tripartism.*

Staff   A term used to describe employees usually on the permanent payroll and who are paid on a weekly, monthly or annual basis.

Statute law   A law that has been made by parliament. Statute laws involve clear minimum conditions on various areas of life, enshrining our rights and regulating our behaviour.

Under the constitution of the country, these include rights such as freedom of worship, freedom of speech, freedom to join an association of one's choice and freedom of movement. Applications and interpretation of these laws are made by the law courts.

Stealing   Every organization must include in its disciplinary code an agreed course of action for dealing with cases of theft. Usually, the decision is one of summary dismissal for cause. In these circumstances, the employee is not entitled to notice or notice pay. However, payment for unused vacation leave and for time worked up to the date of the misdeed must be made. If the employee is a union member the union must be advised, as in other cases of termination.

Strike   (see also **industrial action**)   A stoppage or disruption of work in furtherance of a dispute at the workplace. Various forms of strikes include the following:

S

1. *Work-to-rule:* Doing everything "by the book". No extra or informal systems are used and no overtime is worked.
2. *Go-slow:* A slowing down of all productive activity. This action frustrates production.
3. *Sympathetic strike:* One group of workers takes strike action in support of another group that is already on strike. For example, clerical workers may take strike action in support of production workers.
4. *Token strike:* One-day stoppage in protest against some decision or action by the company's management.
5. *Unofficial strike:* Strike action taken without the knowledge of the union. Employees must therefore stand the consequences of their action. Such strikes may not be illegal when taken in pursuit of disputes between management and workers. However, there is no right to strike in Jamaica or the English-speaking Caribbean. Workers are free to strike, but they may be deemed as having breached their contract of employment as a result of their action. Furthermore, they may be in breach of the law if taken in contravention of any labour law that set procedures to follow in the taking of industrial action. Under the Jamaican Industrial Disputes Act, 1975, workers are required to give the Ministry of Labour certain periods of notice before taking industrial action, and where workers fail to give adequate notice (ten days in essential services), they are in breach of this law and industrial action is therefore unlawful.
6. *Sick-out:* Industrial action taken by the full workforce in the form of absence from work for alleged sickness over a specified time, usually one to two days.

Points to Note

Some possible causes of strikes could be as follows:

- breach of contract
- tardiness in wage negotiation
- failure to implement agreed working conditions
- dismissal of a fellow worker
- poor communication
- victimization
- general dissatisfaction with management
- low morale

S

Payment during Strike Action

Workers are not normally entitled to pay when they have withdrawn their labour. In some forms of industrial action, however, such as work-to-rule or sit-ins, workers ensure that from a technical point of view they have not actually withdrawn their services. Depending on how carefully they have avoided breaching certain rules (that is, the production norms may not have been disturbed to a degree that can be substantiated), workers may be entitled to pay.

A company faced with industrial action in any form may elect to close its doors to protect its products and machinery. Such action, commonly referred to as a "lockout", should not be taken in haste. The situation must be carefully assessed as to whether normal production is being obstructed and whether the ensuing situation is abnormal. The doors may be closed until it is agreed that normality will be restored. Every attempt must be made to follow the established grievance procedure, and to settle the matter as expeditiously as possible at the local level before seeking the assistance of outside parties.

Case: Dispute re Pay During Strike Action (Jamaica)

In 1980, the minister of labour referred to the Industrial Disputes Tribunal (IDT) a dispute arising out of the closure of a "cinema in the wake of a work-to-rule demonstration by the workers" employed to Palace Amusement Company (1921) Ltd, and represented by the Bustamante Industrial Trade Union (BITU). The company submitted that the workers were on go-slow and were, therefore, not entitled to pay for the period during which the business had to be closed. The union contended that no such industrial action had taken place and the workers were to be paid for the time worked. The IDT made no award (meaning that the workers were to be paid for the period of the go-slow). The company appealed to the Supreme Court, which ruled as follows:

1. Every employee is expected to behave fairly to his or her employer and to do a fair day's work for his or her pay. Conversely, every employer is expected to act fairly to his or her worker and to demonstrate reasonableness, foster cooperation and encourage productivity.
2. It is a breach of a term in the contract of service for a worker to wilfully obstruct his or her employer in the course of his or her business. If a worker, with others, takes action to disrupt a business or undertaking so that the resultant effect is to force the employer to cease operations until normality is restored or guaranteed, the workers who participate in the action which forced the cessation are not entitled to receive

any wages during the period of closure. Wages are to be paid for services faithfully performed and not for services producing disruption, chaos and strife.

3. A course of conduct on the part of the workers which tends to frustrate the object for which the contract of service was expressly or implicitly made is a blow aimed at the consensual intention of the parties to the contract. And where the conduct brings about a situation which puts a temporary halt to operation of the business, it is unreasonable for any tribunal to order the employer to pay workers for the period during which the operation of the business ceased.

The Supreme Court upheld the company's appeal against the IDT's award.

Subsistence allowance   An allowance paid in addition to normal wages, usually as a fixed amount in special consideration for extraordinary hours of work. Such an allowance may be paid in the form of a lunch or travelling allowance to employees who are required to work away from base or during unusual hours.

Suspension   The act of temporarily withdrawing the services of an employee for committing a breach of company rules and regulations. Periods of suspension may vary depending on the gravity of the offence. Depending on the gravity of the breach, suspension may best come after the employee has been warned or reprimanded orally or in written form.

Points to Note

1. During suspension, an employee does not suffer loss of seniority.
2. Suspension is without pay or other benefit.
3. On resumption, the employee returns to his or her original position.

T

Take-home pay   This is an expression that describes the average weekly earnings, after deductions from earnings, such as taxes, pension deductions and other statutory deductions. It therefore does not include deductions incurred by or on behalf of the employee to satisfy their personal investments or obligations. For instance, deductions regarding loan repayment or motor car or home mortgage payments on behalf of the employee, though occurring at source or taken from their pay, would be considered part of the take-home package.

Termination for cause (see also **dismissal for cause**)   An employer may terminate an employee's contract of employment for cause without notice. This right must be exercised within four weeks of the employer's recognition of the misconduct that justifies the termination. Failing this, the employer has to give the required notice or pay in lieu of notice.

If an investigation into the cause of dismissal is required, the employee may be suspended from duty without pay pending the actions of the investigation.

Time keeping   As a condition of employment, the company's hours of work must be rigidly observed. Failure to comply with this rule may result in

- a warning being issued, verbally or in writing, or
- either suspension or dismissal for repeated lateness.

Before taking action, however, the employer may give consideration to possible extenuating circumstances that could be discussed in a counselling session with the employee. If the circumstances warrant, the employee may be given time to improve on his or her attendance record.

T

Time off   Company's policies and rules or collective agreements should include provisions for time off with pay under the following conditions:

- educational purposes
- death in the immediate family
- special circumstances at the management's discretion

Such absences and the reasons should be noted on the employee's attendance record.

Total input   *Inputs* are regarded as the factors of production, the basic units which are processed or used in creating or generating finished goods or services. Input factors are usually broadly categorized as *labour* and *capital*. However, in more sophisticated scenarios, other important factors such as *technology, energy, materials* and *management* are disaggregated. Therefore, depending on the degree of sophistication of the business or the level of detail required in making decisions, one or a combination of these factors will be used in measuring input.

Total output   This is the sum of the value of manufactured products (ex-factory value). *Outputs* are quantifiable or countable units or value resulting from the processing of the inputs. Measures of outputs may be gross monetary or value added of the production or business process or the quantity units produced, sales volume and so on.

Some businesses are engaged in single-product or service operations while others have multi-product or service offerings. Where the business is engaged in a single product or service offering, the output will simply be the value of the goods produced, the value added to the goods produced or the total sales for a particular period. However, for multi-product or service entities, output measures for each product or service are converted to a common value such as the total value or value added of all the goods or services produced.

Trade union   An association organized for the purpose of promoting and protecting the rights of employees. In Jamaica, trade unions are registered

T

under the Trade Union Act of 1919 (as amended), and must negotiate in the collective interests of their membership, and in Guyana by the Trades Union Act of 1921. (See Appendix I for a list of registered trade unions in Jamaica.)

The right of every employee to be a member of an organization of choice and to take part at appropriate times in the activities of the organization is enshrined in the Jamaican Constitution and this right, as it applies to trade unions, is set out in detail in the Labour Relations and Industrial Disputes Act, 1975 (Jamaica). The act also protects the employees' membership of a trade union from interference by an employer.

These rights of union membership mean that if an employer dismisses an employee for joining a trade union, that employer would be guilty of an offence. If another employee or trade union prevents another employee from joining a trade union of choice, that individual or trade union would be similarly guilty of an offence. Furthermore, if an employer offers an incentive to employees as an inducement to refrain from joining a trade union, and if that benefit is given only to those who do not join, such an employer would be in breach of the law on the grounds of discriminatory treatment (union busting) against those who do not support the proposal to reject unionization.

Trade union, types   *Industrial* unions draw their membership exclusively from a particular industry or economic activity. The best example of this in the Caribbean would be the Oilfields Workers Union of Trinidad and Tobago. The Jamaica Teachers' Association and the Junior Doctors' Association in Jamaica are perhaps also good examples.

General unions, also referred to as *blanket unions,* are those which represent workers at all levels and across industries. The largest and most powerful unions in the world are the general unions. These unions were developed to help the unskilled workers in industry. Membership of these unions is drawn from several skilled and unskilled classifications and from several different industries. In Jamaica, the principal general unions are the Bustamante Industrial Trade Union (BITU), the National Workers Union (NWU), University and Allied Workers' Union (UAWU) and the Trades Union Congress (TUC). Smaller general unions such as the Jamaica Independent Workers Union are other examples. The Barbados Workers Union and the Guyana Industrial Workers Union are other Caribbean examples.

T

Company unions are those that are formed to and represent only workers in a particular company.

Staff associations, registered or unregistered as trade unions, are bodies that represent the interests of workers in their respective companies.

Craft unions are those formed on the basis of particular skills such as motor mechanics, plumbing or electrical work. This type of union predates the general unions that we know today.

Trade union *bargaining unit* is usually comprised of homogeneous classifications, that is, similar classifications of workers employed in one undertaking who share a common location or workers employed in one undertaking who share a common location or work and a common employer.

Bargaining type: Bargaining can be *separate,* in that, in the event that only one union exists or is recognized at a particular workplace or represents a particular bargaining unit, bargaining is done on a separate or individualized basis. *Joint bargaining* occurs when more than one union represents a set of workers or the same bargaining unit.

Industrial councils are set up to negotiate working conditions on an industry-wide basis where this is deemed beneficial to the industry and the parties. The establishment of these councils arose out of a report from the Whitely Committee (1916) of the British government.

Trade union organizations   Trade unions also form affiliations internationally to garner support from each other as well as to influence development and direction of work-related concerns and provide a counter to employer organizations and their influence at the international level. The following lists important international trade union organizations and trade union support organizations, respectively:

International Trade Union Organizations

ETUC: European Trade Union Confederation, Brussels

FIET: The International Federation of Commercial, Clerical, Professional and Technical Employees

FICSA: Federation of International Civil Servants' Associations (representing international civil servants working at the UN Specialized Agencies)

ICEM: International Federation of Chemical, Energy, Mine and General Workers' Unions

ICFTU: International Confederation of Free Trade Unions, Brussels

ICFTU Asia/Pacific: International Confederation of Free Trade Unions – Asian and Pacific Regional Organization

IFWEA: International Federation of Workers' Education Associations

ITF: International Transport Workers' Federation

ITF–Japan: Japanese branch of ITF

Trade Union Support Organizations

ILO: International Labour Organization

ILO–CEET: Central and Eastern European Team of the ILO

ILO–CIS: International Occupational Safety and Health Information Centre

International Labour Organization: All conventions and recommendations of the ILO on occupational health and safety.

International Commission for Coordination of Solidarity Among Sugar Workers

IFWEA: International Federation of Workers' Education Associations

International Liaison Committee for Workers' International

LaborNet@IGC: A community of labour unions, activists, and organizations using computer networks for information sharing and collaboration with the intent of increasing the human rights and economic justice of workers. LaborNet@IGC seeks to increase awareness among the US labour movement of the different computer networks available to them, and to assist them in coming online through training and technical assistance.

LA Labor News

Labor Neighbor Bulletin Board

Labour Telematics Centre – United Kingdom

UNION-D European Trade Union e-mail discussion group

United Auto Workers New Directions

VGWM – Unit of the Industrial Union FNV. This site provides a vast amount of information and resources on occupational health and safety, some in Dutch and some in English.

T

Training   A prescribed training programme is fundamental to the success of any business activity. Such training should be planned to achieve specific objectives. Training and development of personnel are too often neglected in organizational planning. Too many employers depend on ad hoc training plans for the development of their employees and fail to plan properly for succession, skills development and management training.

In this modern age, training of people must be one of the main objectives of the organization. Personnel must be assessed in terms of their skills and abilities. Weaknesses should be identified and training plans developed to assist personnel in overcoming these weaknesses so that they will become greater assets to the organization. A corollary of an effective training programme is the *performance appraisal* system, which identifies performance, potential and training needs.

Any training in industrial relations should consider the environment, that is, factors in society that influence the relationships between people at the workplace. It should also include discussions on collective agreements, handling of grievances, current trends on the industrial relations scene, safety and hygiene and development of negotiating skills.

Tripartite   The term used to describe equal participation and representation of governments, employers' and workers' organizations in bodies both inside the ILO and at the national and enterprise level – hence tripartism, to describe the decision-making process. (See also **social partners** above.)

U–V

Unemployment benefits (insurance)   This is a programme or provision, usually administered by the state, under which employees are allowed some degree of compensation during periods of unemployment. The insurance or source of income from which benefits/payments are made is usually a levy on employers exclusively for this purpose. However, there are some instances in which employees also pay an amount to the insurance fund. According to the ILO's World Labour Report of 2000, the "great advantage of unemployment insurance is that it provides effective income security. It contributes to consumption smoothing and efficient job search."

There are usually stipulated conditions or qualifications for receipt of unemployment benefits. For instance, benefits are paid out for specified time periods and beneficiaries must not have lost their jobs as a result of having committed any offences. In addition, beneficiaries are expected to make real efforts to find new employment.

Unemployment benefits are mostly evident in developed countries such as in North America and Europe, and are, especially in the latter, part of a wider programme of social welfare. Indeed, "No more than a quarter of the world's 150 million unemployed benefit from some kind of unemployment insurance. The great majority are workers who had contracts in the formal sector. But for those who work in the rural or urban informal sectors, including 750 to 900 million underemployed workers – the working poor – there is hardly any protection at all" (ILO 2000).

The ILO report distinguishes between *high* and *medium* level unemployment protection provider countries. The *high level* protection providers are Austria, Belgium, Denmark, Finland, France, Germany, Iceland, Luxembourg, the Netherlands, Norway, Portugal, Spain, Sweden and Switzerland. Of the various layers of benefits provided by these countries, the first and most important is unemployment insurance paid during the initial period following the loss of a job. Additionally, most of these countries have a second layer of unemployment benefits, called unemployment assistance, which "covers workers who have exhausted their entitlements to unemployment insurance and provides them with a grace period before they come within the purview of less generous social assistance schemes" (ILO 2000).

The *medium level* countries include Australia, Canada, Ireland, Japan, New Zealand, the United Kingdom and the United States. In these countries, fewer of the unemployed receive benefits, which are lower than those available in the high level provider countries. The *World Labour Report* highlights that in Canada, the United Kingdom and the United States, "the duration of unemployment benefit payment is short, with benefits payable for less than 12 months", with no second layer of unemployment assistance available afterwards in Canada and the United States (ILO 2000).

Currently, many questions and debates are raging about the feasibility and longer term viability of unemployment insurance and the broader welfare system, especially in societies in which the age dependency ratio is high.

Almost all OECD countries in the 1990s reduced the protection provided by their unemployment benefit systems as a result of increasing financial strains (and) the publication of various studies . . . which linked the unemployment rate to unemployment benefit variables. . . . Eligibility rules have been tightened, benefit duration and replacement rates reduced and efforts intensified, through active labour market policies, to get unemployed back to work. (ILO 2000)

Summarized details of two unemployment benefit systems, those of the United States and Sweden, appear below.

United States Department of Labor

The US Department of Labor outlines in general the principles and policies governing the administration of unemployment benefits in the United States (http://welfaresecurity.doleta.gov/unemploy/uifactsheet.asp). These are as follows:

Purpose

In general, the Federal-State Unemployment Insurance Program provides unemployment benefits to eligible workers who are unemployed through no fault of their own (as determined under state law), and meet other eligibility requirements of state law.

1. Unemployment insurance payments (benefits) are intended to provide temporary financial assistance to unemployed workers who meet the requirements of state law.

U

2. Each state administers a separate unemployment insurance pro-
    gramme within guidelines established by federal law.
3. Eligibility for unemployment insurance, benefit amounts, and
    the length of time benefits are available are determined by the
    state law under which unemployment insurance claims are
    established.
4. In the majority of states, benefit funding is based solely on a tax
    imposed on *employers*. (Three states require minimal employee
    contributions.)

Eligibility

1. You must meet the state requirements for wages earned or time
    worked during an established (one year) period of time referred
    to as a "base period". (In most states, this is usually the first four
    out of the last five completed calendar quarters prior to the time
    that your claim is filed.)
2. You must be determined to be unemployed through no fault of
    your own (determined under state law), and meet other eligi-
    bility requirements of state law.

Continued Eligibility

1. You must file weekly or biweekly claims (after the week(s) has
    ended), and respond to questions concerning your continued
    eligibility. You must report any earnings from work you had
    during the week(s). You must also report any job offers or refusal
    of work during the week. These claims are usually filed by mail
    or telephone; the state will provide filing instructions.
2. When directed, you must report to your local unemployment
    insurance claims office or one-stop/employment service office
    on the day and at the time you are scheduled to do so. If you
    fail to report as scheduled for any interview, benefits may be
    denied.
3. You must continue to meet the eligibility requirements stated in
    the previous section.

Registering for Work

1. Claimants who file for unemployment benefits may be directed
    to register for work with the state employment service, so it can

U

assist you in finding employment. If you are not required to register, you still may seek help in finding a job from the employment service.

2. The one-stop/employment service office has current labour market information and provides a wide array of re-employment services free of charge.
3. Employment service staff can refer you to job openings in your area, or in other parts of the state or country if you are willing to relocate.
4. They can refer you to various training programmes.
5. If job openings in your field are limited, they can offer testing and counselling to determine other jobs you might like to do and are able to do.
6. If you believe you have special needs or considerations, such as physical needs or other considerations, which may prevent you from getting a job, they can refer you to other agencies for help with those needs.

Disqualification from Eligibility

1. If your reason for separation from your last job is due to some reason other than a "lack of work", a determination will be made about whether you are eligible for benefits.
2. Generally, all determinations of whether or not a person is eligible for benefits are made by the appropriate state under its law or applicable federal laws.
3. If you are disqualified/denied benefits, you have the right to file an appeal. The state will advise you of your appeal rights. You must file your appeal within an established time frame. Your employer may also appeal a determination if he or she does not agree with the state's determination regarding your eligibility.

Benefits

1. In general, benefits are based on a percentage of an individual's earnings over a recent fifty-two-week period – up to a state maximum amount.
2. Benefits can be paid for a maximum of twenty-six weeks in most states.

3. Additional weeks of benefits may be available during times of *high unemployment*. Some states provide additional benefits for specific purposes.

4. Benefits are subject to federal income taxes and must be reported on your federal income tax return. You may elect to have the tax withheld by the state unemployment insurance agency.

The Swedish Model

Sweden's welfare system, including unemployment benefits, is perhaps the most comprehensive to be found anywhere.

"All Swedes, regardless of need, could call upon the government to provide them with the benefits listed below. Most are available at no charge to the individual or family. Some 'subsidized' benefits require persons to pay a partial fee, usually according to one's income" (Constitutional Rights Foundation 1998). Its basic provisions are as follows:

Health and Sickness

1. Subsidized doctor care mainly in county clinics
2. Free public hospital treatment
3. Subsidized dental care; free for children
4. Subsidized prescription drugs; life-saving drugs are free
5. Free abortions and sterilizations
6. Free maternity clinics for prenatal care
7. Cash benefits to compensate for loss of most wages due to sickness; a separate benefit is available for workers injured on the job

Family Support

1. Tax-free monthly payment to parents for each child; single parents receive an additional payment for each child
2. Parents have a right to take a total of twelve months' paid leave from work at near full wages to care for each child up to first year in school
3. Subsidized child care at home or in a government day-care centre
4. One year at a subsidized nursery school
5. Unemployment insurance pays about 80 per cent of previous income

U

Pensions

1. Most retired persons receive three different kinds of old-age pensions paid for by taxes and employer contributions.
2. Full or partial disability pensions; disabled child pension goes to parents until age sixteen and then directly to child
3. Special payment to handicapped persons who are working or in school
4. Surviving spouse and orphan pensions

A few additional kinds of aid are provided only to those who have low incomes. The most important of these are housing subsidies for poor families and elderly pensioners.

Unemployment benefits are not prevalent in Latin America or the Caribbean, except perhaps through severance or redundancy payments. Barbados is the only English-speaking Caribbean country to offer specific unemployment benefits. To be eligible, beneficiaries must be under age sixty-five and be insured for fifty-two weeks; excluded are the self-employed and family labour and permanent government employees. The benefits amount to 60 per cent of average insurable weekly earnings for twenty-six weeks.

Union shop (see also **closed shop**)   A condition of union organization that requires an employee, upon being placed in a job, to join the recognized trade union at the establishment as a condition of employment. This type of trade union organization is not prevalent in the English-speaking Caribbean.

Vacation leave   The Holidays with Pay Law 1973 (Jamaica) (amended) stipulates the minimum vacation leave to be granted and the method of qualifying. The main principle is that a worker earns vacation leave by virtue of working for a certain number of days in a year. The law refers to a "qualifying year", which commences with the employee's date of employment and runs for twelve months thereafter. During each of these qualifying years, leave is earned as follows:

V

1. An employee who has been employed for more than 220 days in any qualifying year is entitled to two normal weeks' vacation with pay.
2. An employee who has worked for 220 days or less, but not less than 110 days, has an entitlement of 1/22 of the number of days worked.

Public holidays falling during an employee's vacation leave are added to the leave as extra days. Vacation leave may be accumulated by mutual agreement.

The law establishes a minimum period of vacation leave. Employers can improve on that period by agreement or if they wish to arrive at a more beneficial formula in negotiating with a trade union. Vacation leave must be planned annually along the following lines:

1. Schedules should be made up and circulated to department heads.
2. Dates should be arranged to avoid overlapping as far as possible.
3. Changes in scheduled vacation leave should be by mutual agreement.

Vacation Leave – Casuals

According to the Holidays with Pay Law 1973 (Jamaica) (as amended), casual employees are entitled to gratuity payments in lieu of vacation leave. As with the permanent employees, however, the casual employees must satisfy certain requirements during each qualifying period. The term "qualifying year" means each twelve-month period starting with the first day of employment.

The minimum gratuity is 3 per cent of the total wages earned by the casual during the qualifying year. Entitlement is earned if a casual:

1. has worked with an employer for at least 110 days during the qualifying year; or
2. in cases where the number of days cannot be ascertained, if wages are equal to 110 times the established daily rate for this category of work; or
3. where the basis of the entitlement cannot be determined as in (1) or (2) above, if the employee's name has appeared on the pay bill for at least twenty weeks during the qualifying year.

V

Holiday Payment for Workers Employed on Piece or Task Rates or on a Commission Basis

These employees are entitled to a minimum daily payment of 1/65 of total wages earned during the thirteen weeks preceding the start of their vacation. These weeks need not be consecutive, but in each one considered the employee must have given the employer full service.

Vicarious liability (see also **employee** and **contractor**)   Where there is a relationship of employer/employee, a situation of *vicarious liability* may arise, namely, A (the employer) may be liable for any damage that B (the employee) may have done to C (another employee).

It is to be noted, however, that the employee in the course of employment must have committed the damage which occurs. The operation of vicarious liability will not be relevant in the instance of an independent contractor operating under a contract for services, unless it can be shown that such an independent contractor owed a duty directly to the employer (such as to take reasonable care) and that duty was broken.

Victimization   The act of penalizing an employee for unjustifiable reasons. When a settlement is reached between the parties following industrial action, the trade unions usually seek inclusion of a clause at the end of the agreement. The clause may read as follows: There will be no victimization on either side as a result of the industrial action taken by workers. This means that the employer will not make a victim of an employee and will not enter the settlement with the intention of deceiving the union or employees. Conversely, the union will not take action against the employer for the role played by the employee during the period of industrial action.

Acts of victimization are difficult to prove because such accusations are based on personal experiences. Usually witnesses cannot be found to substantiate an accusation, nor can clear evidence of victimization be presented.

Victimization is a distasteful occurrence in industrial relations practice and should be severely dealt with wherever it is found.

W

Wage   In ordinary everyday discussion the term or concept of *wage* is used in a restricted sense to refer to the actual hourly, daily, weekly or monthly earnings of a worker, negotiated or otherwise. However, both the concept and the actual wage are a bit more complex. It depends on whether it is being addressed from the point of view of the employee, the employer or the economy.

In another restricted way, the term *wage* is used in reference to the earnings of non-salaried personnel, that is, hourly, daily or weekly paid personnel. Salary is then reserved for monthly paid personnel. In this discussion, wages and salaries are treated as equal in meaning and application.

Wages can be interpreted in three ways:

1. The share of wages in national income and products accounting, usually referred to as *compensation to employees*
2. *Earnings* or the *means of living* of the employee
3. *Labour cost* or the *price of labour* to the employer

Share of Wages in the National Income and Accounts

In this scenario, compensation to employees, operating surplus (profit to employers), fixed-capital consumption/utilization, taxation and subsidies are the principal accounts categories, and are national accounting data.

Appreciating the cost distribution of the gross domestic product (GDP) in relation to these cost categories is a very useful tool in policy analysis. The relative positions of compensation to employees and operating surplus, in particular, are helpful in determining the degree of competitiveness and reinvestment options available to the economy. If compensation to employees is growing at a faster rate than operating surplus, it could indicate a declining competitiveness as well as less resource available for reinvestment purposes.

This is particularly true if the increments in compensation to employees are not related to the productivity of labour but instead to other factors such as inflation and collective bargaining arrangements. For instance, in the developed economies, which tend to have acceptably high levels of labour productivity, compensation to employees tends to be over 50 per cent of GDP and operating surplus below 50 per cent.

W

In light of the above, it is necessary to collect such wage data and compute the necessary ratios and proportions. However, in order to track the changes in compensation to employees over time it is best to use index numbers rather than absolute data.

Earnings of Employees

The concept of wages as earnings addresses the issue of "means of living" by employees. That is to say, it is a measure of the abilities of employees to provide for their families/dependents and themselves. As such, wages refer to the totality of earnings, direct and indirect, which accrue to the employee. The ILO provides a guide to this understanding of wages. The resolution of the Twelfth International Conference of Labour Statisticians (ICLS) (1973) defines the concept of earnings as follows:

   i. The concept of earnings, as applied in wages statistics, relates to remuneration in cash and in kind paid to employees, as a rule at regular intervals, for time worked or work done together with remuneration for time not worked, such as for annual vacation, other paid leave or holidays. Earnings exclude employers' contributions in respect of their employees paid to social security and pension schemes and also the benefits received by employees under these schemes. Earnings also exclude severance and termination pay.

  ii. Statistics of earnings should relate to employees' gross remuneration, i.e., the total before any deductions are made by the employer in respect of taxes, contributions of employees to social security and pension schemes, life insurance premiums, union dues and other obligations of employees. (ILO 1979, 23)

In support of the ICLS resolution, the ILO proposes a set of components that are applicable for compilation of earnings statistics. These are:

  1. Direct wages and salaries (in cash)
   - pay for normal time worked
   - premium pay for overtime and holiday worked
   - premium pay for shift work, night work, and so on, where these are not treated as overtime
   - incentive pay (production bonuses, and so on)
   - other regularly paid bonuses
   - family allowances paid directly by employer

W

- cost-of-living or dearness allowance
- house-rent allowance paid directly by employer
2. Remuneration for time not worked (in cash)
   - annual vacation and other paid leave, including long-service leave
   - public holidays and other recognized holidays
   - other time off granted with pay
3. Bonuses and gratuities (in cash)
   - year-end, seasonal and other one-time bonuses
   - profit-sharing bonuses
   - additional payments in respect of vacation, supplementary to normal vacation pay, and other bonuses and gratuities
4. Payments in kind
   - payments in kind for food and drink
   - payments in kind for fuel (coal, coke, electricity, gas and so on)
   - imputed rental value of free or subsidized housing
   - other payments in kind (for example, footwear, clothing)

Labour Cost/Price of Labour

Wage data are also collected for purposes of determining labour cost, that is, the price of labour to the employer. "In industry, wages account for a large part of the employer's cost of production. Employers consider all expenditure on employing labour, whether in the form of direct wages or fringe or supplementary payments, as well as expenditure on recruitment, vocational training, etc., as part of labour cost" (ILO 1979, 21). Wages here makes a crucial distinction between the real earnings or payments made to employees and what it costs the employer to recruit, maintain and compensate the employee.

The Eleventh ICLS (1966) adopted an International Standard Classification of Labour Cost comprising the following major groups:

- direct wages and salaries
- remuneration for time not worked
- bonuses and gratuities
- food, drink, fuel and other payments in kind
- cost of workers' housing borne by employers
- employers' social security expenditure
- cost of vocational training
- cost of welfare services

W

- labour cost not elsewhere classified (such as cost of transport of workers to and from work, cost of work clothes, and of recruitment)
- taxes regarded as labour cost (for instance, taxes on employment or payroll)

In most companies this aspect of expenditure is assuming greater importance as part of the management of resources. This is true for two main reasons. First, wages (defined in this broad sense) or the wage bill as a proportion of operating expense is averaging above 50 per cent. This is particularly true for labour intensive and service type enterprises.

Second, given the relatively high cost of labour input, productivity, and labour productivity in particular, is significantly affected. As a result, it is imperative that the changes in wages be noted and managed properly.

Unfortunately, notwithstanding the high degree of importance of this version of wages, it is not usually captured in surveys or utilized sufficiently in analysis of performance and productivity of enterprises in Jamaica and the other Caribbean territories. Fortunately, however, the "compensation of employees" version of wages, as discussed above, closely approximates the labour cost version and may be used as a proxy of it.

Wages may be measured by time or piece rates. Wages are intended to remunerate employees for their effort. The wages paid must appear to be at a satisfactory level comparable to those being paid in other companies operating in similar businesses. Wages are as important to an individual as the fundamental freedoms of citizenship. Deductions must not be made without the employee's approval, and wages must show

- equity in the relationship between jobs;
- consistency in terms of the intervals at which they are paid; and
- similar consistency in the reviews of performance that take place to improve wages.

Fringe benefits: Payments which are included in the total pay package of the individual employee. For example, a worker may be given vacation leave with pay, or the employer may contribute to a pension fund, life insurance policy or medical scheme on the employee's behalf. Fringe benefits are usually included as part of the pay package during collective bargaining.

Labour costs: The total cost of the workforce, including all earnings, fringe benefits and payments in kind incurred or afforded by the enterprise.

It comprises payments in the form of gross salaries and wages, bonuses, incentives and other cash allowances; plus payments in kind (discounted products or services) to paid employees; plus salaries and allowances, fees, bonuses and commissions paid to working directors; plus fees and allowances paid to non-working directors for purposes of attending board of directors' or sub-committee meetings, for instance; plus employer's contributions to pension, health, education and the general welfare of employees; plus employment related taxes and statutory payments by the employer on behalf of employees.

Money (monetary) wage: The monetary value of a worker's earnings.

Payment in kind: A form of payment that may be classified under the heading of fringe benefits, whereby no money is actually paid out to the individual worker, but food, travel or housing are provided instead.

Productivity: A concept that is used to measure the output per person or per unit hour. The concept is complex and capable of many interpretations. A commonly used method for measuring productivity is the piece rate system in which an individual's output is measured by the number of units that individual is able to produce per hour. Productivity may be either encouraged or impeded by management practices. Therefore, to determine the level of productivity, one should look at all the factors that influence such output and not only at the actual output itself.

Real wage: The money wages expressed in terms of the price of goods and services that it may purchase. Real wages determine the standard of living of an individual.

Salary: The term used by white-collar workers to define their monthly pay as opposed to blue-collar workers who are paid weekly or hourly and define their pay as wages. The distinction between salaries and wages is really a social one.

Take-home pay: The net amount that the individual receives as pay after deductions have been made.

Wage drift: The percentage difference between basic wages and total earnings. It may be possible for wages to be frozen while at the same time, earnings continue to rise at a rapid rate as a result of shop-floor agreements between management and workers. Earnings may rise through incentive schemes based on productive output, commissions or monetary gifts.

Wage structure: The prevailing structure in a company that identifies the differentials between the rates of pay for skill, ability, responsibility, age, sex and the nature of the job. The structure of wages may be distorted by relative earnings – such as the special rates of pay for people with

W

particular and premium skills as needed in the industry. Male employees may be paid a higher rate than females within the same classification when physical strength is an important requirement for performing certain tasks such as lifting. Furthermore, structures may be distorted where there is a great need to import skills at a premium rate, far in excess of what is paid to similarly qualified local personnel.

Wage index[1]   The passage of time and intervention of extraneous factors, such as inflation, money supply, industrial changes and government policies tend to affect the usefulness of absolute data on wages. Index numbers of wages is a very efficient means by which the effect of externalities is minimized. "Index numbers are the devices by which the trends or changes in the level of wages are measured, and they are useful for the study of secular trends, seasonal variations, business cycles, wage drifts, etc." (ILO 1979, 215).

Purpose Served by Wage Indices

The main purpose that is served by having regular and up-to-date wage indices is that of informing and guiding policy formulation and development in regard to the social and economic impact of changes in wages and salary.

The Social Security Administration of the United States provides a practical example of the use of wage indices. Their National Average Wage Index is used to "index the earnings of individuals for benefit computation purposes . . . and to index several amounts that are important to the operation of Social Security's Old-Age, Survivors, and Disability (OASDI) program" (Social Security Online 2006).

Types of Wage Indices

Almost all situations could make a claim for a wage index. For instance, it is conceivable that wage indices could be derived for managers or clerks in specific economic scenarios such as size-group of enterprise, product or service type, geographic or community location. However, while such disaggregating would be likely to satisfy academic and group interests, it would be too detailed and fragmented for policy formulation on wages.

---

[1] This statement is taken from Hussey 2002.

W

As such, the more feasible and common wage indices are national, regional, industry, occupational, private enterprise and public enterprise. Derivation of these indices is dependent on their practicality or applicability, feasibility and ease of compilation. Indices for these operational contexts may also be for minimum wages or regular wages.

The application of wage indices relate to how they are operationally conceived or the function that they are to serve. The interpretation of wages is discussed under **wage** above.

Wage rate (see also **salary**)   The compensation paid for a given unit of time or effort given by a worker. This is sometimes called salary. However, wage rates are usually expressed in terms of unit of output paid for by the hour or the day, while salaries are stated in terms of rates paid weekly, monthly or annually.

Market surveys to determine comparabilities between rates of pay for similar job classifications give an indication of the rate for the job. These surveys do not address relative levels of performance, ability to pay or skill availability in different categories of jobs. They should be seen as a guide and only a guide on job rates in the marketplace. In the Caribbean, information on executive pay is usually skimpy at best.

There are several rates paid as wages. They include the following:

1. Basic hourly rate – compensation for, say, an hour's work on a job, premiums for overtime, shift differential, bonuses, and so on
2. A minimum job rate – the lowest rate paid for a given job
3. Minimum plant rate – the minimum rate of pay for workers in the lowest paid job in the plant
4. Entry rate – the rate of pay customarily received by a newly hired worker (this may also be a rate paid while on probation)
5. Part-time rates paid to part-time or temporary workers
6. Incentive rates paid where compensation is based upon worker output rather than time worked

---

Warning letter   Issued to an employee as a disciplinary measure when the employee commits a minor offence.

W

White-collar union   These unions represent people in the clerical, professional and administrative fields. An example of a white-collar union is the Union of Technical and Supervisory Personnel, Jamaica.

Winding up   See **liquidation.**

Withdrawal of enthusiasm   See **loss of enthusiasm.**

Women employees   Women are restricted and prohibited from being employed in some industrial undertakings in Jamaica. These conditions are laid down under the Women (Employment of) Act, which states, for example, that women shall not work nights except in such places as hotels, restaurants, theatres or nursing institutions. Night work is defined as being between the hours of 8:00 p.m. and 6:00 a.m.

Another act, the Employment (Equal Pay for Men and Women) Act, 1975, was enacted with the objective of eliminating discrimination in respect of pay for equal work. The act defines equal work, emphasizing that where qualifications, skills, effort and responsibilities are similar, there should be no difference in pay. Aggrieved employees may report discrimination to the minister of labour.

Work-to-rule   A form of industrial action taken by workers in furtherance of a dispute arising out of the contract of employment. Working to rule means performing only those functions deemed basic to the job and not undertaking additional responsibilities normally associated with a job. Sometimes work-to-rule means a "go-slow" where productive output is below acceptable norms.

Workers   There are four different types of workers:

1. *Permanent:* Someone who enjoys all benefits of the company and operates under an ongoing contract of employment for an unspecified period.

2. *Casual:* Any worker employed from day-to-day or who is employed to perform a particular task which cannot be performed in less than one working day.

3. *Temporary:* Usually a worker who is employed to substitute for another worker who is on vacation or sick leave, and so on. Temporary appointments are for a fixed and agreed duration.

4. *Seasonal:* Any worker employed for a minimum of ninety days, or who earns at least the equivalent of ninety days' pay in any season; or whose name appears on the payroll for at least sixteen weeks during a season, mainly in the agricultural sector.

Points to Note

1. Ensure that proper letters of appointment are issued.
2. Record the actual time worked by each worker.
3. Note legal conditions in respect of vacation leave, sick leave, notice of termination.

Working time   This addresses the issue of the statutory or legal number of hours of work in certain contexts or conditions and jurisdictions within which work occurs. The neutral term "normal" hours of work has been used to depict this legal number, while at the same time recognizing that "normal" varies from time to time and from country to country. "Normal" hours of work usually has a reference period of a day, a week, a month or a year. Annualized references are rare even though they have gained currency in recent years, particularly in Europe.

Working hours have been reducing gradually over time, particularly in industrialized countries. However, with the advent of agencies such as the ILO, there have been general attempts towards standardization of working time across countries. For instance, the eight-hour workday and forty-hour workweek have become standard working times for a large proportion of countries today.

Working-time flexibility (flexitime)   Working-time flexibility falls under the general subject or process towards labour market flexibility, which seeks to ensure a more responsive labour market to the new economic realities; more accountability and returns on labour input, variable compensation, multi-skilling, and so on.

W

> In essence, working time flexibility amounts to a departure from traditional working time arrangements, consisting of full-time work during a given number of hours per week (e.g., a straight 40-hour or 48-hour week) or per day (e.g., eight hours). In practice, flexibility means that the number of hours or days of work may vary during a certain period (e.g., a four-day week may be followed by a three-day week or an eight-hour day may follow a five-hour day), provided that total working time during a given period does not exceed certain, often statutory, limits. Such arrangements may sometimes be combined with work on Sundays (where the Sunday is the weekly holiday) or with night work or – and this is a long-standing practice – with shift work. (Schregle 2002, 66)

The overriding reasoning behind the implementation of or recommendation for introduction of working-time flexibility is that it is seen as an important mechanism to assist organizations, enterprises and jurisdictions in becoming more efficient and competitive relative to trading partners and the demands of the market. Its implementation encourages strict time management and reduces absenteeism and overtime arrangements, thereby reducing labour input costs.

Working time flexibility is also proposed as a practical means of assisting in the reduction of high unemployment rates. This would happen if individual workers are restricted to their legal number of hours per week, without overtime, or through the collapsing of the regular working week to three or four working days, and so on, thereby allowing for other persons to be employed in the times saved.

Implementation of flexitime should be undertaken after careful consideration and management to ensure it does not negatively impact on the health and safety of the affected workers and also that the statutory or legal working-time limits are not violated (see Spurgeon 2003).

Y–Z

Y

Year-end bonus A bonus paid at year-end to workers for good performance during a year.

Zero defects The system of rewarding workers who make no mistakes and waste no materials over a given and specific period of time (*International Dictionary of Management*, 1973).

These procedures should be followed:

1. The system must be agreed with employees or the trade union representing them.
2. Measurements should be clearly expressed in precise terms.
3. Rewards should be distributed at frequent intervals to have the best effect – for example, monthly or quarterly intervals.
4. Frequent discussions should be held with workers on performance criteria and operation of the system in order to ensure a clear understanding.

Appendices

Appendix A

PART 1
Industrial Disputes Tribunal, Jamaica

The Industrial Disputes Tribunal of Jamaica was established under the Labour Relations and Industrial Disputes Act (LRIDA) 1975. Many first-timers attend the tribunal with fear and trepidation similar to the anxieties experienced when responding to a summons to a court of law. Such feelings of insecurity, however, are unnecessary as the tribunal conducts its business in a very relaxed manner presided over by a panel comprising a chairman and two members.

The Industrial Disputes Tribunal, commonly known as the IDT, is the final arbiter on all industrial relations disputes in the quasi-public and private sectors of the Jamaican society. Its jurisdiction does not include employees of the Crown. The Labour Relations and Industrial Disputes Act, 1975 (LRIDA), under which the tribunal was created by statute, had as its main features the following:

1. Establishing of a permanent tribunal for the settlement of indus-trial disputes not otherwise settled, that is, by collective bargain-ing procedures
2. Providing for a code of labour relations practices
3. Providing the machinery for the settlement of representational claims
4. Setting out an implied grievance procedure for the settlement of industrial disputes
5. Protecting the rights of workers in respect of trade union mem-bership
6. Underwriting the rights of the worker to his or her employment
7. Providing for the establishment of boards and commissions of enquiry

In order to critically analyse the impact of the IDT in industrial relations in Jamaica, it is important to state some of the important conditions of the LRIDA that are directly related to the role and functions of the IDT.

To avoid the publication of a lengthy statutory law, the preferred option for this book was a summary. The excerpt which follows was extracted (with permission) from the publication *Labour Laws* (1979) by the Jamaica Employers' Federation, a local employer's organization. The section of the LRIDA that deals with the establishment and role of the IDT is summarized below.

The Industrial Disputes Tribunal

The Industrial Disputes Tribunal consists of a chairman and two deputy chairmen and not less than two members representing employers and two representing workers (and such special members as may from time to time be appointed to form a special division of the tribunal). All appointments are made by the minister (with responsibility for industrial relations/labour). The members representing employers and workers are appointed from panels supplied to the minister by organizations representative of employers and workers respectively.

In the case of a special division of the tribunal to settle disputes affecting the national interest, the chairman is appointed by the minister on the joint recommendation of the parties involved and the other two members are appointed respectively on the recommendation of the employer organization and the trade union involved.

Access

All references of disputes to the tribunal must be made through the minister, who shall refer disputes occurring in the prescribed essential services and in the determination of the entitlement of categories of persons to participate in a ballot under the procedure for settlement of representational claims to the tribunal, when other means of settlement have failed to resolve their issue in dispute.

In disputes affecting the national interest the minister shall make a reference to the permanent tribunal where there is failure by the parties jointly to nominate the chairman to be appointed to the special division and to nominate the persons to represent the employers and workers respectively within the seven days allowed by him to the parties for such nomination.

In other disputes, references to the tribunal are made on the *request of all the parties* to the dispute where the minister is satisfied that other means of settlement provided by collective agreement have failed to resolve the issue of dispute.

Industrial Action: Strikes, Lock-Outs, Go-Slows, etc.

In the essential services – health, water, electricity, fire, docks, oil refining and distribution and public passenger transport – industrial action is unlawful unless reference has been made to the minister and he or she has failed to take action within the ten days prescribed.

Any industrial action taken after the minister has acted in the national interest, and has issued directions to the parties to refrain from taking or continuing any industrial action to be served, becomes unlawful.

In any case, the tribunal may, after reference of a dispute, order the cessation of any industrial action related to the dispute referred.

General

The tribunal may be assisted by one or more assessors appointed by the employers and an equal number of assessors appointed by the workers through their trade union.

Grievance Procedure

1. Every collective agreement which is made in writing after the commencement of this act shall, if it does not contain express procedure for the settlement, without stoppage of work, of industrial disputes between the parties, be deemed to contain the procedure specified in subsection (2) of this section referred to as the implied procedure.
2. The implied procedure shall be:
   a. the parties shall first endeavour to settle any dispute or difference between them by negotiation; and
   b. where the parties have tried, but failed to settle a dispute or difference in the manner referred to in paragraph (a) any or all of them may request the minister in writing to assist in settling it by means of conciliation; and
   c. all the parties may request the minister in writing to refer to the tribunal for settlement any dispute or difference

which they tried, but failed, to settle by following the procedure specified in paragraphs 2(a) and (b).

Trade Union Membership

The act embodies the rights of a worker to belong to the union of his choice and protects his right from interference by the employer as well as his right to take part in the activities of his union outside of working hours or by arrangement with or without the consent of his employer.

Right of Worker to His Employment

The act empowers the tribunal, where it finds a worker to have been unjustly dismissed and the worker requests reinstatement, to order the employer to reinstate him with the payment of wages, if any, as the tribunal may determine.

Where the worker does not wish to be reinstated, the tribunal having found him to have been unjustifiably dismissed, shall order the employer to pay the worker such compensation or other relief as the tribunal may determine.

In any other case, the tribunal may, in appropriate circumstances, order that unless the worker is reinstated within a specified period, the employer shall pay the worker such compensation or other relief as the tribunal may determine.

Settlement of Representational Claims

Poll-taking. The act provides for the settlement of claims for bargaining rights by secret ballot.

A ballot shall not be taken if within the period of one year prior to the date of the request such a ballot had been taken, unless the minister is satisfied that during that period new unforeseen circumstances have arisen to justify the taking of the poll requested.

Before proceeding with a poll, the minister must be satisfied that at least 40 per cent of the workers in the proposed bargaining unit are members of the claimant union.

The ballot is taken under the conditions settled for the purpose between the parties concerned. The result is notified to the parties by the minister.

Recognition

Sole Bargaining. If the result of the ballot shows that a majority of the workforce in the bargaining unit wish a particular union to represent them, the employer shall recognize that union for the purpose.

Joint Bargaining. Where the ballot is taken to determine which of two or more trade unions should have bargaining rights and the result shows that each of two or more unions receive not less than 30 per cent of the votes of those eligible to vote, the minister shall at the written request of not less than two of those unions that they wish to be recognized as having joint bargaining rights in the bargaining unit, inform the employer who shall recognize those trade unions accordingly.

Collective Agreements. The minister's decision that a ballot shall be taken shall be subject to the conditions that:

a. any existing collective agreement shall not be affected by the result of the ballot; and
b. no negotiations for the making of a new collective agreement shall be concluded before the ballot is taken.

The Labour Relations Code

A code containing such practical guidance as in the opinion of the minister will be helpful in promoting good industrial relations in accordance with:

a. the principle of collective bargaining freely conducted on behalf of workers and employers and with due regard to the general interests of the public;
b. the principle of developing and maintaining orderly procedures in industry for the peaceful and expeditious settlement of disputes by negotiation, conciliation or arbitration;
c. the principle of developing and maintaining good personnel management techniques designed to secure effective cooperation between workers and their employers and to protect workers and employers against unfair labour practices has been published.

The code is not legally enforceable but failure to observe its provisions shall be taken into account by the tribunal or board of enquiry when determining questions arising in proceedings.

In 1978, the government enacted the first amendment to the LRIDA, which gave the minister of labour power to refer a matter to the permanent tribunal, on request of either party to the dispute. Referrals were not restricted to the essential services, but applied to all sectors. Although the authority of the IDT does not extend to disciplinary issues involving civil servants (such issues are determined by the Public Services Commission), it includes employees of public utilities, that is, the telephone company, electricity supply, water, international communications, and so on, and some quasi-government organizations such as university teachers, hospital workers, and nurses. Its awards may be appealed on the grounds of a breach of law or insanity or insobriety of its members at the time of the hearing.

The objectives of setting up the IDT were as follows:

a. to deal with industrial disputes referred to it by ordering that any industrial action which has begun in contemplation of the furtherance of a dispute shall cease at such time when the tribunal may specify;

b. it may at any time after such reference encourage the parties to endeavour to settle the dispute by negotiation or conciliation and, if they agree to do so, may assist them in their attempt to do so. (LRIDA section 3:12 [v])

Whereas previous laws failed to give powers of reinstatement to arbitrators, the LRIDA gives the IDT specific powers in this regard, and the reference section states:

In any disputes relating to the dismissal of workers, the tribunal in making its award:

1. shall, if it finds that the dismissal was unjustifiable and that the worker wishes to be reinstated, order the employer to reinstate him with payment of so much wages as the tribunal may determine;

2. shall, if it finds that the dismissal was unjustifiable and that the worker does not wish to be reinstated, order the employer to pay the worker such compensation or to grant him such other relief as the tribunal may determine;

3. may in any other case if it considers the circumstances appropriate, order that unless the dismissed worker is reinstated by the employer within such period as the tribunal may specify,

the employer, at the end of that period, to pay the worker such compensation or grant him such other relief as the tribunal may determine, and the employer shall comply with such order. (LRIDA section 3:12 [vi])

Breaches of the LRIDA by employers or employees may be subject to conviction and fines or imprisonment imposed by a resident magistrate in the magistrates' courts of the land.

Awards of the IDT

There is no clear-cut policy on the criteria available for guiding tribunalists in making awards. From time to time, principles such as national interest, financial implications to organizations, effect on the economy, comparability, have been mooted as the guiding principles that led to some awards, but there has been little or no empirical evidence to support these views. Such principles, clearly enunciated, will certainly help negotiators to determine:

1. the parameters of the negotiating mandate; and
2. whether, in view of the differences that separate the parties around the bargaining table, it makes practical sense to seek arbitration services in the event of an impasse or breakdown in negotiations.

Tribunal awards are not given in perpetuity, but in spite of this, no limitation or time frame is set for the effective dates of an award. Parties engaged in collective bargaining assume that the award either expires simultaneously with the existing collective agreement, or when it is amended by the parties during negotiations to amend the collective agreements. This assumption is based on the fact that the award of the IDT is an implied term in the collective agreement.

Rights and Interests

The cases referred to the IDT are either matters of *interests* or matters of *rights* and there may be combinations of both. In interests cases the parties negotiate such items as wages, hours or other conditions of work. On the question of rights issues, these identify situations where one of the parties, usually the trade union, objects to an action by the employer which affects one or several of its members and is or may be in breach of the collective agreement.

Interests awards may be readily incorporated into a collective agreement and subsequently amended whenever an agreement is being amended.

Rights awards, particularly those dealing with union recognition, however, are more difficult to incorporate in a collective agreement as they assume some degree of permanence of recognition which cannot be the case, as union representation is subject to change from contract to contract, and is permissible under the LRIDA. This will be the case especially where the bargaining rights of the union are being challenged by another periodically.

Awards are not retroactive prior to the date on which the dispute first arose. Similarly, awards should stipulate a specific period of enforcement, irrespective of the nature of the award.

Every award must be based on certain guiding principles which should characterize all arbitration proceedings. These principles may be summarized as follows:

1. Equity in respect of the ability of a firm to pay, nature of the job, industry-wide comparability and taking into account the current trends in the cost of living
2. Good conscience, reflecting a clear and unequivocal sense of objectivity and fair play, above and beyond the pale of bias or injudicious interference by politicians, businessmen or trade unionists
3. Merits of the case, which should be determined by the arguments submitted by the parties at the hearings

The tribunalists should demand all relevant information to assist them in arriving at an equitable award. Legal precedents must not be a determining factor in deciding on awards, as the legal condition that led to the judgement/decision of a court of law may, as well as may not, have any relevance to custom and practice of industrial relations, or to the fundamentals of good industrial relations at the workplace. Consequently, a slavish adherence to the dictates of law may be impractical, punitive and even damaging to industrial relations at the workplace. Furthermore, legal precedents militate against moral judgement on issues dealing with work attitudes and behavioural patterns – characteristics that are so fundamental to human relations and yet are so difficult to define and categorize with any accuracy. For instance, a tribunal may find that an employee was wrongfully dismissed, but owing to the prevailing animosity against him in the plant, it would be counter-productive to reinstate him, even though legally he is entitled to reinstatement. In such instances, however, it would be best for all concerned to award some form of financial compensation rather than force an unworkable situation on both parties, simply because the law says that this is how it ought to be.

Interpretation of Awards

Under section 12 (10) of the LRIDA, the tribunal is required to provide an interpretation of an award, if asked to do so, directly to the parties or indirectly through the minister of labour. Of interest, however, is the issue of the Shipping Association of Jamaica versus Trade Unions on Port Bustamante, a case in which the tribunal, in providing an interpretation, substantially changed the award and then refused later to correct the error in the interpretation.

The tribunal feels somewhat reluctant to hear appeals for interpretation. Consequently, important facts that were omitted at the original hearing, and which could be brought out in a hearing called to deal with an interpretation, and could also lead to a more pragmatic and beneficial decision in determining an issue, are ignored completely. Many times, the interpretation given by the IDT may be merely the result of insufficient data, or carelessness in analysing information or ignorance of the tribunalists about the finer points of an industrial relations issue, and results in requests for further interpretations later on. Wherever an award is ambiguous, erroneous or uncertain, it should be corrected through an interpretation by the tribunal in the interest of promoting and maintaining industrial peace. Such interpretation must, of course, have the same binding force as the original award.

No Reasons Given for Awards

The failure of the IDT to give reasons for awards has created difficulties among employers and trade unionists alike, in the interpretation and application of such awards. If the tribunal were to be persuaded, or rather instructed, by the minister of labour to give reasons for its awards, this would help to provide guidelines for management and workers and undoubtedly reduce some of the errors and resulting tensions that result from the implementation of contentious and impractical awards. There have been serious criticisms of the IDT. Some have been constructive and others damaging. The opinions of two legal practitioners who frequently appear before the tribunal may be instructive:

> In recent times the tribunal seems to be losing its effectiveness; some
> of it is due to restrictions placed on the tribunal by the courts . . .
> The courts have handed down a series of judgements which are
> intended to guide the tribunal . . . which the tribunal tends to see
> as interference in their business. (Baugh 1985)

> The tribunal should have its own independent specialist legal advi-
> sor. (Wright 1985)

There is an appalling absence of documentation, information, and critical analyses on IDT procedures and practices. Consequently, the public
at large has scant understanding of the role and functions of the IDT. As
a result, summonses from the tribunal to persons to appear before it, are
regarded with trepidation and grave concern by some and with disregard
by others. These and other reasons result in the non-attendance of key
witnesses at hearings. Ashton Wright (1985), a respected attorney-at-law,
had this to say:

> previous efforts of our tribunal to adopt a set of rules of procedures
> were thwarted by objections from certain workers' representatives
> and by the general indifference of other members. I strongly recom-
> mend the adoption of a set of rules of procedures.

Even though the IDT has powers to subpoena witnesses, it lacks the
force of strong legal action in the event of non-compliance, which may be
enforced through the courts, but few employers would be willing to follow
such a course of action for several reasons, including legal costs, lack of
time, fear of adverse reactions by workers and so forth.

Consequently, some important matters are not properly aired and,
without doubt, some awards suffer from a lack of substantiated findings
and are sometimes impractical in application.

Owing to the fact that many employers and trade unions use the
facilities of the tribunal to resolve routine matters when the process of
collective bargaining is unable to provide a solution, the IDT is sometimes
referred to as the arbitrator of last resort.

PART 2
The Industrial Court, Trinidad and Tobago

Trinidad and Tobago's Industrial Court has a role that is approximately similar to that of Jamaica's Industrial Disputes Tribunal. This court is comprised of two divisions. A chairman presides over each division, which should have at least two additional members. The General Services Division has jurisdiction over matters other than those relating to essential services and the Essential Services Division has responsibility in those cases involving essential services.

The Special Tribunal established under the Civil Service Act and mentioned in other Acts – the Police Service, Fire Service, Prison Service, Education, Supplemental Police, and Central Bank Acts – is supposed to be presided over by "the Chairman of the Essential Services Division and two other members of that Division selected by him, and shall hear and determine disputes arising in" the sectors governed by those acts. Anyone appointed as a member of one division ought not to sit as a member of the other division "unless invited to do so by the Chairman of that other Division".

The Industrial Court, according to the law, should consist of

1. a judge of the Supreme Court "designated, with his consent, by the President of Trinidad and Tobago after consultation with the Chief Justice", or, "a person who has the qualification . . . to be appointed a Judge of the Supreme Court" and is appointed via the same process as in the case of the judge (above);
2. a vice-president who must be a barrister or solicitor with at least ten years' experience and appointed by the president of the country; and
3. other members appointed by the president based on their experience in industrial relations, in economics or accounts, or "who are barristers or solicitors of not less than five years['] standing".

The president of the court should be the chairman of the division to which he or she belongs. If the vice-president is not a member of the division which the president chairs, he or she (the vice-president) would be the chairman of the other division. The vice-president who is supposed to be a barrister or solicitor with at least ten years' experience would be called upon to serve if, for any reason, the president were unable to carry out the task of the presidency.

"In addition to the powers inherent in it as a superior court of record", the court has the authority to:

- hear and determine trade disputes
- register collective agreements and resolve matters relating to such registration
- advise a trade union or other entity, workers or employers to avoid industrial action
- hear and rule on industrial relations offences under the act
- hear and rule on any other matter under its jurisdiction as stipulated in the provisions of the act

Rulings of the Industrial Court are guided by a majority decision. In the absence of a majority, the court should order a new hearing of the issue. The court is mandated to rule or make an award based on what it considers to be "fair and just, having regard to the interests of the persons immediately concerned and the community as a whole".

It is interesting that the court is empowered to arrive at a decision on a dispute if a person or entity which has been summoned to appear before it fails to attend. It can also order any person who it believes is likely to be affected by an order or award to be engaged as a party to the proceedings under consideration.

Source: "Industrial Relations", *Laws of Trinidad*, chapter 88.01.

Appendix B

Sample of Industrial Disputes Tribunal Award

IN RESPECT OF AN INDUSTRIAL DISPUTE BETWEEN XYZ COMPANY LTD AND UNION OF WORKERS

Reference

A. By letter dated 19th April, the Honourable Minister of Labour referred to the Industrial Disputes Tribunal for settlement, the dispute between the Company and the Union in accordance with Section 9 (6) of the Labour Relations and Industrial Disputes Act.

The Terms of Reference to the Tribunal were as follows:

> To determine and settle the dispute between XYZ Company Ltd on the one hand, and the workers employed by that Company to stack pallets in its warehouse, and represented by the Union of Workers on the other hand over:
>
> 1. What constitutes adequate notice prior to cessation of work;
> 2. Short payment for uniform during contract period January '82 to December '83; and
> 3. Sanitary, rest and shelter facilities.

B. By letter dated 19th June, the Honourable Minister of Labour referred to the Industrial Disputes Tribunal for settlement, the dispute between the Company and the Union in accordance with Section 9 (6) of the Labour Relations and Industrial Disputes Act, 1975.

The Terms of Reference to the Tribunal were as follows:

> To determine and settle the dispute between XYZ Company Ltd, on the one hand, and the workers employed by that Company to stack pallets in its warehouse, and represented by the Union of Workers, on the other hand, over the question of payment for the period beginning at 3:00 p.m., Saturday, 8th June to 3:00 p.m., Monday, 10th June.

This dispute arose after the start of proceedings in respect of the dispute at "A" but the parties agreed that both disputes could be consolidated.

The Division of the Tribunal selected in accordance with Section 8 (2) of the Act, was comprised of:

Mr Joe James – Chairman
Mr Michael Phillips – Member, Section 8 (2)(c) (ii)
Mr Ken Thompson – Member, Section 8 (2)(c) (iii)

The Company was represented by:

Mr Lloyd Izett – Attorney-at-Law
Mr Paul Ascot – Managing Director
Mr Louis Reid – Operations Manager

The Union was represented by:

Mr Joe Clunis – Vice-President
Mr Alvin Burroughs – Union Officer

Background to Dispute

Dispute A. This dispute arose out of a claim by the Union for resolution of the following:

1. What constitutes adequate notice prior to cessation of work;
2. Short payment for uniforms during contract period January to December; and
3. Sanitary, rest and shelter facilities.

Discussions at the local level and at the Ministry of Labour failed to resolve the issue as a result of which the matter was referred to the Industrial Disputes Tribunal to be determined.

Dispute B. The dispute arose out of a claim by the Union for payment of the workers for the period beginning at 3:00 p.m. on Saturday, 8th June, to 3:00 p.m. on Monday, 10th June, 1985.

Discussions at the local level and at the Ministry of Labour failed to resolve the issue and consequently it was referred to the Industrial Disputes Tribunal to be determined.

Submissions and Sittings

Written briefs were submitted by the parties on both sides and oral submissions made at eight sittings held on:

23rd April
1st May
3rd June
4th June
6th June
18th June
19th June
3rd July

The Tribunal also paid a visit to the *locus in quo* on 1st July.

Findings

The Tribunal finds with much concern that the existing AGREEMENT between XYZ Company Ltd and Warehousing Ltd to whom the company is contracted is such that the company is not free to operate in the National Interest at all times and without the likelihood of frequent interruptions.

The Tribunal therefore recommends that serious consideration be given to effecting such modifications and/or improvements in the facilities for unloading goods as will reduce or eliminate the present uncertainties to which the workers are constantly exposed.

Award

Dispute A. (1) The Tribunal awards that *adequate notice* constitutes three eight-hour shifts exclusive of the shift (if any) on which the workers would be currently engaged at the time cessation of work is announced. This will allow for 24 hours clear notice being given to the workers – i.e., at the time that cessation of work is announced the notice should allow for three clear shifts (24 hours at least) from the time of announcement; for example, a worker actually engaged on the 6:00 a.m. to 2:00 p.m. shift would be allowed the ensuing three shifts (24 hours) – i.e., 2:00 p.m. to 10:00 p.m.; 10:00 p.m. to 6:00 a.m. and 6:00 a.m. to 2:00 p.m. shifts as NOTICE prior to the effective time for cessation of work.

A worker, however, who has not yet started on a shift would be regarded as having been given adequate notice of three clear shifts beginning from the time of the shift immediately succeeding the one during which the notice was announced; e.g., if the cessation is announced at 9:00 a.m. the notice period would become effective from the commencement of the next regular shift, i.e.:

2:00 p.m. to 10:00 p.m.   } Three clear shifts
10:00 p.m. to 6:00 a.m.   } terminating at 2:00 p.m.
6:00 a.m. to 2:00 p.m.   } the following day.

This award will apply except in cases governed by Clause 7(c) of the existing Agreement between XYZ Company Ltd and the Union of Workers which relates to work being suspended due to storage racks being full, and reads:

Where work is being suspended due to storage racks being full the Union delegates must be advised at least five (5) hours before the suspension of work. The Union Delegates along with a supervisor and a representative of Warehousing Ltd must inspect the storage racks to verify same.

Dispute A. (2) *Short payment* for uniforms during contract period January to December.

The Tribunal makes no award.

Dispute A. (3) *Sanitary rest and shelter facilities.* The Tribunal noted from the visit made to the *locus in quo* that an adequate unit was in place and provided rest and shelter facilities for the workers. The Tribunal also noted that two (2) functional lavatory units were provided for use by the workers.

The Tribunal awards that XYZ Company Ltd continues to maintain the above facilities in satisfactory working conditions for regular use by the workers.

The Tribunal *further* awards that the rooms adjoining the room in which the lavatory units are situated should be updated to provide:

a. immediate shelter for workers (whose duties require them to be on the outside) at any time weather conditions demand immediate shelter.

b. a proper shower for workers who may wish to have a bath at the end of their particular shift.

c. adequate water for drinking or other purposes on the outside from that existing outlet which was seen by the members of the panel on the occasion of their visit.

Dispute B. This dispute relates to the Union's claim for payment for the period extending from 3:00 p.m., Saturday, 8th June to 3:00 p.m., Monday, 10th June, 1985.

The Tribunal makes no award.

DATED THIS 13TH DAY OF SEPTEMBER, 1985

_____   _____

Joe James   Michael Phillips
Chairman   Member

                    Witness: _____

_____   _____

Ken Thompson   Tony Robinson
Member   Secretary to the Division

Appendix C

The Labour Relations Code, 1976 (Jamaica)

Established under the

Labour Relations and Industrial Disputes Act, 1975

Act 14 of 1975

Table of Contents   **Paragraph**

PART I Preliminary

1. Establishment

The code is established in accordance with the provisions of Section 3 of the Labour Relations and Industrial Disputes Act, 1975. Its purpose is to set out guidelines which in the opinion of the minister will be helpful for the purpose of promoting good labour relations, having regard to the following:

    i. the principle of collective bargaining freely conducted on behalf of workers and their employers with due regard to the interest of the public;

    ii. the principle of developing and maintaining orderly procedures in industry for the peaceful and expeditious settlement of disputes by negotiation, conciliation or arbitration;

    iii. the principle of developing and maintaining good personnel management techniques designed to secure effective cooperation between workers and employers and to protect workers and employers against unfair labour practices.

2. Purpose

The code recognizes the dynamic nature of industrial relations and interprets it in its widest sense. It is not confined to procedural matters but includes in its scope human relations and the greater responsibilities of all the parties to the society in general.

Recognition is given to the fact that management in the exercise of its function needs to use its resources (material and human) efficiently. Recognition is also given to the fact that work is a social right and obligation; it is not a commodity; it is to be respected and dignity must be accorded to those who perform it, ensuring continuity of employment, security of earnings and job satisfaction.

The inevitable conflicts that arise in the realization of these goals must be resolved and it is the responsibility of all concerned – management, individual employees, trade unions and employer's associations – to cooperate in its solution. The code is designed to encourage and assist that cooperation.

3. Application

Save where the Constitution provides otherwise, the code applies to all employers and all workers and organizations representing workers in determining their conduct one with the other, and industrial relations should be carried out within the spirit and intent of the code. The code provides guidelines which complement the Labour Relations and Industrial Disputes Act. An infringement of the code does not of itself render anyone liable to legal proceedings. However its provisions may be relevant in deciding any question before a tribunal or board.

4. Revision

In accordance with Section 3 (3) of the Act, the code may be revised by the minister. This will be done in consultation with representative organizations of employers and workers.

This provision is not to be interpreted as inhibiting or restricting the right of the parties to review and improve their own labour management practices as the need arises.

PART II Responsibilities

5. Employers

In keeping with the need for management to be productive and responsive to workers and the society in general, good management practices and industrial relations policies which have the confidence of all must be one of management's major objectives.

The development of such practices and policies are a joint responsibility of employers and all workers and trade unions representing them, but the primary responsibility for their initiation rests with employers.

Employers should therefore ensure that:

i. in the implementation of these policies due regard is paid to their responsibilities to the society;
ii. in addition to discharging their obligations to workers in respect of terms and conditions of employment, they adopt policies for the social and educational improvement of their workers;
iii. they respect their workers' right to belong to a trade union and to take part in the union's activities, which include seeking recognition for negotiation purposes and that they are not averse to negotiating in good faith with such trade union;
iv. adequate and effective procedures for negotiation, communication and consultation, and the settlement of grievances and disputes, are maintained with their workers, and organizations representing such workers;

v. these procedures are understood and applied by all members of the management team;

vi. all supervisory staff have clearly defined responsibilities in the organizational structure, are in charge of manageable work groups, understand their responsibilities and have the necessary qualities, and industrial relations training and exposure to do the job;

vii. supervisors are cognizant of management policies as they affect their individual work groups and that they maintain an effective link between management and members of their work groups.

6. Individual Workers

i. The worker has a responsibility to his employer to perform his contract of service to the best of his ability, to his trade union to support it financially and to vest in it the necessary authority for the performance of its functions efficiently; to his fellow workers to ensure that his actions do not prejudice their general well-being including their health and safety; to the nation to ensure his dedication to the principle of productive work for the good of all. The legal relationship between employer and worker is determined by the individual contract of employment. Often many of its terms are fixed by collective bargaining and contained in collective agreements. The worker should familiarize himself with the terms of his contract, and in particular any procedure for dealing with grievances, and abide by them.

ii. Some workers have special obligations arising out of the nature of their employment. Such workers when acting in the course of their employment should be mindful of those obligations and should refrain from action which conflicts with them.

7. Trade Unions

The main objective of a trade union is to promote the interest of its members, with due regard being paid to the interest of the total labour force and to the greater national interest. To achieve this aim, trade unions have a duty to maintain the viability of the undertaking by ensuring cooperation with management in measures to promote efficiency and good industrial relations.

Trade unions should therefore:

i. where appropriate, maintain jointly with management and other trade unions effective arrangements at industry or local levels for negotiation, consultation and communication and for settling grievances and disputes;

ii. take all reasonable steps to ensure that their officials and members observe all arrangements;

iii. provide for the training of delegates in the scope of their powers and duties and the day-to-day operation of the union;

iv. provide adequate educational opportunities for the advancement of their members;

v. be properly staffed to serve the needs of their members, and allow for effective lines of communication between such staff and the rank and file membership;

vi. encourage members to take part in their activities by adopting such means as would best allow them to do so, including the compilation and distribution of information;

vii. make available information pertaining to the rules and policies of the unions;

viii. provide adequate advisory services for their members and in particular assist them to understand the terms and conditions of their employment;

ix. identify trends in industrial relations to help their members to anticipate and keep abreast of change.

8. Employers' Associations

The principal aim of employers' associations is to promote the interests of their members, with due regard being paid to the interest of the total labour force and to the greater national interest.

Employers' associations should therefore:

i. cooperate with trade unions for the establishment at industry level, where appropriate, of procedures for the negotiation of terms and conditions of employment and the settlement of disputes and grievances;

ii. encourage their members to establish effective procedures in consultation with trade unions recognized by them, for the settlement of disputes and grievances at the local level;

iii. take all reasonable steps to ensure that their members pursue those procedures which are established;

iv.   collect, analyse and distribute information in the industrial rela-
       tions field;

v.   identify trends in industrial relations to help their members to
       anticipate and keep abreast of change;

vi.   provide adequate advisory services for their members;

vii.   encourage their members to provide adequate educational oppor-
       tunities for the advancement of their workers;

viii. encourage their members to take an interest in their association
       and be prepared to contribute to its resources.

PART III Personnel Management Practices

9. Employment Policies

Clear, comprehensive and non-discriminatory employment policies are
an indication of the efficiency of an undertaking. The initiation of such
policies is primarily the responsibility of employers, but they should
be developed in consultation or negotiation with workers or their
representatives.

Employment policies should:

i.   provide for proper recruitment and selection, having regard to
       the qualification and experience needed to perform the job;

ii.   have regard to the need for workers to advance themselves in
       the undertaking and so consider filling vacancies by promotion
       or transfers;

iii.   make clear to the workers the requirements, terms and condi-
       tions of employment, including *inter alia* –

       a.   general conditions of employment;

       b.   job requirements and the person to whom the worker is
            directly responsible;

       c.   disciplinary rules and the procedures for the examination of
            grievances;

       d.   opportunities for promotion and training;

       e.   social welfare services, such as medical care, canteens,
            pensions;

       f.   occupational safety, health and welfare regulations;

       g.   methods of consultation;

       h.   any trade union arrangements;

       i.   the company's personnel and industrial relations policies.

iv. provide induction training both as to the actual job performance and as to the policies and procedures existing in the undertaking, encouraging their adoption particularly as they relate to safety, health and welfare matters;

v. ensure that workers are kept abreast of changing job techniques by on the job training or by approved courses;

vi. not be influenced by conditions relating to age, sex or other personal factors except where relevant to the job;

vii. make provision for workers to further their educational standard if they so desire, by granting time off for such purposes;

viii. be carried out by competent staff and be subject to periodic review to ensure efficiency.

10. Manpower Use and Planning

Proper manpower utilization policies are essential to efficiency. Such policies should:

i. be given high priority and be integrated with other aspects of planning in the undertaking;

ii. assess existing manpower resources based on adequate and up-to-date personnel records;

iii. identify future manpower needs and formulate and implement policies for their fulfilment;

iv. seek to avoid unnecessary fluctuation in the workforce and, where such fluctuations are necessary, ensure that there is a minimum of disruption to the workers concerned;

v. ensure that the undertaking operates in an efficient manner by identifying such problems as absenteeism and high incidence of labour turn-over, recording such information and taking steps in consultation with workers or their representatives to correct them.

11. Security of Workers

Recognition is given to the need for workers to be secure in their employment and management should in so far as is consistent with operational efficiency:

i. provide continuity of employment, implementing where practicable, pension and medical schemes;

   ii. in consultation with workers or their representatives take all reasonable steps to avoid redundancies;

  iii. in consultation with workers or their representatives evolve a contingency plan with respect to redundancies so as to ensure in the event of redundancy that workers do not face undue hardship. In this regard management should endeavour to inform the worker, trade unions and the minister responsible for labour as soon as the need may be evident for such redundancies;

  iv. actively assist workers in securing alternative employment and facilitate them as far as is practicable in this pursuit.

12. Working Environment

Various Acts of Parliament lay down minimum standards in respect of working conditions.

A. Management in consultation with workers or their representatives should seek to improve these standards.

Management has a duty to:

   i. furnish, equip and otherwise provide factories, workshops, offices and other places where work is to be performed with such facilities as meet the reasonable requirements of safety, health and welfare regulations and to adopt suitable measures for the workers' protection, and the prevention of the spread of epidemic or infectious disease;

  ii. organize work in such a manner as to provide in so far as is practicable and best a guarantee for the workers' safety and health;

  iii. adopt the statutory and other suitable measures for the prevention of accidents at the workplace and to keep at all times such medication and therapeutic materials as are necessary for the administration of effective first aid;

  iv. ensure that personnel are trained in first aid techniques, and in such numbers, as to provide for the presence of at least one such trained worker during working hours;

  v. display in conspicuous positions at the workplace rules and regulations, statutory or otherwise, concerning safety and health precautions.

B. The worker has a duty to:

    i. ensure that he understands and observes the safety and health regulations;

   ii. make use of all protective equipment provided;

  iii. cooperate with management and fellow workers in the development and implementation of all safety, health and welfare measures.

13. Payment of Wages

The question of payment for work done is often a contentious area in industrial relations. Wage systems should be agreed and should not be in contravention of any statute.

    Wage systems should also:

    i. ensure that the agreed wages and rates are paid;

   ii. be kept in simple terms so that workers can understand them;

  iii. be kept under review to ensure their applicability to changing circumstances.

PART IV Workers' Representation and the Collective Bargaining Process

14. Trade Union Recognition

    i. The Labour Relations and Industrial Disputes Act, and Regulations 1975, set out the conditions and procedures for the taking of ballots to determine bargaining rights on behalf of workers. This does not, however, preclude employers and trade unions from voluntarily determining claims for bargaining rights where:

       a. there are no other trade unions representing or claiming to represent the workers in question;

       b. the employer is satisfied that the majority of workers in the proposed bargaining unit are members of the applicant union;

   ii. where recognition is accorded voluntarily the employer should immediately so inform the Ministry of Labour and Employment stating the name of the trade union, the date of recognition and the composition of the bargaining unit;

  iii. the employer and the recognized trade union should agree on procedures for resolving disputes and differences and should conduct negotiations in good faith;

iv. trade unions recognized for bargaining purposes should be allowed reasonable facilities to properly represent their members.

15. Representation at Place of Employment (Delegates)

To ensure the proper representation of all workers, delegates are appointed from the workforce to represent the interest of the workers. In doing so, cognizance must be taken of the size and distribution of the workforce as well as the organization of the establishment.

   i. Trade unions should:
   a. specify the conditions of eligibility for the selection and appointment of delegates, and define the manner in which they can be removed;
   b. provide delegates with written authority setting out their responsibilities, particularly with regard to industrial action;
   c. notify management promptly in writing when delegates are appointed, the period for which they hold office, the work groups they represent and any changes among delegates;
   d. in consultation with management, provide for the proper training of delegates and seek to agree on remuneration whilst they attend training courses;
   e. consider the selection of a chief delegate to co-ordinate activities and, where there is more than one union, seek agreement with management and that other union for the coordination of delegate activities.
   ii. Management should:
   a. notify delegates of its employment and industrial relations policies;
   b. consult with delegates on proposed changes in work programmes and methods of any other matter directly affecting the workers;
   c. cooperate with delegates in the performance of their duties and in particular agree on reasonable time off with pay to carry out these duties. Where such time off has not previously been agreed on, a request by delegates should be made of the immediate supervisor and should not be unreasonably withheld;
   d. make available to delegates a list of new workers and staff changes of particular interest to the bargaining unit, and offer reasonable facilities to acquaint workers with union matters.

16. Collective Bargaining

   i. Collective bargaining is the process whereby workers or their representatives and management negotiate with a view to reaching agreement on the terms and conditions of employment of the workers concerned. It should be conducted in an atmosphere of reasonableness and good faith, and management and unions should take all steps to ensure that their representatives conduct themselves during negotiations in a manner which will avoid undue acrimony and facilitate the peaceful and orderly conduct of the negotiations. There should be a determination to abide by the terms agreed and due regard should always be paid to the interest of the community.

   ii. Collective bargaining is more meaningful if the parties are informed on the matters being negotiated. The parties should aim to meet all reasonable requests for information which is relevant to the negotiation in hand and, in particular, management should make available information which is supplied to their shareholders or published in annual reports.

   iii. Collective bargaining may take place in relation to the industry as a whole, or a particular undertaking, or in relation to a particular group of employees within an establishment.

   iv. Where negotiations take place at more than one level, their extent and scope should be clearly defined and properly confined to matters which can appropriately be dealt with at those levels.

17. Bargaining Units

   i. Section 2 of the Labour Relations and Industrial Disputes Act, 1975, defines a bargaining unit as "those workers or categories of workers of an employer in relation to whom collective bargaining is or could appropriately be carried on". The regulations made under that act lay down certain factors to be considered in the event of a dispute in relation to workers who should comprise the bargaining unit. In addition to these factors, consideration may be given to the following:

     a. the composition of bargaining units should be as wide as practicable so as to avoid a multiplicity of units within the same establishment, as too many small units make it difficult to ensure that related groups of employees are treated consistently;

    b. the practice of having separate bargaining units for management and supervisory personnel and excluding them from other bargaining units;

    c. that negotiation arrangements may need periodic review but this must be balanced against the need to avoid disruption of existing bargaining units which are working well.

  ii. Where a dispute exists over any matter concerning the bargaining unit, the parties should endeavour to settle the matter by direct negotiation.

Failing agreement, the parties should utilize the conciliation services of the Ministry of Labour.

18. Collective Agreements

The major aim of the collective bargaining process is to arrive at terms and conditions acceptable to both employers and workers. These terms and conditions are usually enshrined in collective agreements, and often contain procedural and substantive provisions.

  i. Procedural provisions should cover:

    a. arrangements for negotiating terms and conditions of employment and provision for their re-negotiation;

    b. grievance procedures for settling collective disputes and for dealing with disciplinary matters;

    c. facilities for trade union activities in the establishment, and the appointment and functions of delegates;

    d. provisions for joint, permanent and ad hoc consultative committees.

  ii. Substantive provisions should state:

    a. the duration of the agreement;

    b. all matters relating to remuneration;

    c. normal hours of work, provision for overtime and shift work;

    d. provisions for vacation, sick, maternity and casual leave;

    e. compensation for job-related injuries;

    f. provisions for dealing with redundancies, temporary layoff and re-hiring;

    g. provisions for determining job performance, job evaluation and job classification;

    h. provisions for deduction by management from the pay of members of trade unions, contributions duly authorized by such members.

iii. Where practicable, collective agreements should be concluded on an industry-wide level, as this ensures uniformity and consistency throughout the particular industry. The matters suitable to such agreement may cover:
   a. terms and conditions of employment of general application;
   b. general guidelines as to how and within what limits any negotiations at the level of an undertaking should be conducted.
iv. Collective agreements should be in writing, and management should send copies of such agreements to the Ministry of Labour and Employment for their records.

PART V Communication and Consultation

19. Communication and Consultation

Communication and consultation are necessary ingredients in a good industrial relations policy as these promote a climate of mutual understanding and trust which alternately result in increased efficiency and greater job satisfaction. Management and workers or their representatives should therefore cooperate in promoting communication and consultation within the organization.

A. Communication

Communication is a two-way flow of information between management and workers or their representatives. There should likewise be scope for a cross-flow of information between various departments of management:

   i. management should, following consultation with workers or their representatives, take appropriate measures to apply an effective policy of communication;
  ii. such measures as are adopted should in no way prejudice the position of recognized workers' representatives or management and supervisory representatives;
 iii. a communication policy should be adapted to the nature of the undertaking, its size and composition and the interest of the workers;
  iv. the most important medium of communication is word of mouth through personal contact between management and workers or workers' representatives. However, personal contact should be supplemented where necessary by means such as:

    a. written information by way of house-journals, bulletins, notice-boards

    b. meetings for the purpose of exchanging views and information

    c. media aimed at permitting workers to submit suggestions and ideas on the operation of the undertaking

    d. proper orientation courses

v. the matters of interest to be communicated include the operation and future prospects of the undertaking especially as they affect the workers. Information regarding training, prospects of promotion, general working conditions, staff welfare services, safety regulations, social security schemes, transfers, termination of employment, job description and procedure for the examination of grievances is a matter which management is expected to have readily available in easily understandable form. Management should undertake to explain decisions which are likely to affect directly or indirectly the situation of the workers in the establishment provided the disclosure of such information is not damaging to either of the parties.

B. Consultation

Consultation is the joint examination and discussion of problems and matters affecting management and workers. It involves seeking mutually acceptable solutions through a genuine exchange of views and information. Management should take the initiative in establishing and regularizing consultative arrangements appropriate to the circumstance of the undertaking in cooperation with the workers or their representatives.

  i. Management should ensure that in establishing consultative arrangements:

    a. all the information necessary for effective consultation is supplied;

    b. there is adequate opportunity for workers and their representatives to expose their views without prejudicing their positions in any way;

    c. senior members of management take an active part in consultation;

    d. there is adequate opportunity for reporting back.

  ii. Where formal arrangements exist the rules and procedures as well as the subjects to be discussed should be agreed between representatives of management and workers.

PART VI Grievance, Dispute and Disciplinary Procedures

20. Disputes Procedure

Disputes are broadly of two kinds:
- a. disputes of right, which involve the application and interpretation of existing agreements or rights, and
- b. disputes of interest, which relate to claims by workers or a proposal by management as to the terms and conditions of employment.

Management and workers' representatives should adopt a procedure for the settlement of such disputes which:

- i.   should be in writing;
- ii. states the level at which an issue should first be raised;
- iii. sets time limits for each stage of the procedure and provides for extensions by agreement;
- iv. precludes industrial action until all stages of the procedure have been exhausted without success;
- v.   have recourse to the Ministry of Labour and Employment conciliation services.

21. Individual Grievance Procedure

All workers have a right to seek redress for grievances relating to their employment and management in consultation with workers or their representatives should establish and publicize arrangements for the settling of such grievances. The number of stages and the time allotted between stages will depend on the individual establishment. They should neither be too numerous nor too long if they are to avoid frustration. The procedure should be in writing and should indicate:

- i.   that the grievance be normally discussed first by the worker and immediate supervisor – commonly referred to as the "first stage";
- ii. that if unresolved at the first stage, the grievance be referred to the department head, and that the worker delegate may accompany the worker at this stage – the second stage – if the worker so wishes;
- iii. that if the grievance remains unresolved at the second stage, it be referred to higher management at which stage it is advantageous that the worker be represented by a union officer; this is the third stage;

    iv. that on failure to reach agreement at the third stage, the parties agree to the reference of the dispute to conciliation by the Ministry of Labour and Employment;

    v. a time limit between the reference at all stages;

    vi. an agreement to avoid industrial action before the procedure is exhausted.

22. Disciplinary Procedure

    i. Disciplinary procedures should be agreed between management and workers' representatives and should ensure that fair and effective arrangements exist for dealing with disciplinary matters. The procedure should be in writing and should:

        a. specify who has the authority to take various forms of disciplinary action, and ensure that supervisors do not have the power to dismiss without reference to more senior management;

        b. indicate that the matter giving rise to the disciplinary action be clearly specified and communicated in writing to the relevant parties;

        c. give the worker the opportunity to state his case and the right to be accompanied by his representatives;

        d. provide for a right of appeal, whenever practicable, to a level of management not previously involved;

        e. be simple and rapid in operation.

    ii. The disciplinary measures taken will depend on the nature of the misconduct. But normally the procedures should operate as follows:

        a. the first step should be an oral warning, or in the case of more serious misconduct, a written warning setting out the circumstances;

        b. no worker should be dismissed for a first breach of discipline except in the case of gross misconduct;

        c. action on any further misconduct, for example, final warning, suspension without pay or dismissal, should be recorded in writing;

        d. details of any disciplinary action should be given in writing to the worker and to his representative;

        e. no disciplinary action should normally be taken against a delegate until the circumstances of the case have been discussed with a full-time official of the union concerned.

Appendix D

Sample of Claim by Trade Union for Recognition

To_____
(Name of Employer)

_____
(Address)

The _____
(Name of Trade Union)

Of _____
(Registered Address)

Hereby claims bargaining rights in respect of your employees specified in the particulars hereto appended.

PARTICULARS

1. Address of the employer's establishment/s involved:

_____

2. General nature of business at the establishment:

_____

3. Description of the category/categories claimed

_____

Dated this _____ day of _____ 20__

Signature _____

Office _____

of _____

cc Ministry of Labour

Appendix E

Sample Ministry of Labour Letter to Advise Firm of Ballot-Taking

BY HAND

Dear Sir,

Re: Claim for Bargaining Rights dated 1st September by the Bustamante Industrial Trade Union on XYZ Co. Ltd.

I am to inform you that a ballot in respect of the abovementioned claim will be conducted on Friday, 14th November between 10:00 and 12:30 p.m. at (name of venue) for the purpose of determining bargaining rights in respect of Clerical and Maintenance workers.

The Ministry requests that you provide, in accordance with Regulation 7 of the Labour Relations and Industrial Disputes Regulations 1975, suitable accommodation for the taking of a ballot at (name of venue).

An officer of this Ministry will inspect the accommodation to determine its suitability on or before the commencement of the voting period.

You are to nominate an official agent for the purpose of representing your interest at the proposed ballot and to inform me of the name of the said agent, prior to the holding of the ballot. The agent should have due authorization to present to the Presiding Officer on the day of the ballot.

The ballot will be counted at the Ministry of Labour, 1F North Street, Kingston on Monday 17th November at 10:00 a.m. and a representative of your Company is invited to be present.

Yours faithfully,

_____

for Permanent Secretary

Appendix F

Sample Ministry of Labour Certificate Setting Out Ballot Results

BY HAND

Dear Sir,

> Re: Representational Rights Ballot involving XYZ Ltd, the Company, and W.U., the Union, held at (venue) on Friday November 14, 1986

I hereby certify that the result of the abovementioned ballot is as follows:

Total number of persons eligible to vote	–	35
The number voting	–	21
The number voting union I	–	NIL
The number voting union II	–	21
The number who did not vote	–	14
The number of rejected vote(s)	–	NIL

Yours faithfully,

_____

Permanent Secretary

Appendix G

Authorization for Deduction of Dues (Name of Union)

_____ THE UNDERSIGNED OF

_____ EMPLOYED AS _____ HEREBY

REQUEST AND AUTHORIZE MESSRS _____ (NAME OF EMPLOYER)

_____ TO DEDUCT FROM MY WAGES

ON WEEK ENDING _____ THE SUM OF _____

MADE UP AS FOLLOWS:

ENTRANCE FEE _____ WEEKLY DUES _____

AND TO DEDUCT FROM MY WAGES/SALARY EACH WEEK AS FROM WEEK ENDING

_____ THE SUM OF ONE DOLLAR ($1.00) OR HEREAFTER ANY OTHER AMOUNT THAT MIGHT BE DETERMINED BY THE MANAGING EXECUTIVE COMMITTEE OF THE UNION FROM TIME TO TIME AND REMIT SAME MONTHLY TO THE

_____ UNION

AS LONG AS THIS AUTHORIZATION REMAINS IN FORCE.

WITNESS _____ SIGNATURE _____

DATE_____

Appendix H

Revocation of Authorization
for Deduction of Dues

I _____ THE UNDERSIGNED

OF _____ HEREBY REVOKE MY

AUTHORIZATION TO MESSRS _____ (NAME OF COMPANY)

FOR THE _____ (NAME OF UNION)

FOR THE DEDUCTIONS OF UNION DUES FROM MY WAGES.

THIS REVOCATION IS EFFECTIVE FROM _____

SIGNED _____

WITNESS _____

DATE _____

Appendix I

List of Registered Trade Unions in Jamaica

NAME	REG. NO.
Bustamante Industrial Trade Union	9
The Shipping Association of Jamaica	11
Machado Employee Union	37
Master Printers and Allied Trades Association of Jamaica	44
Independence Port Workers Union	47
Trade Union Congress of Jamaica	49
National Workers Union	53
Jamaica Gasolene Retailers Association	55
The Jamaica Association of Professional Builders and Draftsmen	60
The Water Commission and Allied Workers Union	64
Hardware Merchants Association	65
The Jamaica Federation of Musicians Union	68
The Jamaica Employers Federation	69
The Jamaica Dry Cleaning and Laundry Employers Association	71
The Importers and Distributors Association of Jamaica	73
United Port Workers and Seamen's Union	78
Western Seamen's Union	83
St Mary Farmers Union	84
Jamaica Independent Workers Union	85
Port Supervisors Union	87
The Jamaica Federation of Labour	88
Motor Owners Contractors Union	89
Domestic Workers Union	90
Rural Bus and Stage Carriage Truck Operators Association	91
Jamaica Congress of Labour	92
The Jamaica Phonographic Record Retailers Association	93
Union of Technical, Administrative and Supervisory Personnel	94
Northern Taxi-Cab Association	95
The Jamaica Car Transport Organisation	96
Jamaica Maritime Union	97
Printers and Allied Workers Association of Jamaica	98
Jamaica Omnibus Service Workers Association	99

NAME	REG. NO.
Municipal and Parish Councils Workers Union	100
Service Station Attendants Union	101
Sheraton Contract Carriers Association	102
The Jamaica Workers Union	103
The Electrical and Construction Workers Union	104
Independent Trade Union Action Council	105
The Sugar Producers Federation of Jamaica	106
University and Allied Workers' Union	107
Jamaica Union of Public Officers and Public Employees	108
Jamaica Banana Growers Union	109
Jamaica Farmers Union	110
Association of Supervisors, Surveyors, Engineers and Technicians	111
Voluntary Organisation of Women	112
The West Indies Group of University Teachers	113
Refrigeration and Appliance Workers Association	114
Dockers and Marine Workers Union	115
The Justice Liberal Union of Jamaica	116
The Jamaican Union of Bank Employees	117
Union of Journalists and Allied Employees	118
Jamaica Forklift and Equipment Association	119
Carpenters and Allied Workers Union	120
Frome WIS Co. Staff Association	121
Newspaper Delivery Contractors Association	123
Southern Clarendon Truckers Association	124
University of Technology Academic Staff Union	125
Barclays Bank of Jamaica Limited Staff Association	126
United Taxi Drivers Association	127
The British American Insurance Co. Ltd Salesmen's Association	128
The Jamaica Elevator Technical and Allied Workers Association	129
The Jamaica Auto Parts Dealers Association	130
The National Union of Democratic Teachers	131
Jamaica Telephone Company Executive and Allied Staff Association	132
Jamaica Public Service Managers Association	133
Association of Jamaican Airline Pilots	134
The Jamaica Kerosene Distributors Association	135
National Housing Trust Staff Association	136
Jamintel Management and Allied Staff Association	137
The Desnoes and Geddes Monthly Paid Staff Association	138
Carreras Staff Association	139

NAME	REG. NO.
Union of Schools Agricultural and Allied Workers	140
JAMAL Staff Association Union	141
United Union of Jamaica	142
Stage Carriage Mini-Bus Operators Association	143
The Jamaica Red Cap Porters Association	144
The Insurance Companies of Jamaica and Allied Workers Union	145
The Maxi Taxi Association	146

Appendix J

Sample Disciplinary Code

No.	Offence	First Offence	Second Offence	Third Offence	Fourth Offence
1	Punching in before changing into uniforms	Warning	Warning	Discharge	
2	Punching out after changing uniforms	Warning	Warning	Discharge	
3	Being habitually late or absent without reasonable cause (three times in thirty-day period)	Warning	3 working days off	10 working days off	Discharge
4	Early quitting or lateness	Warning	3 working days off	10 working days off	Discharge
5	Absent without leave after commencing work	Warning	3 working days off	10 working days off	Discharge
6	Absent without leave	Warning	3 working days off	10 working days off	Discharge
7	Absent from work without leave for seven consecutive working days without cause	Liable for discharge			
8	Fraudulent use of sick leave provision or tampering with sick leave provision or tampering with sick leave certificate	Discharge			

No.	Offence	First Offence	Second Offence	Third Offence	Fourth Offence
9	Contributing to unsanitary conditions or poor housekeeping	Warning	3 working days off	10 working days off	Discharge
10	Unauthorized possession of firearms or other weapons on premises	Discharge			
11	Smoking in restricted areas	Warning	3 working days off	10 working days off	Discharge
12	Drinking any alcoholic beverage on company's premises while on duty or company's time	5 working days off	Discharge		
13	Bringing alcoholic liquor on the job without permission	Discharge			
14	Coming to work under the influence of liquor	Sent home	Sent home or discharge depending on severity	Discharge	
15	Punching in or out for another employee – party or parties involved	Discharge			

No.	Offence				
16	Vending, soliciting or collecting contributions for any purpose at any time unless authorized by management	3 working days off	Discharge		
17	Distributing written or printed matter of any description on company's premises unless authorized by management, or unless it is a pamphlet authorized by the trade union	3 working days off	Discharge		
18	Failing to observe safety regulations, endangering life	3 working days off	5 working days off	Discharge	
19	Failing to be neat and tidily attired in uniforms while on duty: female staff are required to wear hairnets, nail polish is not permitted and nails must be kept short and clean; the wearing of jewellery, except wedding bands, is not permitted	Warning	3 working days off	7 working days off	Discharge

No.	Offence	First Offence	Second Offence	Third Offence	Fourth Offence
20	Eating in areas other than the prescribed lunch room	Warning	3 working days off	Discharge	
21	Failing to take lunch time assigned by a foreman	Warning	3 working days off	Discharge	
22	Posting on, or removing any matter from bulletin boards or other company's property unless authorized by management	1 working day off	3 working days off	Discharge	
23	Gambling or engaging in lottery on company's premises	Discharge			
24	Stealing, or removing company's property or any employee's property unless authorized	Discharge			

		1st	2nd	3rd	4th
25	Misusing, destroying or damaging any company's property or airline's property or the property of any employee:				
	a. Causing damage, minor negligence	Discharge warning	3 working days off	Discharge	
	b. Failing to report damage	3 working days off	Discharge		
26	Making false, vicious or malicious statements concerning any employee, the company or its products	Warning	3 working days off	1 working week off	Discharge
27	Provoking or instigating a fight or fighting during working hours or on company's premises between fellow workers	Suspension or discharge			
	a. Fighting with supervisor or foreman	Discharge			
28	Immoral conduct (sexual)	Discharge			

No.	Offence	First Offence	Second Offence	Third Offence	Fourth Offence
29	Entering other departments without authority	Warning	1 working day off	3 working days off	Discharge
	a. absence from workplace without permission	Warning	1 working day off	3 working days off	Discharge
30	Sleeping on the job	Warning	Discharge		
31	Failing to report for overtime work without good reason after being assigned to work according to overtime policy	Warning	3 working days off	1 working week off	Discharge
32	a. Operating, using machines, tools or equipment to which employee has not been assigned	Suspension or discharge	Discharge		
	b. Performing other than assigned work	Warning	3 working days off	Discharge	

33	Causing material or products to be scrapped due to carelessness		3 working days off		Discharge
34	Mistake due to carelessness	Warning	3 working days off	1 working week off	Discharge
35	Insubordination	Suspension or discharge			

Note: For the purpose of this schedule, the term "days off" shall be interpreted to mean suspension from work.

Appendix K

Constitution of the Joint Industrial Council for the _____ Industry

1. Name:

The name of the Council shall be the Joint Industrial Council for the _____ Industry of Jamaica (hereinafter referred to as "The Council").

2. Scope:

All which are owned by members of the _____ Association (hereinafter referred to as the "Association") shall be within the scope of the Council, subject to any exemption which may subsequently be agreed upon by the Council.

(1) The objects for which the Council is established are:

(i) To secure cooperation between management and labour engaged in the _____ industry with a view to the general improvement of the conditions of all engaged therein as aforesaid.

(ii) To consider and determine upon all matters relating to wages, hours and working conditions on _____.

(iii) To encourage such practices as will ensure the avoidance of industrial disputes in connection with work on _____ and the speedy settlement of such disputes as may occur.

(iv) To represent the needs and opinions of management and labour engaged in _____ to the Government, Government Departments and other authorities.

(v) To cooperate with other industrial councils on problems of common interest where necessary.

(2) In the interpretation of this clause the objects, powers and duties and functions assumed by or conferred on the Council by any sub-clause shall not be restricted by reference to any other sub-clause, and in the event of any doubt or ambiguity this clause and every sub-clause hereof shall be construed in such a way as to widen and not restrict the powers of the Council.

3. Membership and appointments:

(1) The Council shall consist of 10 representatives, one-half by trade unions in the following allocations:

Name of Organization		Number of Representatives
a. The _____ Association		_____
b. (i) The _____ Union		_____
(ii) The _____ Union		_____
(iii) The _____ Union		_____

(2) The Association or any constituent Trade Union shall have and may exercise the right at any time to withdraw a representative and to appoint another in his or her place; provided that such a change shall not be effective until notice in writing, as hereinafter provided, shall have been given to the Secretary.

(3) The Association or any constituent Trade Union shall have and may exercise the right to appoint a proxy to sit and vote at any particular meeting in the place of a representative who is unable to attend. The appointment shall be in writing under the hand of a registered officer of the Association or the Trade Union and shall be handed to the Secretary before the commencement of, or at, the meeting at which the proxy is to sit.

4. Retirement and reappointment:

(1) The first Council shall remain in office unless or until changed as hereinafter provided.

(2) Members of the Council shall hold office for one year and shall be eligible for reappointment by the Association and the respective Trade Unions as the case may be.

(3) Casual vacancies shall be filled by the Association or by the Trade Union concerned. A member appointed to fill a casual vacancy shall sit until the end of the current year.

5. Notifications:

Immediately following the appointment of members of the Council the Association and the constituent Trade Unions shall furnish the Secretary with the names and addresses of their representatives.

6. Officers:

(1) At its first meeting and thereafter at the first meeting held each year after the nomination of representatives, each side of the Council shall

elect one of its members to serve as Co-Chairman for the ensuing year. The Chairman shall not be from the same side of the Council for two (2) consecutive meetings. In the absence of both Co-Chairmen, the side whose turn it is to provide the Chairman shall have the right to elect a Chairman for the meeting in substitution for the Co-Chairman.

(2) The Council shall appoint a Secretary and may appoint a Treasurer, upon such terms and for such periods as the Council may think fit.

7. Meetings:

(1) *Ordinary:* Ordinary meetings of the Council shall be summoned on 21 days' notice and shall be held as often as necessary and not less than once every six months. Copies of the Agenda shall accompany such notice.

(2) *Special:* Special meetings shall be summoned on the requisition of the Association or any of the constituent Trade Unions. At least 14 days' notice shall be given and the Agenda shall accompany such notice, and only such matters as are on the Agenda may be discussed.

(3) *Emergency:* Emergency meetings shall be called within 48 hours. Such meetings shall be summoned on the request of any one of the constituent parties after consultation with the Co-Chairman of the side not making the request for the emergency meeting. Notice of this meeting shall be deposited at the Headquarters of any of the constituent parties.

(4) *Annual:* Annual meetings shall be held in the month of September of each year.

(5) All meetings shall be summoned by the Secretary.

8. Quorum:

The quorum shall be three members on each side of the Council, provided that at least two unions are represented on the quorum.

9. Committees:

(1) The Council may appoint an Executive Committee and may appoint such other standing or sectional committees as may be necessary.

(2) The Council appoints Committees for special purposes.

(3) The reports of all Committees shall be submitted to the council for confirmation.

(4) The Council may make rules to govern its own procedure for the determination of its business or for the guidance of any Committee appointed by it.

10. Co-opted members:

The Council shall have the power to appoint an Executive Committee or to authorize the Committee to co-opt such persons of special knowledge not being members of the Council as may serve the special purposes of the Council; provided that so far as the Executive Committee is concerned:

(a) the two sides of the Council shall be equally represented;

(b) any appointed or co-opted members shall serve only in a consultative capacity and shall not have the right to vote.

11. Voting:

The voting in Council and in Committees shall be by show of hands or otherwise as the Council may from time to time determine. No resolution shall be regarded as Carried unless it has been approved by a majority of the members present on each side of the Council. The Chairman shall exercise an original vote only.

12. General:

(1) All matters coming within the scope of the Objects of the Council as set out in Clause 3 shall be referred to the Council for recommendations as the Council shall consider appropriate and neither the Association nor any constituent Trade Union shall deal with such matter or take any section thereon before the Council shall have had a reasonable opportunity of considering and reporting on the same.

(2) A concise record of every decision or recommendation of the Council shall be sent by the Secretary by registered mail to the Association and the constituent Trade Unions within seven days of the same having been made and such decision or recommendation shall be binding unless within a further period of seven days, the Association or any of the constituent Trade Unions give notice of objection thereto, in which case the decision or recommendation shall not be binding on the Association or any of the Trade Unions and in such case the matter shall be treated in all respects as if the Council had been unable to agree upon a recommendation, and in such a case the matter shall be regarded as falling under section 3 (i) and (ii) hereunder.

(3) (i) The Council shall discuss in full with a view to settlement any matter of dispute referred to it. If in relation to any matter submitted to it, the Council, after having been offered a reasonable opportunity for full discussion, is unable to agree upon the recommendation for

settlement to be made by it to the constituent bodies, the matter may, at the request of either side, be referred to the Permanent Secretary of the Ministry of Labour within 10 days of failure to arrive at such settlement.

(ii) In the event of a deadlock and on the agreement of the Council, alternative methods of settlement shall be:

(a) reference to a Board of Enquiry on the request of either party; or

(b) reference to arbitration on the agreement of both sides.

(iii) In so far as the enquiry is concerned it shall be subject to the same terms and conditions as set out in 4 (ii) and (iii) below, substituting "enquiry" for "arbitration" and "impartial person" for "arbitrator".

(4) If the agreement of the parties to the dispute is reached on the reference to arbitration, such arbitration shall be in accordance with the following provisions:

(i) The reference shall be to a single arbitrator appointed by the Council or to an arbitrator appointed by the Council and assessors appointed in equal numbers by each side of the Council.

(ii) The date, time and place for the holding of the arbitration shall be fixed by the arbitrator, who shall notify the parties accordingly through the Ministry of Labour.

(iii) Upon the failure of the parties to agree to the procedure to be adopted at the hearing it shall be determined by the arbitrator.

(iv) In all cases, the decision of the arbitrator alone shall be final and binding on all parties; and in all cases of dispute over the interpretation of the arbitrator's award, the award shall be referred back to the arbitrator for clarification or interpretation at the request of either party to the dispute and such clarification or interpretation shall be final and binding on all parties.

(v) The constituent Trade Unions undertake to use their best efforts to avoid slow-downs and/or strikes and the Association undertakes to use its best efforts to avoid lockouts, and in no case shall either party resort to such practices until the Council has had an opportunity for discussion of the issue. In cases where a dispute is apprehended or has occurred on the request of any constituent party to the Secretary, a meeting of the Council shall be held within 48 hours of the receipt of the request.

(vi) The right of the workers to strike and of the employers to lockout may be exercised, subject to the provisions of Clause 12 (4) (v) above.

(vii) Every member of the Council shall be wholly free in the performance of his or her duties as a member thereof and shall not be discriminated against, either by the Association or by any of the constituent Trade Unions, as the result of any action appropriately undertaken by such member in good faith in his or her capacity as a member of the Council.

13. Amendment of Constitution:

The Council may from time to time by resolution duly passed in accordance with Clause 11, repeal, add to, alter or amend this constitution as it may think fit.

We the undersigned, approve and adopt the above Constitution and agree to put the same into operation with effect from _____

Dated this _____ day of _____ 20__

Signatories _____

Appendix L

Wage Guidelines in Jamaica: A Short History

Pay or wage guidelines in Jamaica over the years have evolved from the period of the 1970s when the intent was not only to contain salaries but to achieve parity to the point where it became expedient to remove them. During the latter part of the 1970s the Michael Manley administration sought to clamp down on companies who, at the time, were awarding significant increases to management employees. The 1976 guidelines were predicated on a cost of living increase which was to be calculated on the difference between the consumer price index and the percentage increase of the last contract. The only stipulation was that it was not to exceed J$10 per week and rates were established for different income groups, starting from J$7,000 where the maximum calculable rates were applicable, to a maximum of J$16,000 where no increases were to be granted. This obviously incurred the wrath of those within this income group who responded by reclassifying and creating a number of new posts.

It became evident that a percentage figure had to be set if government were to keep the disparity between salary increases at ten to one. Consequently, the guidelines in the ministry paper of 1977 set a ceiling on wage increases and attempted to seek preferential increases for workers at the lower end of the scale. The guidelines of 1979–81 were to be actually a sharing of the wage fund in a prescribed manner with those at the bottom gaining more, not an across-the-board increase. These guidelines also included a price control policy aimed at maintaining prices at rates commensurate with wage increases.

On 16 May 1979 pay guidelines which stipulated a maximum ceiling for salary increases were tabled in the house of representatives as Ministry Paper No. 23. They outlined the principles which would govern the proposed wage increase ceiling for all categories of workers.

The ministry paper also outlined the rationale behind the imposition of these guidelines. It stated that these were part of broader economic objectives aimed at achieving:

1. improvement in the balance of payments, which would be reflected in the achievement and maintenance of a desirable level of liquid foreign exchange reserves;
2. achievement of a 3 per cent growth rate in GDP during 1979 and a real growth rate of 4 per cent by 1981; and
3. the fastest possible reduction in the rate of unemployment during the 1979–81 period and the achievement of a level of employment which is consistent with an equitable distribution of income as well as the maintenance of social stability.

The guidelines as they were then introduced would be based on a maximum permissible increase in salaries of 10 per cent per annum. This was defined as straight time, overtime pay and the money value of allowances, fringe benefits – for example, commissions, bonuses, insurance schemes, cost of living and lunch allowances, leave provisions and any benefit resulting from a reduction in a forty-hour workweek. The last two were of particular interest, as the thinking that pay in lieu of leave and the attachment of a monetary value to reduction in working hours representing part of a company's wage fund, was somewhat austere. It, however, did not include employer's contributions to the National Insurance Scheme, the National Housing Trust and *approved* pension schemes as well as other reimbursable expenditure (for example, genuine travelling allowance, provision for uniforms, tools and equipment) carried out in the performance of one's job. Increases arising from general promotion of entire groups or categories would be included as part of the wage fund and, as such, subject to a 10 per cent guideline. Workers who operated on a piece rate or task rate were also to be embraced by the wage guidelines.

Certain provisions were made for the successful application of these guidelines. The wage fund to be calculated was to be based on the total pay bill as mentioned earlier but, in instances where different bargaining units existed within a company, provision was made for it to be calculated on the basis of the total pay bill within each unit. The ministry paper also stipulated that provision was to be made for those at the lower end of the scale, who were supposed to receive preferential treatment in negotiations. Each employee's increase was supposed to be calculated by the unit he or she belonged to and this suggested differing levels of increase within companies.

Provisions were made for increased benefits to employees in the form of productivity incentive schemes. Prior approval for these schemes had to be obtained from the Ministry of Labour with regard to the basis of the scheme, the method of calculation and payment dates. Established objectives of these schemes were to (1) increase employment; and (2) maintain an increase in the rate of inflation to a maximum of 10 per cent per annum over the next two years.

All contracts were established for a period of two years and the effective date was 31 May 1979. Contracts negotiated before this period were not subject to these guidelines and companies were encouraged to conclude negotiations within three months after 31 May 1979. Retroactivity was calculated from the commencement date of the new contract.

Ability to pay was in the context of the maximum 10 per cent increase. Remembering that this was a ceiling and not an absolute figure, it was therefore quite possible for a company to plead inability to pay 10 per cent to their employees. Earlier guidelines had stipulated that this ability to pay must in no way be subsidized by price increases.

Compliance was ensured by a combination of factors:

1. Section 11 of the LRIDA was amended, making it possible for the minister to refer disputes to the tribunal for settlement on:
   a. the request in writing of any or all of the party or parties to an industrial dispute;
   b. the minister's own initiative to resolve an impasse. Before any of this was done, the minister had to be satisfied that there was no other recourse at the local or conciliation level of the Ministry of Labour.
2. The second mechanism related to the reporting of the wage fund and settlements. The fund had to be reported to the Ministry of Labour at least fourteen days before the commencement of negotiations and, likewise, the settlement at least fourteen days after the agreement or award was made. The ministry decided whether or not the increase fell within the specified limit. Where a breach existed the settlement was not registered, which meant that a certificate was not issued and therefore not permissible for income tax relief or price adjustment purposes. The ministry, in turn, notified the Income Tax Department about the nature of such awards and suggested recourse. In order to give the act some teeth, the Income Tax Law was to be amended to exclude any adjustment over the stipulated amount from allowable deductions from profits or income for the purpose of computing income tax.

Guidelines were re-introduced in 1987 and showed very little difference from those that had previously existed. During this period, that is, from 1981 to 1987, wage increases revolved around a 15 per cent average, and it is argued that those guidelines helped to dampen the excessive rash of wage increases, which the pay guidelines of the late 1970s sought to address. Under the guidelines as tabled in Ministry Paper No. 6 of January 1987, no mention was made of "the relative deprivation of the lower paid staff" and their receiving preferential treatment in wage increases. Also, in the case of what was referred to as "bona-fide promotion", this was not to be included in the total wage bill. Ability to pay was not tied to the conditionality of no price increases, which was a constant theme throughout all previously existing pay guidelines.

Successive wage guidelines include those of 1988–89 and 1990–91. With the exception of the latter, where the ceiling was increased from 10 per cent to 12 per cent, the form and content has been the same as the re-introduced guidelines of 1987–88. In 1990, government saw the need to increase the guidelines based on inflationary measures and this figure was actually predicated on keeping the exchange rate fixed. Many at the time wondered how government would manage such a feat in view of excessive demand for foreign exchange and the demands this would create within the system.

On 9 May 1991, wage guidelines were removed from private sector wage negotiations after years of lobbying by nearly every sector or interest group in Jamaica. Ability to pay was the main criterion in wage negotiations. The government felt that this was to be tempered by "gains in productivity, as any rash of increases not commensurate with this factor would price our goods and services out of the international market". This somewhat brought to mind the Pay Guidelines of 1977 in which the issue of relevant factors was expounded. These included the degree of mechanization vis-à-vis other similar businesses, the location of the business, levels of compensation within the same industry for comparable work, and the nature of the goods – whether import or export, or both. Unions were urged to exercise caution in their claims as this could lead to reductions and layoffs.

The guidelines negotiated under the Edward Seaga–led regime of the 1980s did not take this into consideration and responded more to inflationary measures. International Monetary Fund (IMF) negotiation had stipulated reintroduction of wage guidelines with the hope of containing inflation.

Wage guidelines, in whatever shape or form, have drawn criticisms from all unions and, depending on the government that instituted them, the two major unions have come out strongly against them. They have contended that workers should share the brunt of IMF policies, as unregulated incomes have been blamed for causing inflation. They have also contended that productivity had not improved as envisaged by the guidelines nor has there been any improvement in employment. Based on this, they saw no reason to continue with guidelines. Industrial relations practitioners have been arguing for the removal of wage guidelines because they impinge upon and frustrate free collective bargaining.

So great were the pressures on government to remove the guidelines and relax the laws which governed them that very few companies were actually compliant. Companies started by granting massive increases on non-taxable allowances to the extent that government had to change the law to bring these into the tax net. Companies had also begun to give employees across-the-board sums and to embrace the establishment of more incentive schemes in their thrust to give employees more. A survey carried out by Carl Stone of the University of the West Indies in 1990 showed that only 32 per cent of companies surveyed gave pay increases of between 12.5 per cent. As much as 26 per cent gave 20 to 25 per cent, with 2 per cent giving 30 per cent and over, reflecting the scant regard for wage guidelines.

With an inflation rate running in excess of 30 per cent and the gradual removal of subsidies, the pressure intensified to the point where guidelines in the private, and to an extent in the public sector (where a wage fund exists), were finally removed in mid-1991.

Appendix M

ILO INSTRUMENTS: OCCUPATIONAL SAFETY AND HEALTH International Occupational Safety and Health Information Center (CIS)

ILO Conventions and Recommendations concerning occupational safety and health
Occupational Safety and Health Convention, 1981, No. 155
Occupational Safety and Health Recommendation, 1981, No. 164

Occupational Health Services
Occupational Health Services Convention, 1985, No. 161
Occupational Health Services Recommendation, 1985, No. 171

Major Hazard Control
Prevention of Major Industrial Accidents Convention, 1993, No. 174
Prevention of Major Industrial Accidents Recommendation, 1993, No. 181

Working Environment
Working Environment Convention, 1977, No. 148
Working Environment Recommendation, 1977, No. 156

Toxic Substances and Agents
Anthrax Prevention Recommendation, 1919, No. 3
Asbestos Convention, 1986, No. 162
Asbestos Recommendation, 1986, No. 172
Benzene Convention, 1971, No. 136
Benzene Recommendation, 1971, No. 144
Chemicals Convention, 1990, No. 170
Chemicals Recommendation, 1990, No. 177
Radiation Protection Convention, 1960, No. 115
Radiation Protection Recommendation, 1960, No. 114
White Lead (Painting) Convention, 1921, No. 13

Occupational Cancer
   Occupational Cancer Convention, 1974, No. 139
   Occupational Cancer Recommendation, 1974, No. 147

Particular Branches of Activity
   Health Protection and Medical Care (Seafarers) Convention, 1987, No. 164
   Hygiene (Commerce and Offices) Convention, 1964, No. 120
   Labour Inspection (Agriculture) Convention, 1969, No. 129
   Labour Inspection (Agriculture) Recommendation, 1969, No. 133
   Labour Inspection (Seafarers) Convention, 1996, No. 178
   Labour Inspection (Seafarers) Recommendation, 1996, No. 185
   Marking of Weight (Packages Transported by Vessels) Convention, 1929,
      No. 27
   Medical Advice at Sea Recommendation, 1958, No. 106
   Medical Examination (Fishermen) Convention, 1959, No. 129
   Medical Examination (Seafarers) Convention, 1946, No. 73
   Occupational Safety and Health (Dock Work) Convention, 1979, No. 152
   Occupational Safety and Health (Dock Work) Recommendation, 1979,
      No. 160
   Plantations Convention, 1958, No. 110
   Prevention of Accidents (Seafarers) Convention, 1970, No. 134
   Prevention of Accidents (Seafarers) Recommendation, 1970, No. 142
   Protection against Accidents (Dockers) Convention, 1929, No. 28
   Protection against Accidents (Dockers) Convention (Revised), 1932,
      No. 32
   Safety and Health in Construction Convention, 1988, No. 167
   Safety and Health in Construction Recommendation, 1988, No. 175
   Safety and Health in Mines Convention, 1995, No. 176
   Safety and Health in Mines Recommendation, 1995, No. 183
   Safety Provisions (Building) Convention, 1937, No. 62
   Safety Provisions (Building) Recommendation, 1937, No. 53
   Ships' Medicine Chests Recommendation, 1958, No. 105

Guarding of Machinery
   Guarding of Machinery Convention, 1963, No. 119
   Guarding of Machinery Recommendation, 1963, No. 118

Maximum Weight
   Maximum Weight Convention, 1967, No. 127
   Maximum Weight Recommendation, 1967, No. 128

Employment of Women
  Maternity Protection Convention, 1919, No. 3
  Maternity Protection Convention (Revised), 1952, No. 103
  Maternity Protection Convention (Revised), 2000, No. 183
  Maternity Protection Recommendation (Revised), 2000, No. 191
  Night Work (Women) Convention (Revised), 1948, No. 89
  Night Work (Women) Protocol, 1990, No. 89
  Underground Work (Women) Convention, 1935, No. 45

Employment of Children and Young Persons
  Medical Examination of Young Persons (Industry) Convention, 1946,
    No. 77
  Medical Examination of Young Persons (Non-Industrial Occupations)
    Convention, 1946, No. 78
  Medical Examination of Young Persons (Sea) Convention, 1921, No. 16
  Medical Examination of Young Persons (Underground Work) Conven-
    tion, 1965, No. 124
  Minimum Age Convention 1973, No. 138
  Minimum Age (Agriculture) Convention, 1921, No. 10
  Minimum Age (Sea) Convention, 1920, No. 7
  Night Work of Young Persons (Industry) Convention (Revised), 1948,
    No. 90
  Night Work of Young Persons (Non-Industrial Occupations) Conven-
    tion, 1946, No. 79
  Worst Forms of Child Labour Convention, 1999, No. 182
  Worst Forms of Child Labour Recommendation, 1999, No. 190

Migrant Workers
  Migrant Workers (Supplementary Provisions) Convention, 1975, No. 143

Labour Protection
  Labour Inspection Convention, 1947, No. 81
  Labour Inspection Recommendation, 1947, No. 81

Appendix N

Selected Industrial Relations Cases

Case 1: Unfair/Unjustifiable Dismissal (Gross Disrespect and Insolence)
GSB Clerks' Cooperative Credit Union (GSB) v. Bustamante Industrial Trade Union (BITU) (Jamaica)

Case 2: Unjustifiable Dismissal (Failure to Resume Work)
The Village Resorts Limited/Grand Lido Negril v. the Bustamante Industrial Trade Union (BITU), and the Industrial Disputes Tribunal (IDT) (Jamaica)

Case 3: Fair-Play (Fairness and Equity)
The Jamaica Civil Service Association (JCSA) v. the Government of Jamaica Tribunal Award of February 14, 2001 (Jamaica)

Case 4: Unfair Dismissal (Redundancy)
The Jamaica Flour Mills Limited (the Applicant) v. the Industrial Disputes Tribunal (the Respondent) (Jamaica)

Case 5: Unfair/Unjustifiable Dismissal (Quashed by the Court)
Institute of Jamaica and the Jamaica Civil Service Association Tribunal (1999) The Institute of Jamaica v. the Industrial Disputes Tribunal/Coleen Beecher (Jamaica)

Case 6: Unjustifiable Dismissal (Criminal Charge)
Salada Foods v. the National Workers Union (Jamaica)

Case 7: Calculation of Redundancy Payments
Mariner's Negril Beach Club (MNBC) v. Bustamante Industrial Trade Union (BITU) (Jamaica)

Case 8: Bargaining Rights (Eligibility for Union Representation)
The National Commercial Bank (Jamaica) (NCB) Limited v. the Bustamante Industrial Trade Union (BITU) (Jamaica)

Case 9: Pay Disparity/Anomaly
Ministries of Health (MOH), and Finance and Planning (MOFP) v. the Union of Technical and Supervisory Personnel (UTASP) (IDT 1/2003) (Jamaica)

Case 10: Bargaining Rights (Eligibility for Union Representation)
Canadian Imperial Bank of Commerce (Jamaica) Ltd (CIBC) v. Bustamante Industrial Trade Union (BITU) (Jamaica)

Case 11: Recovery of Funds Paid to Employees (Overpayment): Unauthorized Deductions
Jamaica National Heritage Trust (JNHT) v. the Bustamante Industrial Trade Union (BITU) (Jamaica)

Case 12: Job Evaluation Market Reference and Calculation of Retroactive Payments
Jamaica Public Service Company Limited (JPSCo) v. the Bustamante Industrial Trade Union (BITU) and the National Workers Union (NWU) (Jamaica)

Case 13: Dismissal Due to Insubordination, Disrespect and so on
Employee (Michael Browne) v. T. Geddes Grant (Barbados)

Case 14: Grievance Procedure Regarding Performance Appraisal: Personnel Records
TD No. 48/92 (Date of Award/"Delivery" – 18 January 1993)
University of the West Indies (St Augustine Campus) v. University and Affiliated Workers Union (Trinidad and Tobago)

Case 15: Dismissal, Breach of Contract of Employment, Job Abandonment, Compensation
TD 130/91, Trinidad and Tobago (Date of Award/"Delivery" – 12 May 1993)
Employee v. Romeo's Gas Station (Trinidad and Tobago)

Case 16: Summary Dismissal (Insolence and Wilful Disrespect)
Trinidad and Tobago Trade Dispute No. 82 of 2001
National Union of Domestic Employees v. K. Allen and Sons Funeral Directors Limited (Trinidad and Tobago)

Case 1: Unfair/Unjustifiable Dismissal
(Gross Disrespect and Insolence)

GSB Clerks' Cooperative Credit Union (GSB) v. Bustamante Industrial Trade Union (BITU) (Jamaica)

This case involved the dismissal of Ann Marie Allen-Orgill, a receptionist with GSB Credit Union, who was dismissed on the basis of the attitude that she displayed particularly towards Miss Beverley Johnson, Operations Manager, regarding interpretation of office security arrangements. The differences arose in relation to a specific incident involving whether a member of the credit union should have been allowed to enter for service after the office had been closed for service for the day on 12 February. The member was allowed to enter after the manager (Miss Johnson) discussed the matter with the general manager.

The employee had raised questions about the decision to admit a member to the offices after closure for the day, and had mentioned that such access was not allowed under the existing regulations.

There were discussions between the receptionist and the manager about the status of the rules and whether they had changed. In one instance there was a "spirited exchange between the two women" and one of their colleagues requested that they "tone down" (IDT 11/2003, 4). On the following day the manager (Miss Johnson), in an effort to clarify what had occurred, held meetings with persons who were directly or indirectly involved in the matter.

The receptionist (Mrs Allen-Orgill) and her immediate supervisor participated in one meeting. During the meeting, the receptionist reportedly "became angry and loud". She said that a security guard had behaved disrespectfully towards her; that Miss Johnson had told her that she need not inform her (the receptionist) of the policy change; and that she (the receptionist) was operating within instructions from the general manager, who said that staff needed to be flexible.

The meeting ended abruptly as Miss Johnson objected to the receptionist's behaviour (IDT 11/2003, 5).

The operations manager and general manager decided to dismiss the employee (receptionist) "for *gross disrespect* and *insolence*" under the guidelines of the Employee Code of Conduct. A letter of dismissal issued to the employee on 14 February raised, for example, questions about "trust and confidence to perform . . . duties" on the part of the receptionist/employee (IDT 11/2003, 4–5).

Failure of the credit union and the Bustamante Industrial Trade Union which represents the credit union's workers to resolve the dispute led to the Ministry of Labour and Social Security referring it in October, that year, to the Industrial Disputes Tribunal (IDT) for arbitration. Among the union's contentions were that it had not received a copy of the dismissal letter; the Employee Code of Business Conduct was not followed; the employee was not afforded a hearing or trial, thereby resulting in a breach of natural justice; and the manner of dismissal "was unwarranted, unjustifiable" and hasty.

The Tribunal's Findings and Award

The tribunal noted that the dismissed employee's supervisor "had never had a problem with her", that there "was no evidence to suggest that she had work related problems" with persons at her place of work, and that her "behaviour could not be deemed abusive" and she "seemed genuinely upset by the behaviour of a disrespectful security guard, and a manager who told her that she had no right to know if there was a change in policy regarding flexibility of the staff in dealing with members of the credit union as told by the deputy general manager" (IDT 11/2003, 12).

The tribunal found that the employee had expressed her concern inappropriately; that there was no evidence that she had offended prior to that incident and that "the infraction was not in keeping with paragraph 22 . . . of the Labour Relations Code" (see Appendix C). It further decided that the employee had not been offered the "opportunity to state her case and the right to be accompanied by her representative which is inconsistent with" the "Disciplinary Action Employees Code of Business Conduct and Paragraph 22 . . . of the Labour Relations Code" (IDT 11/2003, 15).

In keeping with section 12, the tribunal ordered the credit union to reinstate the employee "with effect from the 14th February with seventy-five percent (75%) of her wages up to the 14th May (following year) or the date on which she" resumed "her duties", whichever was earlier, "and full wages thereafter" (IDT 11/2003).

Lessons Learnt

1. Managers should ensure that they act fairly and equitably, in accordance with existing codes of conduct and the details of the particular events leading to their decisions for disciplinary action against employees.

2. Employees should endeavour to relate their concerns in a civil manner in dealing with supervisors/managers and at the work-place in general.

3. Policy changes should be put in writing and circulated to all employees.

4. On matters involving union members the trade union must be consulted at some stage of the process of handling the disciplinary matter.

Source: IDT 11/2003.

Case 2: Unjustifiable Dismissal (Failure to Resume Work)

The Village Resorts Limited/Grand Lido Negril v. the Bustamante Industrial Trade Union (BITU), and the Industrial Disputes Tribunal (IDT) (Jamaica)

Since 1991, Grand Lido Hotel employees were represented by a staff association. The association had signed a collective labour agreement with the employer, Grand Lido Hotel, Negril, on behalf of the workers on 30 June 1991. The agreement was amended and renewed and the expiry date was March 1997. In December 1994, the Bustamante Industrial Trade Union (BITU) sought bargaining rights on behalf of the employees but the employers refused to hold discussions with the union.

Several workers were dismissed in the period from January to 28 March 1995. On 29 March, a leading BITU officer (Vice-President Pearnell Charles) visited the hotel and requested a meeting with the general man-ager and the request was denied but the union officer nevertheless addressed the workers on the hotel's premises without the manager's consent. On that day, workers on the 7:00 a.m. shift punched their work cards and waited for the general manager, a Mr James, to meet with and address them, having been advised by their staff association's president. Unsatisfied with the content of the address, the workers did not immedi-ately resume working.

Later that day the management issued written instructions to workers, ordering an immediate resumption of work and warning of disciplinary charges if they did not. He also offered to meet a representative of their association on their resumption but the workers did not resume. They later stated, for example, that they would return to work if management promised not to victimize them. Up to late that day a solution had not been arrived at and letters of dismissal were prepared late that night and issued to workers on their arrival at work during the course of the following morning (March 30).

The case was referred to the Industrial Disputes Tribunal for hearing.

The Tribunal's Findings and Award (dated 22 November 1995)

The tribunal directed that the 225 employees were unjustifiably dismissed and should be reinstated. It explained that blame could not be laid solely on the workers; management's attitude was a contributory factor, and it was therefore "unreasonable and unfair" to impose such an extreme punishment on the workers.

The Supreme Court's Position

An application was made by the company to the Supreme Court for an "order of certiorari" to quash the tribunal's award.

Legal representatives for the company based their application on the argument that the tribunal "misdirected itself in law, in the interpretation of Section 12 (5)(c)" of the LRIDA and especially regarding the interpretation of the word "unjustifiable", and in having made the award in favour of the workers even in light of their refusal to "resume their contractual duties".

In the Supreme Court, Justice J. Ellis, for instance, noted the applicant's argument that the tribunal had acted outside the law when it interpreted "unjustifiable" as being synonymous with "unfair". The court, nevertheless, reiterated that the tribunal was not constrained within the bounds of the common law as its task was to assess whether workers had been unjustifiably dismissed in the light of Section 12 (5)(c) of the LRIDA.

The court upheld the tribunal's award but concluded that workers had been misguided and had contravened their employment contract when they learnt at some stage during the crisis that the general manager "would not be meeting and addressing them as they had been led to believe". It also noted that workers had lost confidence in the ability of their association to represent them, and had been "excited and unduly influenced by the presence" of the BITU representatives, and that the management had not exercised the "understanding and compromise which the conflict required" (Suit No. M98 of 1995, 31).

The Appeal Court's Position

The company took the case to the Court of Appeal but the appeal was dismissed by a majority vote. A central theme in the court's assessment was that, although the company's dismissal of the workers might have been lawful, it was not so much the legality as whether the dismissal was unjustifiable.

Lessons Learnt

1. Workers should be aware of their contractual obligations and be guided by them.
2. Employers should explore all possible options before taking extreme disciplinary action against workers.
3. Both employers and workers should take into account the wider consequences of their action in the interest of maintaining peace and harmony in the work environment.
4. Note the subtle difference between a "lawful dismissal" and an "unjustifiable" one. Employers and workers may enjoy the legal right to terminate a contract of employment if the reason is justifiable, that is, if it is a misdemeanor warranting dismissal.

Source: Supreme Court Civil Appeal No. 66/97, Suit No. M98 of 1995.

Case 3: Fair-Play (Fairness and Equity)

The Jamaica Civil Service Association (JCSA) v. the Government of Jamaica Tribunal Award of February 14, 2001 (Jamaica)

A dispute about revision of motor vehicle upkeep allowances and mileage travelling rates remained unresolved. The Ministry of Labour and Social Security referred the dispute to the tribunal for its ruling.

The tribunal awarded to civil servants on 14 February 2001, new travel upkeep allowances and rates per kilometre for the use of their motor vehicles. However, whereas the Jamaica Civil Service Association (JCSA) was in agreement with the "kilometre travelling rate", it felt that the award had not sufficiently accounted for the true cost of travel in the case of the "upkeep" allowance. In fact, JCSA felt that the award meant that the cost of travel would be greater than the monthly allowances members would receive from the government. The Ministry of Labour referred the dispute to the Industrial Disputes Tribunal, and the following award – which the JCSA found unsatisfactory – was made.

The Tribunal's Award

The tribunal ruled that

1. full upkeep at the rate of J$180,000 per year (J$15,000 monthly), should be effective from 1 October 2000, and that
2. a kilometre travel rate of J$10.35 should prevail.

The association contested the level of the "upkeep" allowance stipulated by the tribunal, stating that both the association's experts and the government's had presented higher figures for the "real costs incurred . . . for upkeep and travelling" than those reflected in the tribunal's award. The tribunal's award for "upkeep" was equivalent to J$15,000 monthly whereas the association's experts placed costs at J$16,886.67 monthly and the government's at J$18,500. In awarding J$15,000, the tribunal, according to the association, had acted "contrary to the evidence placed before it and therefore the award" was "bad in law and unsupported by the evidence".

The association responded by applying for a writ of certiorari and took the case to the Supreme Court.

The Supreme Court's Ruling

The Supreme Court ruled in favour of the JCSA. It noted that the government's budgetary "considerations were inappropriately led before the tribunal and seemed . . . to have unduly influenced the monthly award . . . of $J15,000.00 per month".

The court further noted that the national interest would not be served by failing to reimburse workers in full for money they had spent, and reminded that protection from "arbitrary deprivation of property" is enunciated in the constitution.

Lessons Learnt

1. Vigilance should be exercised in ensuring that employees receive benefits that are due to them and are adequately compensated.
2. Evidence should be carefully scrutinized when decisions are being made on industrial relations issues.
3. Equity and fair play are important tenets in the management/worker relationship.

Source: Supreme Court (Suit No. 36 of 11 October 2001).

Case 4: Unfair Dismissal (Redundancy)

The Jamaica Flour Mills Limited (the Applicant) v. the Industrial Disputes Tribunal (the Respondent) (Jamaica)

The Jamaica Flour Mills, on 13 August 1999, made three positions redundant and the affected employees were offered payment instead of notice without prior consultation with them (two of whom had served thirteen years and the third, twenty-eight years) or their trade union representatives (National Workers Union). Other workers took strike action to support their redundant colleagues. The case was referred to the tribunal for arbitration.

The Tribunal's Award

By majority decision, the tribunal ordered the reinstatement of the three dismissed workers with effect from 13 August 1999 – the date on which the redundancies/dismissals took effect. It called for full wages for one worker who had not collected his cheque up to the time of the hearing, and 60 per cent for the other two "up to the 21st of October 2000, or the date on which the Company re-engages them and they resume duties, whichever is earlier and full wages thereafter".

The Supreme Court's Ruling

The Jamaica Flour Mills appealed against the award in the Supreme Court in an effort to have it quashed.

The company based its case on the main grounds that the tribunal had not properly appreciated or applied the Employment (Termination and Redundancy Payments) Act (especially Section 5), whereby the employer had a right under clause 21 of the Collective Labour Agreement to make redundancies for technological change, and the employer also had jurisdiction over the direction and control of its workforce (Suit M105 of 2000, 3–4).

The court argued that there may be grounds for redundancy but that it may be viewed as unfair or unjustifiable, depending on the manner in which it is carried out. The court drew from Paragraph 19 of the Labour Relations Code which refers to the importance of consultation as a central element in good industrial relations policy. The code also advises that management should, in the relevant circumstances, endeavour to avoid redundancies, that management should have a contingency plan related to redundancies to minimize hardship on the part of workers, and should inform the various parties – workers, trade union and the minister – where the need for redundancies arises.

The Rulings of the Courts

The Supreme Court upheld the tribunal's ruling.

The Court of Appeal dismissed the company's appeal in noting the injustice in the dismissals and that workers had wished to be reinstated.

Lessons Learnt

1. In effecting redundancy, consultation and adequate preparation are important.
2. Employers/management should be sensitive to/cognizant of workers' plight even in cases where redundancies have to be carried out.

Source: The Supreme Court of Jamaica (Suit No. M105 of 2000); (Appeal Court) Supreme Court Civil Appeal No. 7/2002.

Case 5: Unfair/Unjustifiable Dismissal (Quashed by the Court)

Institute of Jamaica and the Jamaica Civil Service Association Tribunal (1999)
The Institute of Jamaica v. the Industrial Disputes Tribunal/Coleen Beecher (Jamaica)

Mrs Beecher, who had joined the staff of the Institute of Jamaica as an administrator on 1 March 1996, had her employment terminated. She was employed on a full-time basis but permanent employment had to be ratified by the Council of the Institute. Up to the time of her dismissal, permanent status had not been confirmed. The dismissed employee had not been given an effective hearing and the employee had committed the offence of removing the Institute's staff chart without approval.

The letter (dated 15 January 1999) advising Mrs Beecher of the termination of employment had, attached to it, a cheque which was intended to cover a month's salary in lieu of notice and sixty-five days' outstanding vacation leave. A letter, dated 14 December 1998 referred to unsatisfactory performance at her job and "unpleasant confrontations with staff". The appellant (the Institute of Jamaica) also advised that Mrs Beecher was told of unsatisfactory performance in the summer of 1998 (Civil Appeal 9/2002, 7).

The dispute between the Institute of Jamaica and the Jamaica Civil Service Association was referred by the Ministry of Labour to the Industrial Disputes Tribunal on 17 November 1999 for settlement, after other channels had failed to resolve the issue.

The Tribunal's Award

The tribunal ruled that the employee should be reinstated as an officer of the Institute of Jamaica: "The tribunal finds that the termination of the services of Mrs Coleen Beecher was unjustifiable and accordingly rules that she be reinstated within three weeks of the date of this AWARD and that she be paid nine months' salary up to the time of reinstatement."

In this award, dated 31 May 2000, it noted that a request from the Cabinet Office to the Institute of Jamaica's executive director to have the employee's position "regularized" had been ignored and that the employee had not been "afforded a proper hearing". This request did not have a significant effect because it was not binding on the executive director as the executive director was the officer with the right to determine, for instance, the quality of the employee's performance. However, the tribunal also noted that the employee had committed a serious offence by removing the staff chart from the Institute's records without approval.

The Court of Appeal's Ruling

The Court of Appeal felt that the IDT ought to have considered the employer's submissions on the merits of reinstatement. In failing to interpret the act (Section 12 [5][c]) correctly and to give a hearing to the appellant on the question of reinstatement, the IDT made two legal errors. "The law on industrial relations is designed to strike a fair balance between the rights of the worker and the rights of the employer" (Civil Appeal 9/2002, 30). The ruling of the appeal court prevailed and stipulated that the award of the Industrial Disputes Tribunal of 31 May 2000 ordering reinstatement and payments be quashed, that the dismissal was justifiable, and offered costs to the appellant, the Institute of Jamaica in the Court of Appeal and the court below.

Lessons Learnt

1. Employers should observe the conditions under which they employ workers, legal as well as physical and psychological.
2. Workers should avoid committing breaches of regulations which may be inimical to their employment and the organization, and should endeavour to perform at the levels expected within the terms of their employment, even when on probation.

3. Reinstatement may not be the best course of action for an employee or employees who are dismissed.
4. Rules and regulations must be in writing; and read and understood by all.

Source: Supreme Court, Suit No. M105 of 2000; (Court of Appeal) Supreme Court Civil Appeal 9/2002.

Case 6: Unjustifiable Dismissal (Criminal Charge)

Salada Foods v. the National Workers Union (Jamaica)

Background

Salada Foods Jamaica Limited claimed that Mr Lascelles Forsythe, who had served the company for more than twenty-three years, was searched by police in the presence of the company's chief security officers on 8 September 1995, and found with sachets of Salada's coffee ("in his pockets and work helmet"). The Hunts Bay police in Kingston counted 124 sachets.

The employee was acquitted of the larceny charge in the resident magistrate's court on 5 March 1996, but when the union wrote to the company shortly after the acquittal requesting the reinstatement of the employee, Salada Foods refused to do so.

At the Tribunal

The union stated that it was not suggesting innocence but rather that by failing to comply with the company's disciplinary code, Salada's management had acted unreasonably in dismissing the employee. It explained that, because Salada's management failed to investigate the allegation against the employee, the employee had the right to call for reinstatement. The union requested that the tribunal order that the employee be reinstated and be paid his wages from 8 September 1995.

The Tribunal's Award

In handing down the award on 29 August 2003, the tribunal noted management's inattention to the rules of *natural justice*. The tribunal stated that it had no evidence suggesting that the company had allowed the employee to defend himself before being dismissed.

The tribunal ordered reinstatement but also instructed that there should be no retroactive wages for the period prior to the date on which the award was made.

Lessons Learnt

1. The rules of natural justice – in this case the worker's right to be given a hearing – should always be observed.
2. Employees should be aware of the consequences of their actions relating to the handling of company property.

Case 7: Calculation of Redundancy Payments

Mariner's Negril Beach Club (MNBC) v. Bustamante Industrial Trade Union (BITU) (Jamaica)

Background

The company stated that Mariner's Resort acquired the operations of the Negril Beach Club. The new owners endeavoured to introduce a new brand and, in doing so, changed the name of the operations to Mariner's Negril Beach Club. A decision to transform to a three-star/all-inclusive hotel required that workers be made redundant. Mariner's informed the BITU and carried out this redundancy process by 18 December 1998.

In spite of some differences and misunderstandings between the company and the union/workers on the guidelines for payments, as subsequent statements suggested, redundancy letters and initial cheque payments from the company were handed to workers on 19 December.

The union challenged the decision and reported the matter to the Ministry of Labour, Social Security and Sports. In a letter dated 8 March 1999, the ministry referred the dispute to the tribunal with the following terms of reference: "To determine and settle the dispute between Mariner's Negril Beach Club . . . and certain workers formerly employed to the company and represented by the Bustamante Industrial Trade Union . . . over calculation of redundancy payments for the said workers" (IDT 5/99, 1).

At the Tribunal

The company stated that workers and their union representative met on 18 December and discussed payment plans which would be in accordance with the guidelines of the Employment (Termination and Redundancy Payments) Act and Regulations and would be payable in ten installments. Additionally, workers were to receive full pay instead of notice as well as pay for any outstanding vacation leave. On the following day the workers collected their redundancy letters and initial cheques.

The company also stated that it heard nothing further from the union or the workers until it learnt that the union had referred a dispute to the Ministry of Labour, Social Security and Sports. It also stated that its decision to pay other installments was based on management's decision to wait until the dispute was settled.

The union informed the tribunal that unionized workers at the Negril Beach Club were retained by Mariner's Negril Beach Club in December 1998 and served with letters of redundancy later that month. The workers were paid one-tenth of the payment calculated in keeping with the provisions of the Employment (Termination and Redundancy Payments) Act and the Employment (Termination and Redundancy Payments) Regulations of 1974.

Payments, the union emphasized, should have been based on the Collective Labour Agreement (for the two-year period from 1 May 1997 to 30 April 1999), dated 7 October 1997. Paragraph five of that agreement states, for example, that a worker with five years of continuous service would receive two weeks' pay per year from year one whereas a worker who served more than ten years continuously should obtain five weeks' pay per year from the first year.

The Tribunal's Award

After eight sittings during the period 21 June 1999 to 10 August 2000, the tribunal directed, in its award of 5 October 2000, that each of the workers who was issued a redundancy notice should be given the balance of the redundancy payment mentioned "in his/her redundancy notice less the installment included in the cheque issued to and negotiated by him/her" (IDT 5/99, 4).

Subsequent Union Action

The BITU successfully sought an order of certiorari to have the Supreme Court quash the tribunal's award and an order of mandamus directing the tribunal to grant an award based on the provision for severance payment contained in the Collective Labour Agreement arrived at between the union and the company on the 7 October 1997. Under the agreement, workers had been granted increased wages and allowances mainly in two stages from May 1997 and May 1998.

Supreme Court's Ruling

The court overruled the tribunal and handed down an award which favoured calculations based on the Collective Labour Agreement.

Lessons Learnt

1. A change of name does not free a company from the liability of redundancy obligations or other payments due to workers.
2. Parties in industrial relations should be knowledgeable and constantly abreast of regulations and guidelines governing their relationships, especially when matters (for example, redundancy) with far-reaching implications for the parties and others, such as workers' families, are involved.
3. The Industrial Disputes Tribunal, a key arbiter in industrial relations, may be challenged on specific issues of law and rights of individual workers.

Source: IDT 5/99.

Case 8: Bargaining Rights (Eligibility for Union Representation)

The National Commercial Bank (Jamaica) (NCB) Limited v. the Bustamante Industrial Trade Union (BITU) (Jamaica)

Background

In June 2000 the BITU sought bargaining rights for certain categories of NCB staff but the company disagreed with the proposed inclusion of these categories. The categories that the union put forward for the ballot included executives and senior managers. The company wrote on 28 July 2000 to the Ministry of Labour and Social Security arguing that executives and senior managers should not be included as they were responsible for company policies and strategies and had particular functions and that their inclusion in a ballot would conflict with their duties to the company. Additionally, the company argued that such a scenario would leave the company without an impartial individual to negotiate with a union that had bargaining rights.

The matter remained unresolved and the ministry referred the dispute to the Industrial Disputes Tribunal on 28 August 2000.

The union argued that the Jamaica Constitution and the Labour Relations and Industrial Disputes Act (LRIDA) stipulated that persons were allowed the right to join the trade union of their choice. Members of the bank's senior management, the union also stated, were interested in exercising that right.

The company pointed to misinterpretation of the LRIDA, which was used as a basis for the union's demand. However, the union responded, for example, that when the workers sought representation they were not involved in policymaking and that this was more apparent after 1995, the year it applied for bargaining rights.

The Tribunal's Award

The tribunal ruled in favour of the union by directing that the disputed categories of persons be included in the ballot.

Lessons Learnt

1. Proper interpretation of industrial relations laws and regulations and adherence to them are important in maintaining peace in the industrial relations environment.
2. Timing is important in resolving disputes.
3. Claims arising between a worker and manager must be clear and specific if misinterpretation is to be avoided.

Source: IDT 21/2000

Case 9: Pay Disparity/Anomaly

Ministries of Health (MOH), and Finance and Planning (MOFP) v. the Union of Technical and Supervisory Personnel (UTASP) (IDT 1/2003) (Jamaica)

The defined roles of medical technologists (MTs) suggested that they carried out tests on which doctors based their treatment. Entry level qualification was a diploma in medical technology. Scientific officers (SOs), by job description, carried out other duties and required at least a natural science degree (IDT 1/2003, 15).

Medical technologists had been restive from 1996 about disparities and anomalies relating to their salaries and those of SOs. When under an agreement that became effective on 1 April that year their rate of pay remained substantially lower than that for SOs, MTs pointed out that in some cases they had to supervise SOs. A new MOH review that combined salaries and allowances became effective on 1 April 2000. In the review, some MTs were placed in a marginally higher pay range than SOs.

Two subsequent reclassifications – effective April 2001 and October 2002 – awarded significant increases that offered a higher salary range to SOs.

The union felt that the prevailing arrangement was inconsistent with the advice in the final report of the Health Sector Pay Review Project. The job evaluation had been conducted within the MOH and the final report was submitted in March 1999.

In a letter addressed to the MOH in December 2002, the union noted that it was disappointed that after a year the MTs' salary structure had not been adjusted, that both categories of workers were performing similar duties, and that MTs were "restive" and had "decided that the adjustments should be made on or before 31 December 2002". The union also warned of "confrontation" without further notice if that deadline were not met (IDT 1/2003, 9).

The MOH replied with a letter, dated 27 December 2002, which implied that the deadline could not be met, and stated in it, for example, that in future SOs would be employed at the National Public Health Laboratory on the condition that they did not perform the duties of MTs.

Failure to resolve the impasse led to the MTs taking strike action on 2 January 2003. Conciliation meetings, held at the Ministry of Labour and Social Security on 3 January, were unsuccessful. However, the workers returned to work on 6 January. With no further progress, the ministry referred the dispute to the tribunal on 14 January 2003 (IDT 1/2003, 10–11).

The Tribunal's Award

The tribunal, in its award dated 24 July 2003, ruled that a reclassification of the MT group should be conducted by 31 December 2003 and "there should be full implementation of the financial benefits by 1 March 2004, retroactive to 1st January 2001". Second, "all Chief Medical Technologists 1 and 2 who were required to supervise Scientific Officers shall be paid the additional Sum of Twenty One Thousand Dollars (J$21,000.00) per month effective 1 January 2001 until this arrangement ceases" (IDT 1/2003, 27).

Lessons Learnt

1. Workers are entitled to equal pay for equal work with few exceptions. Proper classification and deployment of workers are required for good order and stability.
2. Where anomalies or disparities exist they should be addressed and resolved amicably in order to ensure minimum disruption in organizations and work.
3. Unnecessarily drawn-out/protracted negotiations are inimical to a good industrial relations environment.

Source: IDT 1/2003.

Case 10: Bargaining Rights (Eligibility for Union Representation)

Canadian Imperial Bank of Commerce (Jamaica) Ltd (CIBC) v. Bustamante Industrial Trade Union (BITU) (Jamaica)

Background

This case concerns the eligibility of persons for participation in a ballot as part of the BITU's claim for bargaining rights.

CIBC, a Canadian-based commercial banking company, had twelve branches in Jamaica. In addition, it had a trust and merchant bank and a building society as part of its business portfolio. It had a total of 500 employees. The bank's name was changed to First Caribbean International Bank (Jamaica) Limited on 11 October 2002, as part of the regional merger between CIBC and Barclays Bank PLC.

In May 2002, the union had served the bank notice that it wished to be recognized as the bargaining agent for 362 members of staff in sixty-nine categories.

The bank objected to the inclusion of 62 staff members – who were in broadly, administrative and supervisory categories – in a poll to be taken. The bank felt, for example, that these employees should be placed in a separate poll because they exercised discipline over workers in other categories and members of the categories exercising such discipline were also privy to confidential information.

The union's opposition, based on its experience of representing employees in several banks, was partly buttressed by the fact that one poll had already been conducted, after which discussions were held and several bargaining units were formed as necessary.

The Tribunal's Award

The tribunal explained that the central issue for its attention was about which categories of employees should be involved in the ballot. It disagreed with the bank's interpretation of Regulation 4 of the Labour Relations and Industrial Disputes Act (LRIDA), and ordered the inclusion of the disputed sixty-two workers in the representational rights ballot.

Lessons Learnt

1. Precedents are relevant in industrial relations practice. The union's experience of having conducted a single poll for relevant employees in each of the other banks it represented was a significant deciding element in its argument.

2. Administrative and supervisory personnel need not be separated in a ballot as the division into bargaining units after a poll provides an appropriate structure. However, there may be implications for industrial peace if one union represents all categories of workers. A separation is strongly advised.
3. Proper interpretation of relevant regulations is important.

Source: IDT 20/2002.

Case 11: Recovery of Funds Paid to Employees (Overpayment): Unauthorized Deductions

Jamaica National Heritage Trust (JNHT) v. the Bustamante Industrial Trade Union (BITU) (Jamaica)

The Jamaica National Heritage Trust (JNHT), a public sector entity, learnt through an audit, dated 19 December 2001, that payments had been made inappropriately as advances and subsistence allowance to employees. The JNHT sought to recover advances for subsistence allowance paid to employees by deductions from their salaries on 25 August 2002. Workers took strike action and failure to reach agreement led to the Ministry of Labour and Social Security referring the matter to the Industrial Disputes Tribunal.

The tribunal was directed to determine whether the JNHT acted appropriately in deducting money from the employees' salaries to recover subsistence allowance paid in relation to (1) a Stony Gut project (St Thomas) and (2) other projects.

A 19 December 2001 audit received by the JNHT stated that, in some situations, subsistence allowances were being paid to members of staff simultaneously with payment of (for) actual expenses. This contravened the 1976 Staff Orders. It also stated that the JNHT's senior officers were unaware of the regulations and requested the recovery of money paid for allowances from the officers.

The union wrote to the JNHT on 22 August 2002, asking for an urgent meeting and for a delay in making deductions from retroactive salary payments. The JNHT, however, deducted various amounts on that day (August 22). A work stoppage ensued after which the case was handed over to the tribunal.

At the Tribunal

The union stated that "there was an agreed procedure that the Trust would pay for accommodation directly to Hotels involved and pay employees by way of an advance to cover the cost of their meals where meals were not affected by the Hotels". With regard to the Stony Gut project, the union further stated, "the evidence presented was that *accommodation only* was provided" by a resort and "the employees had to make other arrangements for their meals for which they were given an advance and that it was only after the Auditor's Report that they were required to provide bills for their meals". It was "difficult to provide those bills" (IDT 21/2002, 8).

The JNHT contended at the tribunal that it acted based on the audit, which stated: "Accommodation and subsistence allowances were paid simultaneously to officers on assignment. It should be noted that the officers were entitled to subsistence or payment for accommodation and meals whichever is greater and not both" (IDT 21/2002, 8).

The Tribunal's Award

The tribunal noted that the JNHT, in making deductions other than statutory and other agreed deductions, acted inappropriately but also noted that deductions relating to "past projects" would "be appropriate where documentary evidence makes it abundantly clear that the officers concerned were provided with Accommodation and Meals and at the same time were paid Subsistence Allowance in respect of the same period" (IDT 21/2002, 10).

Lessons Learnt

1. Unauthorized deductions from employees' salaries are unlawful and may undermine good industrial relations practice.
2. Officers should be aware of the regulations governing deductions from employees' salaries
3. Appropriate management and supervision of deductions and payments must be in place to prevent disagreements and disruptions of the business process.
4. In cases such as this, discussion with employees over the issue rather than immediate action to recover funds might have prevented conflict.

Source: IDT 21/2002.

Case 12: Job Evaluation Market Reference and Calculation of Retroactive Payments

Jamaica Public Service Company Limited (JPSCo) v. the Bustamante Industrial Trade Union (BITU) and the National Workers Union (NWU) (Jamaica)

Background

In 1990, the management of JPSCo decided to carry out a job evaluation exercise aimed at making the company more competitive and at attracting skilled workers as well as retaining skilled ones. The evaluation "was to establish an internal alignment of compensation packages payable to position holders within the bargaining unit and to enable the company to be generally competitive in the labour market" (IDT 3/2003, 3). The management envisioned the building of a world-class company.

The company, the NWU, which represented the clerical staff, and the BITU, which represented the hourly paid staff, reached an agreement for the period 1 January 2000 to 31 December 2001. They agreed that the job reclassification and evaluation exercise would be conducted by Trevor Hamilton and Associates (THA) and that THA's recommendations would be binding on the company and the unions (IDT 2/2003, 3–4).

In April 2001, Mirant Corporation, a US energy company based in Atlanta, acquired majority shares in the company. The new president supported the ongoing job evaluation, which was not completed by the originally scheduled date of 31 March 2001, but rather in February 2002, the evaluation having been delayed because of an expansion in its scope. The completed evaluation was considered a success, and the compensation levels for the company "were placed within a 5–10 percentile of the market for the benchmarked companies surveyed" (IDT 3/2003, 3).

Eleven local companies, against which the company's salaries were benchmarked, participated in the survey. Peat Marwick and Partners Management Consultants, contracted to carry out the salary survey, confirmed that based on the index of basic pay and allowances, JPSCo was among the top four, "with all four bargaining units being compensated at above market" (IDT 3/2003, 5).

The union contended that the company had taken a unilateral stand to compensate workers on the basis of an average of the eleven companies surveyed (a middle position in the market) rather than an average of the top four (top position) in which (four) the JPSCo was included. It felt the company's approach was unfair because, in arriving at a compensation package based on that formula, it would make itself uncompetitive.

The union also contended that management's refusal to "pay retroactively any financial gains from the job evaluation and compensation review exercise was not in keeping with the spirit and intent of the 2000–2001 collective agreement and established principles regarding retroactivity" (IDT 3/2003, 6).

The company had mentioned that its compensation policy did not recognize the principle of retroactive pay. However, as "a show of good faith" it proposed a retroactive date of 1 October 2001. The company later agreed on 1 April but the union insisted on 1 January 2001 (IDT 3/2003, 6).

The Ministry of Labour and Social Security reported the matter to the Industrial Disputes Tribunal after the parties failed to resolve the matter. The tribunal was asked to decide on the salary structure following the job evaluation and compensation review, and decide on the date when the new rates would be effective.

The Tribunal's Award

In its award of 29 August 2003, the tribunal directed that the salary structure to be implemented following the job evaluation and compensation exercise should be one which was consistent with and maintained the established compensation policy and philosophy agreed on by the parties in the 1990–91 Heads of Agreement which was "based on a formula of the top 5–10 percentile of the benchmarked market" (IDT 3/2003, 19).

The tribunal further directed that the effective date of payment of the new rates should be 1 January 2001 (19).

Lessons Learnt

1. Job evaluations must be conducted properly, with all relevant parties or their representatives agreeing to the steps and stages, and effective dates.
2. Agreements should be honoured by the parties involved in the interest of maintaining good industrial relations.
3. Change of ownership or control does not necessarily have to lead to change of industrial relations policy/philosophy.

Source: IDT 3/2003.

Case 13: Dismissal Due to Insubordination, Disrespect and so on

Employee (Michael Browne) v. T. Geddes Grant (Barbados)

An employee of T. Geddes Grant was fired in July 2000 on the grounds of "insubordination, refusing to carry out instructions, and referring to his supervisor as a 'stupe'". Two warnings for similar behaviour had been issued to the employee during the same year. The employee, a former forklift operator, sued the company over the dismissal.

The Employee's Position

The employee, through his lawyer, challenged the dismissal on the basis that the circumstances did not suggest insubordination and that even if they did, summary dismissal was uncalled for. He argued that in the case of longstanding employees "the law was clear that . . . not every trifling act justifies summary dismissal". The plaintiff had worked with T. Geddes Grant for about twenty-four years.

The Lower Court and Appeal Court

Information provided to the court indicated that on 15 July 2000, the employee, rather than follow his supervisor's instruction to get a forklift had instead complained to another supervisor that his immediate supervisor was "behaving like a 'stupe'". The comment was made in the presence of the employee's supervisor.

The lower court agreed with the employer's decision to dismiss the worker, having heard that the employee had been warned two times for similar behaviour and had been suspended and given a final warning on 20 August 1999.

The Supreme Court felt that the employee had been "given a lawful and reasonable order" which "he never carried out". It felt that the substance of insubordination was "disobedience" and "defiance of authority". The employee's action was one of insubordination which justified the decision to dismiss him.

Lessons Learnt

1. The employer has rights and obligations in managing the affairs of the enterprise.
2. The employee should obey instructions and directions given by the supervisor, which are in keeping with the job functions.

3. The right of appeal against any unreasonable instructions should be excluded in the grievance procedure of the company.
4. Any objections to a legitimate instruction must be pursued through the company's grievance machinery.
5. Being disrespectful to anyone is not acceptable in the workplace.

Source: Barbados Employers' Consortium (BEC) @ Work 4, no. 5 (October 2004): 3. See also "Company Right to Sack Worker", *Daily Nation* (Barbados), 8 June 2004.

Case 14: Grievance Procedure Regarding Performance Appraisal: Personnel Records

TD No. 48/92 (Date of Award/"Delivery" – 18 January 1993)
University of the West Indies (St Augustine Campus) v. University and Affiliated Workers Union (Trinidad and Tobago)

Unfavourable comments were allegedly lodged against a worker by his head of department at the University of the West Indies (St Augustine campus) in a document referred to as the "annual staff appraisal report" for the period from 1 November 1989 to 31 October 1990.

The head of department had added the following comment: "The worker is becoming a very difficult employee. He seems to have a problem accepting the authority of his supervisor. A change of attitude is needed. However, he has the technical ability to perform his duties well."

The worker alleged that the comments were not included in the annual staff appraisal report when he was allowed to view it.

The Employer's Position

The university alleged that adding the comments amounted to a lapse in procedure and stated that the report was not adverse.

The Union's Position

The trade union involved – the University and Affiliated Workers Union – alleged that the comments were written in the annual staff appraisal report without the worker's knowledge and that such an act was not only against the worker's terms and conditions of service laid out in the collective agreement but also "contrary to the principles and practices of good industrial relations".

The Industrial Court's Award

The court felt that the matter should have been resolved at an earlier stage – that is, prior to reaching the court. It also felt that the comments were adverse and maintained that the worker should have been allowed to read them before they were placed on his personnel records. The university extended the wrong, the court argued, by denying the union's request that they be removed from the employee's records. The court therefore ordered that the comments by the head of department should be removed from the employee's file and personnel records by 25 January 1993 and that evidence of the removal should be provided to the union. The court also warned that future breaches of that kind could attract a cost.

Lessons Learnt

1. Communication is an important element in the pursuit of organizational efficiency and good industrial relations practice.
2. Observations about workers' attitudes and performance should be discussed with the relevant parties, including the worker, in order to arrive at a solution that is in the interest of all parties and the organization.
3. Failure to share positive or adverse comments which have an important bearing on an employee's or employees' personnel records with the employee or employees has consequences for both those directly involved and the organization.
4. Best-practice systems require accuracy in documenting information in the personnel files of employees.

Source: Employers' Consultative Association, *Industrial Relations Trends and Practices in Trinidad and Tobago* (summary of 1993 Industrial Court Judgements) (Port of Spain: ECA, 2004), 71.

Case 15: Dismissal, Breach of Contract of Employment, Job Abandonment, Compensation

TD 130/91, Trinidad and Tobago (Date of Award/"Delivery" – 12 May 1993)
Employee v. Romeo's Gas Station (Trinidad and Tobago)

While working as an attendant at Romeo's Gas Station during the period 1985 to 1990, the employee at the centre of this case took temporary employment elsewhere in December 1990, against her employer's wishes.

The Employer's Position

The employer did not recall the employee to her job but also did not specifically inform her that she was dismissed. According the employer, the worker committed a fundamental breach of contract by abandoning the job but also stated that the worker's performance had been satisfactory.

The Worker's Position

The worker admitted that she did not obtain permission from her employer at the gas station to take temporary employment elsewhere.

The Court's Ruling

As a legal concept in industrial relations, *abandonment* "has never been clearly defined".

The court was made aware that the worker's absence lasted no more than two days after which she was told not to appear at the work site. The court also noted that the employer knew of the worker's location and that the worker always indicated her intention to return to her substantive job. However, the court further observed that the hours of work overlapped (8 a.m. to 4 p.m. at the gas station and 7 a.m. to 11 a.m. at the temporary job).

A direct warning from the employer, the court advised, might have made his position clear, and it found that the circumstances in which the worker was dismissed were not consistent with good industrial relations practices. In addition, it advised that some blame also rested with the worker.

The court ruled out reinstatement as a useful option and also "any compensation for alleged loss of earnings or any other claim". However, it awarded the worker two weeks' compensation per year for the first four years that she was employed to the gas station and three weeks' compensation per year for the last five years of employment. After a deduction of 45 per cent, the payment was to be made by 31 May 1993.

Lessons Learnt

1. An employer should clearly communicate workers' obligations to them.
2. A worker should be mindful of contravening the conditions of his or her employment. Knowingly committing a breach does not guarantee reinstatement in cases where a worker accepts temporary employment which conflicts with his or her full-time commitment.

3. All decisions concerned with acts of indiscipline or breaches of conduct should be conveyed simply and explicitly in writing.

Source: Employers' Consultative Association, *Industrial Relations Trends and Practices in Trinidad and Tobago* (summary of 1993 Industrial Court Judgements) (Port of Spain: ECA, 2004), 34.

Case 16: Summary Dismissal (Insolence and Wilful Disrespect)

Trinidad and Tobago Trade Dispute No. 82 of 2001
National Union of Domestic Employees v. K. Allen and Sons Funeral Directors Limited (Trinidad and Tobago)

Background

An employee of the company named above was dismissed on 2 November 2000 after protest action and the use of abusive language to her employer.

The Union's Position

The union stated that the worker had begun working with the company on 12 May 1998 and had worked as a mortician until the time of her dismissal.

The Worker's Position

The worker, who was the only witness, stated that she had enjoyed a good working relationship with the managing director until August 2000 when he received a petition (on which her signature was also listed) from workers, based on perceived poor working conditions. According to her, he called all workers who had signed the petition "to the front of the building and he started getting really abusive". She said she had been victimized thereafter, unfairly suspended in September 2000, and received a letter informing her that her temporary employment would end in March 2001.

The Company's Position

The company stated that the worker had been a satisfactory employee when she joined the company but had subsequently acquired a poor attitude which manifested itself in several ways, including unsanitary practices and a refusal "to say good morning to staff" and being "verbally abusive to customers". Another employee who was her supervisor stated that she refused to comply with his instructions, behaving as though she was his supervisor.

On the morning of 2 November, the worker used very abusive language to her employer, the managing director, who stated that he had had enough of her behaviour and insolence. He told her that she was fired and she requested a letter of dismissal. He denied that he had victimized her after the workers' petition was submitted.

The Court's Findings

The Industrial Court also learnt that on 2 November 2000 the worker went to her job against advice that she should first speak with the managing director. The managing director appeared shortly afterwards and "verbally abused the worker over her (alleged) ill-speaking him with a competitor, with whom she had earlier sought employment". The worker denied this but, not convinced of her sincerity, the managing director suspended her.

The worker was found to be abusive to her employer and suspension was unwarranted. "It is our finding . . . that the language used by the worker [to her employer on 2 November 2000] was improper, unacceptable, foul and obscene." The court stated that the dismissal was "fully merited".

Source: The library, Employers' Consultative Association of Trinidad and Tobago.

References

Asian Productivity Organization. *Labour-Management Cooperation: Promoting Labour Market Flexibility.* Tokyo: Asian Productivity Organization, 2002.

Baugh, R. 1985. "Revision of the Industrial Relations System in Jamaica". Typescript.

Constitutional Rights Foundation. 1998. "Bill of Rights in Action". 14, no. 3. http://www.crf-usa.org/bria/bria14_3.html

Döding, G. 1976. *Co-Determination: The German Model.* Bonn: Friedrich Ebert Stiftung.

Downes, A.S. 1997. "Wage Developments in the Caribbean". *Journal of Eastern Caribbean Studies* 22, no. 1: 32–44.

———. 2003. *Productivity and Competitiveness in the Jamaican Economy.* Bridgetown, Barbados: Inter American Development Bank.

Fraser, J.M. 1977. *Principles and Practice of Supervisory Management.* London: Nelson.

Gershenfeld, W.J. 1974. *Compulsory Arbitration in Jamaica 1952–1959.* Kingston: Institute of Social and Economic Research, University of the West Indies.

Goolsarran, S.J. 2003. *The System of Industrial Relations in Guyana.* Port of Spain: International Labour Office (Caribbean).

Green, G.D. 1987. *Industrial Relations.* 2nd ed. London: Pitman.

———. 1991. *Industrial Relations.* 3rd ed. London: Pitman.

Handy, C. 1992. "Making Career Sense of Labour Market Information". http://workinfonet.bc.ca/lmisi/making/chapter2/SHIFT1.htm.

Hussey, B.H. 1995. "Employee Attitude Surveys: An Aid to Organizational Efficiency". In *Human Resource Management: A Caribbean Perspective,* ed. N. Cowell and I. Boxill, 237–45. Kingston: Canoe Press.

———. 2000. "Final Report on IADB Regional Project in Non-Traditional Skills for Low-Income Women, Labour Market Information System Component". Typescript.

———. 2002. "Labour Market Reform Support to Jamaica's Economic Reform Programme: Design and Development of a National Wage Index". Paper prepared for the Planning Institute of Jamaica, Kingston.

Hussmanns, R., T. Mehran and V.J. Verma. 1990. *Surveys of Economically Active Population, Employment, Unemployment and Underemployment: An ILO Manual on Concepts and Methods.* Geneva: International Labour Organization.

Interlock Employee Assistance Program. 2005. "What Is an Employee Assistance Program?" http://www.interlock.org/whateap.html (accessed in 2005).

International Labour Office. 1995. *Law on Freedom of Association: Standards and Procedures.* Geneva: International Labour Office.

International Labour Organization. 1979. *An Integrated System of Wages Statistics: A Manual of Methods.* Geneva: International Labour Organization.

———. Trade Union Advisory Committee. 1996. *Labour Standards in the Global Trade and Investment System.* Geneva: International Labour Organization.

————. Bureau of Statistics. 1997. *Resolution Concerning Statistics on Strikes, Lockouts and Other Action Due to Labour Disputes*. Geneva: International Labour Organization.

————. 1999. *Key Indicators of the Labour Market: Country Profiles*. Geneva: International Labour Organization. http://www.ilo.org/public/English/employment/strat/kilm/ (accessed in 1999).

————. 2000. *World Labour Report*. "Unemployment Benefit Systems". http://www.ilo.org/public/english/bureau/inf/pkits/wlr2000/wlr00ch3.htm

Jamaica Employers' Federation. 1979. *Labour Laws*. Kingston: Jamaica Employers' Federation.

Johannsen, H., and G.T. Page. 1975. *International Dictionary of Management*. London: Kogan Page.

Joint Trade Unions Research Development Centre (JTURDC). 1986. *Pension Schemes: An Introductory Manual for Workers*. Kingston: Joint Trade Unions Research Development Centre.

Kirkaldy, S.G. 1979. *An Introduction to Industrial Relations and Labour Law in Jamaica*. Kingston: Trade Union Education Institute, University of the West Indies, 1979.

Los Angeles County. 1989. "Los Angeles County Board of Supervisors Policy Manual: Policy Number 09.090: Telecommuting Policy".

National Productivity Corporation. 2001. *A Glossary of Productivity and Quality Terminologies*. Petaling Jaya, Malaysia: National Productivity Corporation.

————. 2003. *National Productivity Report*. Petaling Jaya, Malaysia: National Productivity Corporation.

Nurse, L.A. 1992. *Trade Unionism and Industrial Relations in the Commonwealth Caribbean: History, Contemporary Practice and Prospect*. Contributions in Labor Studies, no. 40. Wesport: Greenwood.

Okpaluba, C. 1975. "Statutory Regulation of Collective Bargaining: With Special Reference to the Industrial Stabilisation Act of Trinidad and Tobago". *Law and Society in the Caribbean*, no. 5. Kingston: Institute of Social and Economic Research.

Phillip, G. 1986. *A–Z of Industrial Relations Practices at the Workplace*. Kingston: Kingston Publishers.

"A Ponzi Problem: US Dependency Ratio, Social Security Solvency, and the False Panacea of Immigration". http://www.fairus.org/html/publications.html

Poole, M. 1984. *Industrial Relations in the Future*. London: Routledge and Kegan Paul.

Rogovsky, N., and E. Sims. 2002. *Corporate Success through People: Making International Labour Standards Work for You*. Geneva: International Labour Organization.

Salmon, M. 1998. *Industrial Relations: Theory and Practice*. 3rd ed. Hampstead: Prentice Hall Europe.

Schregle, J. 2002. *Global Views and Experience in Labour Management Cooperation: Promoting Labour Market Flexibility (A Forum Report)*. Tokyo: Asian Productivity Organization.

Social Security Online. 2006. "Automatic Increases: Average Wage Index Series". http://www.ssa.gov/OCAT/COLA/AWIgrowth.html

Spurgeon, A. 2003. *Working Time: Its Impact on Safety and Health.* Geneva: International Labour Office.

Stone, C. 1983. *Work Attitude Survey: A Report to the Jamaican Government.* Task Force on Work Attitude Report. Kingston: Jamaica Information Service.

Stoppi, M.J. 2001. *Commercial Arbitration in the Caribbean: A Practical Guide.* Kingston: University of the West Indies Press.

Strachan, G. Preface. *The System of Industrial Relations in Guyana,* by S.L. Goolsarran. Port of Spain: International Labour Office (Caribbean).

US Department of Labour (Employment and Training Administration). "State Unemployment Insurance Benefits." http://welfaresecurity.doleta.gov/unemploy/uifactsheet.asp

Vincent, M. 1983. Introduction. *Industrial Relations.* London: Heinemann.

Wallace, M.J., Jr., J. Marc and C.H. Fay. 1988. *Compensation Theory and Practice.* 2nd ed. Boston: PWS-Kent.

Wolfe, Lensley H. 2001. Foreword. *Commercial Arbitration in the Caribbean: A Practical Guide,* by M.J. Stoppi. Kingston: University of the West Indies Press, 2001.

Wright, A. 1985. "Role of the IDT in Industrial Relations". Typescript.